WILD NEW YORK

Margaret Mittelbach
& Michael Crewdson

Wild NEW YORK

A Guide to the Wildlife, Wild Places,
& Natural Phenomena
of New York City

A Peter N. Nevraumont Book
Crown Publishers, Inc.
New York

Copyright ©1997 by Margaret Mittelbach and Michael Crewdson
Maps copyright © 1997 by Mark Stein Studios
Illustrations © 1997 by Patricia Wynne

All rights reserved. No part of this book may be reproduced or transmitted in any form or by any means, electronic or mechanical, including photocopying, recording, or by any information storage and retrieval system, without permission in writing from the publishers.

Published by Crown Publishers, Inc., 201 East 50th Street, New York, New York 10022.
Member of the Crown Publishing Group.

Random House, Inc. New York, Toronto, London, Sydney, Auckland
http://www.randomhouse.com/

CROWN is a trademark of Crown Publishers, Inc.

Printed in the United States of America

Library of Congress Cataloging-in-Publication Data is available on request.

ISBN 0-517-70484-6

10 9 8 7 6 5 4 3 2

Credits accompanying color photographs are an extension of this copyright page.

Black-and-White Photography Credits: *page 2:* Seal of New Netherland, New York City Municipal Archives; *13:* Hurricane Edourd, National Oceanic and Atmospheric Administration; *15:* October 1996 Nor'easter, National Oceanic and Atmospheric Administration; *16:* Empire State Building hit by lightning, Underwood Photo Archives, San Fransisco; *23:* Hudson River Palisades, Palisades Interstate Park; *26:* Gneiss and Manhattan schist, American Museum of Natural History; *27:* Subway excavation, New York Transit Museum Archives; *28:* Cretaceous leaf fossil, Staten Island Museum of Arts and Sciences; *30:* Central Park outcrop, American Museum of Natural History; *33:* Subway garnet, American Museum of Natural History; *38:* American Mastodon, American Museum of Natural History; *52:* Sand tiger shark, New York Aquarium for Wildlife Conservation; *80:* Jackrabbit at John F. Kennedy Airport, Don Riepe; *160:* Camperdown Elm, Laura Nash; *172:* "Major" the coyote, Daniel Hack.

Slightly different versions of the essays, "D-Day for Gotham's Rarest Bird," "Return to the Hudson River: The Running of the Shad," and "Grasslands," originally appeared in *Newsday;* parts of the "Ice Age" and "Peregrine Falcons" were first printed in *Brooklyn Bridge;* and a version of "The Oldest Love Story in the Book: The Mating of the Horseshoe Crabs" was first printed in the *New York Daily News.*

Jacket and book design by Jaye Zimet

Created and Produced by Nevraumont Publishing Company
New York, New York
Ann J. Perrini, President

This book is dedicated to Frank and Carole Crewdson for their enthusiastic support and optimism and to Frank and Sari Mittelbach for nurturing the idea.

Contents

INTRODUCTION, *IX*

Chapter 1
PLANET NEW YORK

LOCATION, LOCATION, LOCATION, *2* - HEAVENLY BODIES, *3* - WEATHER AND CLIMATE, *6* - A SHOW OF FORCE: NATURE TAKES CONTROL, *8* - IT CAME FROM THE SEA, *11*

Chapter 2
THE ANCIENT APPLE

PRIMORDIAL MOUNTAINS AND SEAS, *21* - HOT ROCKS, *25* - NATURE: THE GREAT ARCHITECT, *30* - THE ICE AGE, *34*

Chapter 3
STRANGE NEIGHBORHOODS
The City's Ecosystems

THE HUDSON ESTUARY, *42* - SALT MARSHES, *44* - FORESTS, *48* - BEACHES, *51* - FRESH WATER, *54* - GRASSLANDS, *57*

Chapter 4
CITY ANIMALS

PEREGRINE FALCONS, *61* - EGRETS—WE HAVE A FEW, *65* - PIGEONS: BIRDS WITH A PAST, *67* - D-DAY FOR GOTHAM'S RAREST BIRD, *70* - WARBLER MANIA, *73* - LOCAL HEROES—SQUIRRELS, *75* - RAT NATION, *77* - COYOTES: "NEW YORK CITY OR BUST," *80* - REPTILES AND AMPHIBIANS, *81* - COCKROACHES: THE GUESTS THAT WOULDN'T LEAVE, *85* - FISH AND OTHER UNDERWATER CREATURES, *88*

Chapter 5
PUTTING DOWN ROOTS
The City's Plants

THE CITY'S TREES, *97* - FLOWERS, *104* - THE NEW YORK UNDERWORLD: MUSHROOMS AND FUNGI, *107* - HAY FEVER HELL, *109* - THERE *IS* A SEASON: FALL COLORS, *110*

Chapter 6
RITES AND MYSTERIES
The City's Natural Phenomena

THE ATLANTIC FLYWAY, *113* - THE RUNNING OF THE SHAD, *117* A LITTLE ROMANCE: THE MATING OF THE HORSESHOE CRABS, *120* THE FLIGHT OF THE MONARCHS, *122* - THE BROOD: THE EMERGENCE OF THE 17-YEAR CICADAS, *124*

Chapter 7
WILD PLACES
Exploring Nature in New York City

MANHATTAN: THE WILD HEART, *128* - JAMAICA BAY, *143* - BROOKLYN, *158* THE BRONX, *166* - QUEENS, *177* - STATEN ISLAND: COUNTRY IN THE CITY, *185*

INDEX, *195*

MAPS

WINTER SKY, *4*
GET MY DRIFT? (CONTINENTAL DRIFT), *22*
CAMERON'S LINE, *24*
GEOLOGY AND THE NEW YORK CITY SKYLINE, *31*
NEW YORK CITY DURING THE LAST ICE AGE, *36-37*
HUDSON RIVER ESTUARY, *42*
MANHATTAN: BEFORE AND AFTER (LANDFILL), *46*
HARBOR HERONRY, *65*
CITY FISHING SITES, *91*
ATLANTIC FLYWAY ROUTES, *114*
CENTRAL PARK, THE RAMBLE (WILD WALK), *132*
CENTRAL PARK, THE GREAT NORTH (WILD WALK), *135*
INWOOD HILL PARK (WILD WALK), *138*
JAMAICA BAY AND THE ROCKAWAYS, *145*
JAMAICA BAY WILDLIFE REFUGE (WILD WALK), *147*
FLOYD BENNETT FIELD (WILD WALK), *150*
BREEZY POINT TIP, *152*
FORT TILDEN, *154*
PROSPECT PARK (WILD WALK), *161*
BROOKLYN BOTANIC GARDEN, *165*
PELHAM BAY PARK (WILD WALK), *168*
VAN CORTLANDT PARK (WILD WALK), *170*
NEW YORK BOTANICAL GARDEN, *174*
ALLEY POND PARK (WILD WALK), *178*
FOREST PARK, *182*
THE STATEN ISLAND GREENBELT (WILD WALK), *186*
CLAY PIT PONDS STATE PARK PRESERVE, *190*
GREAT KILLS PARK, *192*

COLOR PHOTO SECTION FOLLOWS PAGE 84

INTRODUCTION

When we first told people we were writing a book about nature in New York City, many of them asked, "Is there any?" Over the last three years of researching and writing, we learned that, not only is there nature and wildlife in New York City, there is too much for us to cover in one book.

During our research, which took us from Coney Island to the top of the Empire State Building, we were repeatedly amazed by what we encountered: By the beautiful landscapes and ecosystems that we never knew existed. By the variety of life that survives here. And by the unique and sometimes otherworldly natural phenomena that continue to occur in this, one of the most populated and extravagantly built-up cities in the world.

In 1954, the poet Frank O'Hara wrote that "One need never leave the confines of New York to get all the greenery one wishes." We are happy to report that his observation still holds true today. *Wild New York* discusses climate, geology, ecosystems, flora, and fauna. It also offers descriptions of more than 30 wild places throughout the five boroughs, from seashores and salt marshes to forests and woodland ponds. While some of these natural areas are on the city's edges, many are right in its heart—and we encourage readers to explore them. Wherever you live, nature is lurking not far from your door.

As part of the process of creating *Wild New York*, we interviewed hundreds of New Yorkers who have devoted their time and energy to preserving the wilder side of the city's environment. They graciously shared their knowledge with us, and without them—wildlife biologists, environmental advocates, park rangers, and naturalists—this book could never have been written. In particular, we would like to thank Don Riepe, Chief of Resource Management at the Gateway National Recreation Area, and Michael Feller, Chief Naturalist at the

Natural Resources Group for the Department of Parks and Recreation. Their color photographs, all taken within New York City, enrich this book beyond words.

We would also like to thank the following individuals and organizations for contributing their insights:

David Taft, Robert Cook, and Mary Hake of the National Parks Service; Andrew Greller, Queens College; David Burg, Marcia Fowle, Peter Mott, and Norman Stotz of the New York City Audubon Society; Christopher Letts, John Waldman, and Nancy Steinberg of the Hudson River Foundation; Paul Sieswerda, New York Aquarium for Wildlife Conservation; C. Lavett Smith, Joe Peters, and Sidney Horenstein of the American Museum of Natural History; Ron and Jean Bourque, GRAMP; Melissa Ennen and Joe Fodor, *Brooklyn Bridge* magazine; Reg Gale and Martha Miles, *New York Newsday*; Steven Clemants and Lori Dugan-Gold, the Brooklyn Botanic Garden; Captain Joseph Shastay Jr., New York Harbor Sportfishing; Jenny Worsnopp, Lynn Darsh, and John Marshall of the Amateur Astronomers Association of New York; Mark Kramer, Meteorological Evaluation Services; Nicholas Coch, Queens College; Gary Conte, National Weather Service; Robert Grumet; Charles A. Baskerville, U.S. Geological Survey; Chris Nadareski, Scott Chessman, Eileen Schnock, Mike Greenberg, Thomas Brosnan, and Marie O'Shea of the New York City Department of Environmental Protection; Cathy Drew, the River Project; Stephen V. DeSimone of DeSimone, Chaplin and Dobryn Consulting Engineers; Charles Merguerian, Hofstra University; John Sanders, New York Academy of Sciences; John Puffer, Rutgers University; Neil Tyson, the Hayden Planetarium; John Bender; Deborah Kirschner, Marianne Kramer, and Neal Calvanese of the Central Park Conservancy; Tupper Thomas, Ed Toth, Barbara McTiernan, and Ed Christian of the Prospect Park Alliance; Ed Johnson and Ray Matarazzo, Staten Island Institute of Arts and Sciences; Richard Lynch; Sam Sadove and Kim Durham, Okeanos Ocean Research Foundation; Micky and Barbara Cohen, Bayswater State Park; Jack Cashman; Richard Rosenbloom; Robert Schmidt, Simon's Rock College; Tom Burke, Rare Bird Alert;

Barbara Toborg, the American Littoral Society; Chip Taylor, University of Kansas, Monarch Watch Project; Guy Tudor, the New York City Butterfly Club; Dick Buegler, the Protectors of the Pine Oak Woods; Bob Zaremba, the Nature Conservancy; Josephine A'mato and William Hansen; Paul Kerlinger; Steve Walter; Vivian Sokol; Sharon Freedman; Sammy Chevalier; Hanna and Artie Richard; Andrew Stone, the Trust for Public Land; Steven Garber, the Port Authority of New York and New Jersey; Mike Greenman, New York City Department of General Services; Gary Lincoff, New York Mycological Society; Robert Bartolomei, Wayne Cahilly, Robert Cardeiro, Karl Lauby, Nancy Ross, and Wayt Thomas of the New York Botanical Garden; Karl Anderson, Naomi Dicker, and Patrick L. Cooney of the Torrey Botanical Society; Randy Dupree, New York City Department of Health; Betty Farber, the Liberty Science Center; Les Sirkin; Arthur Johnsen and James Peek, New York Department of Environmental Conservation; Alan Benimoff, College of Staten Island; Mari Muki; Judy Sklar; South Street Seaport Museum; Nancy Wolf, Environmental Action Coalition; Joe Vietri, the Army Corps of Engineers; Bill Fink, Battery Park City Parks Corp.; John Behler, Michael Klemens and Ed Spevak of the New York Zoological Society; David Nowak, USDA Forest Service; Allen Salzberg, New York Turtle & Tortoise Society; Joe Cunningham; the "Outings Party" Crew; Alexis Rockman, Mark Dion and Bob Braine; Daniel Hack; Laura Nash; Susan Weiner; Gregory and Natasha Crewdson; Cathy and Liebes Clarke, Julie Rose, Karen Bender, Cameron McWhirter; Paul, Gabrielle, and Stella Mittelbach; Sam and Julie Rubin; John McGreivey, Richard Sandman, John Denaro, John Porter, Kevin Saumell, Anabel Ressner; the staff of the New York Department of Environmental Conservation Division of Marine Resources; Chris Simon, University of Connecticut; Peter Hearn and Lenny Speregen, Pan Aqua Diving; Klaus Jacob and John Armbruster, Lamont-Doherty Earth Observatory of Columbia University; Bill Evans and Martha Fischer, Cornell University Laboratory of Ornithology; the Brooklyn Public Library; the New York Public Library; Jack and Lois Baird, Friends of Blue Heron Park; Edward DeFreitas, Empire Pest Control; and Mark McDonnell, Bartlett Arboretum.

We would especially like to thank the staff of the New York City Department of Parks and Recreation, including Commissioner Henry Stern, David Kunstler, Parke Spencer, Marc Matsil, Todd Miller, Carl Alderson, Jane Schachat, Josephine Scalia, Fiona Watt, Tony Emmerich, Kathy Nutt, Ricardo Hinkle, Ron Zych and Marc Maratea. The assistance of the Park's Department's Natural Resources Group and the Urban Park Rangers was invaluable.

Finally, we want to thank Peter N. Nevraumont and Ann J. Perrini of the Nevraumont Publishing Company for believing in this project from the very beginning; Peter St. John Ginna at Crown Publishers for putting his faith in *Wild New York*, Allison Arieff at Crown for her thoughtful comments on our first draft; Patricia Wynne for her original illustrations; Stephanie Hiebert for copyediting the final manuscript; Mark Stein for his wonderful cartography; and Jaye Zimet for her elegant design.

Chapter 1

PLANET NEW YORK

New York City is the center of the universe. True or false? Any poll would reveal that most New Yorkers agree with this statement, and in many ways they're right. New York is a (if not the) global center for art, fashion, publishing, advertising, news, theater, and finance.

From a geographic standpoint, however, New York City is just another point on the grid, at 40 degrees and 47 seconds north of the equator and 73 degrees and 58 seconds west of the prime meridian. New York City is built on a series of islands, perched on the rim of the Atlantic Ocean. A dot on the planet where the sun rises each day and goes down each night.

The fact that New York is part of Earth—subject to climate, the motions of the heavens, and even earthquakes—often goes unremarked. Few city residents awake to see the sunrise. Almost no one notices the daily rise and fall of the tides on the Hudson River. And the weather—hot or cold, stormy or clear—is viewed askance, not as a meteorological phenomenon, but as a hindrance to the morning commute.

Though New Yorkers convince themselves that the city is too fast paced to bother with such trivia, most people have no idea how fast paced things really are. Every day, New Yorkers travel 19,176 miles as they whirl around Earth's axis, and every year the city travels 584 million miles around the sun. Even now, New York City is hurtling through space at a rate of 66,600 miles per hour.

LOCATION, LOCATION, LOCATION

Looking up at the World Trade Center—the embodiment of the city's financial power—it's hard to believe that New York City was ever exploited for its natural resources. But it's true. The residents of the five boroughs once lived off the land. Less than 400 years ago, roughly 1,000 Native Americans who spoke Munsee, a dialect of the Delaware language, lived rather bucolic lives here. They fished in the Hudson River, ate oysters from the harbor, hunted ducks on Jamaica Bay, and made dug-out canoes from the tall, native tulip trees.

In 1609, however, the area's natural attractions drew outside interests. When the explorer Henry Hudson first sailed up the river that now bears his name, he was looking for the fabled Northwest Passage. Instead, his attention was captured by a fashion detail. While the people at the river's mouth (in what is now the financial district) wore deerskin clothing, the tribes farther upriver wore beaver pelts. In Europe, beaver skins were an expensive luxury item. Yet Hudson and his crew could buy these furs from the Native Americans for just a few trinkets.

The beaver—whose fur was popular for making coat linings, muffs, and broad-brimmed hats during the seventeenth century—is what gave New York City its start. Although Hudson never personally profited (he was set adrift by mutineers in 1611 and never seen again), within just a few years of his visit, hundreds of fur traders were paddling up and down the Hudson River, and Lower Manhattan had become their premier trading post.

Why set up shop in Manhattan? Why not Atlantic City? Fire Island? Poughkeepsie? It turned out that Lower Manhattan had one natural resource even more valuable than beavers—its location. On the edge of the Atlantic Ocean and at the mouth of the Hudson River, New

---

Wild Fact

BEAVER TALE

When New York City was first permanently settled by the Dutch in 1626, beaver furs were its chief commodity and export. That year, 7,246 beaver pelts were shipped back to the Netherlands, and by 1671, 80,000 furs were being exported annually. Eventually, beavers were even used as money in New Amsterdam, with one beaver valued at 16 Dutch guilders.

Though beavers no longer make their home in New York City, it is a tribute to their early fame that there is still a Beaver Street in Manhattan, just one block south of the New York Stock Exchange. It is also fitting that this toothy creature—the largest rodent in North America—is and always has been pictured on the official seal of the city of New York.

York City had one of the best natural harbors in the world. In size—17 miles from the tip of the Battery to the open waters of the Atlantic—it was as large as the ports of London, Liverpool, and Amsterdam combined. It was deep and easily navigable. And its waters were calm, shielded against gales and fog by the arms of the Rockaway Peninsula, Sandy Hook, and the Verrazano Narrows. In addition, via the Hudson River, the harbor offered direct access to the hinterland. In an era when water travel was the only way to go, Lower Manhattan was supremely situated for commerce.

Even after the Northeast's beavers had all been hunted, the preeminence of the harbor continued to fuel the city's growth. In 1678, 18 vessels were reported registered at the port of New York. By 1741, this number had grown to 530, and by 1883 to 20,000. By 1930, New York was the world's busiest port, and at least one ship arrived or departed every 10 minutes. All this traffic had a dramatic effect on the city and the nation. During the nineteenth century, more than 60 percent of the country's imports came through the port of New York. And between 1820 and 1920, 23 million new immigrants arrived by boat and entered the United States through New York Harbor.

> ### *Wild Fact*
>
> ### THE VIEW FROM VERRAZANO
>
> *At the end of a hundred leagues we found a very agreeable location situated within two prominent hills, in the midst of which flowed to the sea a very great river, which was deep at the mouth.*
>
> This is what Giovanni da Verrazano, the explorer who beat Henry Hudson to the Hudson River by 85 years, had to say when he discovered the narrow entrance to the upper harbor, never imagining that one day a 4,260-foot-long suspension bridge bearing his name (with a $7 toll) would span the "two prominent hills"—now known as Brooklyn and Staten Island.

HEAVENLY BODIES

If the city's skies were entirely dark, about 2,000 stars would be visible to the naked eye. But such a complete view of the heavens has been visible only once in recent years—during the New York City blackout in the summer of 1977. While some New Yorkers used this massive snuffing of the lights as an opportunity for looting and arson, a handful of astronomy buffs climbed to their rooftops to observe such usually obscure stellar phenomena as the Milky Way and the signs of the zodiac.

On average nights, New York City isn't the world's best place for stargazing. The glittering skyline and bright street lamps create so much light pollution that they tend to outshine the stars. But that doesn't mean the stars aren't out there; it just means we're limited to contemplating the heavy hitters—such as the sun, moon, five of the planets (Mercury, Venus, Mars, Jupiter, and Saturn), and about 100 of the most luminous stars.

Located 3,100 miles north of the equator, New York is presented with a unique view of the heavens that changes as the night and the year lengthen. (The only other cities that have the same sky show are those that share New York's latitude—40 degrees north—such as Beijing and Madrid.) And while winter may not be the best time of year to be outside, it is—because of the position of the celestial globe—the best season for stargazing.

During the city's colder months, the southeastern sky above the East River presents an array of bright and colorful stars. In winter the brightest star in all the sky—Sirius, the Dog Star—shines on the horizon, flashing dazzlingly as its light slices through Earth's turbulent atmosphere. Above Sirius is the famous constellation Orion, the hunter. Best known for the stellar threesome Orion's Belt, Orion is also home to the red supergiant Betelgeuse, which marks Orion's left shoulder, and the blue giant Rigel, which marks the hunter's right knee.

Although most stars in the sky look pretty much the same to the naked eye, Betelgeuse and Rigel offer something to ponder. The seventh brightest star in the sky, Betelgeuse is tremendously far away (1.8 quadrillion miles) and enormous beyond our comprehension, larger in diameter than the orbit of Venus around the sun. Yet, because it is an old star, and dying, Betelgeuse glows a tepid reddish orange that can be observed even from New York City.

By contrast, Rigel—the fifth brightest star in the New York sky—is three times farther away from Earth than Betelgeuse, yet even brighter than the red giant. Why? Because Rigel is young and hot and huge. One hundred times larger than the sun, Rigel burns twice as hot, at a temperature of about 18,000°F. This hyperhot glow is what gives Rigel its striking blue light in the winter sky.

In summertime, thanks to the tilt of Earth on its axis, the city is treated to a completely different view of the heavens. High overhead, three bright stars—Vega, Altair, and Deneb—form the Summer Triangle. Less than 30 light-years away, Vega and Altair are relatively close neighbors, and the third and eighth brightest stars, respectively, in the city sky. Meanwhile, Deneb—the third member of the trio and the 13th brightest star—is 1,800 light-years away, meaning that the starlight that reaches us from Deneb started its journey during the height of the Roman Empire. One of the most distant of all stars visible to the naked eye, Deneb is so bright because it is a supergiant like Rigel. According to astronomers, if Deneb were as close to Earth as Vega and Altair are, it would appear 10,000 times brighter than it does now.

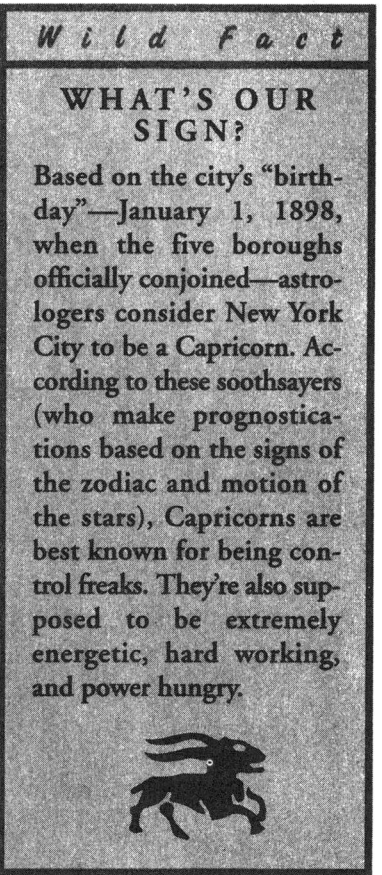

Wild Fact

WHAT'S OUR SIGN?

Based on the city's "birthday"—January 1, 1898, when the five boroughs officially conjoined—astrologers consider New York City to be a Capricorn. According to these soothsayers (who make prognostications based on the signs of the zodiac and motion of the stars), Capricorns are best known for being control freaks. They're also supposed to be extremely energetic, hard working, and power hungry.

LOCAL COLOR

Some people travel thousands of miles to see beautiful sunsets—to Key West or the California coast. However, the waterways along New York City's edge offer some stunning light shows of their own. On clear days with light, wispy clouds high above New York Harbor, the sunset tints the entire western sky in luminous pale pinks and oranges.

What gives our sunsets such delicate colors? As the sun approaches the horizon, sunlight shines sideways through the troposphere—the thickest layer of Earth's atmosphere—bouncing off particles in the air. These particles—whether droplets of moisture, pollution, or even dust blown here from the Sahara Desert—reflect red, yellow, and orange light. In one extreme example, when Mount Pinatubo erupted in the Philippines in 1991, the volcano spewed particles into the atmosphere, causing unusually red sunsets in New York City for more than a year.

To find the city's best sunsets, atmospheric scientists recommend visiting any place with a good view to the west, preferably overlooking the Hudson River or New York Harbor. Some of the best views can be seen from the observation deck on the 102nd floor of the Empire State Building, the Promenade along the East River in Brooklyn Heights, the Battery Park City Esplanade with a view of the Statue of Liberty, the lower promenade in Riverside Park, and the Brooklyn-bound drive along the Brooklyn-Queens Expressway, where you can see the sunset reflected off the glass towers of the New York City skyline.

Where can all these heavenly bodies best be viewed? Local astronomers recommend climbing to rooftops above the street lights, or heading for one of the city's less light-polluted areas, such as Central Park in Manhattan, Floyd Bennett Field in Brooklyn, and Great Kills Park on Staten Island. On clear nights, New York City's sky can be surprisingly awe inspiring.

"When you look at the sky, you see yourself as being a small person on a very large planet that's spinning in space," says Lynn Darsh, president of the Amateur Astronomers Association of New York. "That's a perspective that we normally don't have, because we're focused more on looking down at the sidewalk than up at the stars."

WEATHER AND CLIMATE

New York is one of those places where talking about the weather is more than just chitchat. Storms can tear the city's beaches apart. Heavy snowfall can shut the city down. And the hot, humid summers can tax human patience to the limit. Even good weather is something to talk about—since it's often so fleeting.

How do you explain such a contrary climate? Although New York technically has four seasons, it seems to be dominated by two: broiling, almost tropical summers, and cold, unpredictable winters. In between, the city celebrates a brief spring and a blessedly lingering fall, often called the city's champagne season because—in comparison to the wilting summers—it feels dry and effervescent.

What happened to the picture-perfect four seasons that the Northeast is famous for? About halfway between the equator and the North Pole, New York City is seemingly positioned to have four seasons of equal duration. But the city's location on the even-temperatured Atlantic Ocean moderates such distinctions. Whereas land temperatures are quickly affected by seasonal change, ocean temperatures respond more slowly. At the end of summer, as the days shorten and the sun provides less heat, the ocean holds on to its warmth, warding off the cold season and prolonging New York City's autumn. By the same token, once it has cooled down in winter, the ocean is loathe to warm up again. That's why spring in the city is slow in coming and sometimes painfully short. The nearness of the Atlantic also affects the character of the city's two major seasons by saturating the air with moisture. It is because we live in a port city that we experience such sticky summers and raw-feeling winters.

Year to year, and even day to day, however, the weather is always changing. New York City is on the track of almost every major weather system in North America. We are blasted by frigid winter air from Canada, struck by coastal storms from North Carolina, parched by heat waves from the Midwest, and even bombarded by hurricanes that start off of the coast of Africa.

To top things off, the city has the audacity to make its own weather. If you look at an infrared satellite picture of the Northeast—particularly at night—New York City shows up as a "heat island," as much as 20°F hotter than the surrounding suburbs. The pavement, concrete, asphalt, and metal of the city center trap solar radiation faster than

---

Wild Fact

HOT TOWN

New York City's hottest day ever was July 9, 1936, when the official temperature was 106°F and the unofficial temperature—recorded in Times Square—reached 115°F in the shade. By late afternoon, midtown's busy shopping streets were so soft that crosswalks became dotted with the heels of women's shoes caught in the asphalt. By nightfall, thousands of people were sleeping in Central Park in an effort to escape the relentless heat. The following day, the newspapers reported that the ovenlike weather had blown in from the drought-parched Great Plains, then experiencing the worst years of the Dust Bowl.

> ### Wild Fact
>
> ### HOW LOW CAN WE GO?
>
> Brought on by a fast-moving cold front called a Canadian Clipper, the most shivery day in New York City was Friday, February 9, 1934, when the city woke up to a temperature of −15°F. By midmorning, local hospitals were jammed with hundreds of schoolchildren suffering from frostbite. During the day, six men were found frozen to death on the street, on subway platforms, and in unheated buildings. Meanwhile, wealthy New Yorkers booked a record number of flights to Florida to escape the subzero weather.

wooded parks and suburbs do and cool off more slowly, radiating a furnacelike heat.

Although this heat island effect can warm things up in winter (even lowering heating bills), in summer it's a nightmare. One August, scientists from Cornell University measured temperatures along Columbus Avenue: While the air temperature was 86°F in Central Park, it was 108°F on the street on the Upper West Side.

A SHOW OF FORCE: NATURE TAKES CONTROL

New Yorkers have been trying to conquer the obstacles imposed by the natural world ever since the city was founded. Engineers have spanned the rivers that divide the city with hundreds of miles of tunnels and bridges; blasted through bedrock, 180 feet deep, to build its subways; and filled in the waters around Manhattan to create more real estate. Still, New York City can't always beat Mother Nature.

SNOWBOUND

Snowfall in the city is erratic and unpredictable, ranging from just a few inches to more than 5 feet in any given winter. One year, New Yorkers may see nothing but a few pathetic snowflakes that melt as soon as they hit the pavement. Then, just when we're lulled into a false sense of security, we get walloped by a snowstorm that shuts the city down.

That's what happened on Sunday, January 7, 1996, when a blizzard—in the form of a huge nor'easter from South Carolina—tracked up the Atlantic seaboard and dumped 20 inches of snow on New York in just 48 hours. At the storm's peak overnight, high winds of 51 miles per hour were recorded at La Guardia Airport, with gusts of 46 miles per hour whipping into Manhattan.

Although the city's self-proclaimed "largest snow-fighting force in the nation" was at the ready—with 200,000 tons of stockpiled rock salt and 1,600 snowplows—it wasn't nearly enough to keep up with the storm. On Monday

WHAT'S NORMAL? NEW YORK CITY WEATHER AVERAGES FROM CENTRAL PARK, 1869–1995

	Average Daily Temp. (°F)		Average Monthly Precipitation (inches)		Average Number of		
	High	Low	Rain	Snow	Rainy or Snowy Days	Partly Cloudy Days	Sunny Days
January	38	25	3.4	7.6	11	9	8
February	40	27	3.3	8.5	10	9	8
March	50	35	4.1	5	11	10	9
April	61	44	4.2	0.9	11	11	8
May	72	54	4.4	Trace	11	12	8
June	80	63	3.7	0	10	12	8
July	85	68	4.4	0	11	13	9
August	84	67	4	0	10	12	9
September	76	60	3.9	0	8	10	11
October	65	50	3.6	Trace	8	10	12
November	54	41	4.5	0.9	9	10	9
December	43	31	3.9	5.5	10	9	9

morning, with the snow still falling heavily, Mayor Rudolph Giuliani declared New York City officially closed. All three major airports, the public schools, the libraries, the U.S. mail, several subway lines, and thousands of businesses were shuttered. Streets were barred to all traffic but emergency vehicles, and normally crowded thoroughfares like Broadway in Manhattan became silent playgrounds for cross-country skiers and pedestrians wandering down the middle of the road.

On a typical January day, such a snowstorm wouldn't stand a chance in New York City. We're too close to the warming influence of the Atlantic Ocean and what weather forecasters call the rain/snow line. Four out of five times, when a winter storm is blanketing inland areas such as Buffalo and Syracuse with the white stuff, the same storm system is pelting the city with slushy, disappointing rain. It takes a raging storm combined with a

Wild Fact

AND THE WINNER IS . . .

For all their bluster, the Great Blizzard of 1888 (21 inches) and the Blizzard of 1996 (20.2 inches) were only the city's second and third largest snowstorms. The biggest snowstorm in New York City's history struck the day after Christmas in 1947, when a "snow cloudburst" dropped 26.4 inches of wet, fluffy snow and covered the city in a white cloak weighing an estimated 99 million tons.

> ## Wild Fact
>
> ### IN LIKE A LION AND OUT WITH A POTHOLE
>
> New York City is the nation's pothole capital, with each spring heralding about 35,000 new potholes. Here's how a pothole is born: During the winter, rain and melting snow seep into cracks in the street and freeze, causing the cracks to expand. When the ice melts, it leaves cavities beneath the street's surface that grow bigger and bigger, thanks to the city's yo-yoing freeze-and-thaw cycles. Then all that's required to turn the city into a cratered obstacle course is for cars and trucks to squash down the top layer of pavement.
>
> Depending on the level of seasonal slush, some pothole years are worse than others. The snowy, rainy winter of 1993–1994 proved to be a record maker: In one 10-day period, the city's Department of Transportation filled 100,000 potholes, including 16 "superpotholes"—some the size of small cars.

powerful cold front—such as a mass of frigid Arctic air dropping down from Canada—to lay Big Snow on New York City. Though such double-threat conditions are rare, they were exactly what caused the Blizzard of 1996.

Normally, New York City gets the most snow in February—an average of 8½ inches—when the nearby Atlantic Ocean reaches its coldest temperatures of the year, about 36°F. These cooler ocean temperatures persist into early spring, so even though the city is receiving more springtime sunshine, storms can still bring a raw mix of either rain or snow. This climatic fickleness makes spring weather the toughest for forecasters to predict.

In fact, the most treacherous snowstorm in the city's history—and one about which entire books have been written—took place just when spring seemed about to dawn. The weather forecast for Monday, March 12, 1888, had predicted fair weather, but unbeknownst to the city's meteorologists—who usually received their data via telegraph and carrier pigeon—a mammoth storm was tracking up the Atlantic coast, sucking in cold air from Canada and dumping record snowfalls over Washington, D.C. When New York City's residents awoke that Monday, they were greeted not by fair weather, but by driving snow and hurricane-force winds—what later came to be known as the Great Blizzard of 1888.

Unaware of the blizzard's true ferocity, many New Yorkers tried to go to their jobs that day. With wind gusts of 70 miles per hour, however, pedestrians were literally knocked off their feet. Horse-drawn trolleys were blown onto their sides. And hundreds of people had to be rescued from the storm's clutches.

The blizzard raged unabated for 40 hours, and by the next day, 21 inches of snow had fallen. The weight of the snow pulled down telegraph lines, and the city was completely cut off from the outside world. In downtown Manhattan, high winds built snowdrifts that reached two stories in height, and Brooklyn's Gravesend neighborhood boasted the biggest snowdrift of all: a 52-foot-tall white behemoth. Many victims were buried alive in these giant drifts. In total, 200 New Yorkers perished, making the Great Blizzard of 1888—in terms of cost to human life—the worst natural disaster in the city's history.

IT CAME FROM THE SEA...

Thanks to a wall of mountains to the west, New York City is somewhat protected from most major storms that track across the northern United States. However, with 578 miles of waterfront, the city is exposed to the full force of the elements along the coast. In fact, most of the city's really severe storms come in from the Atlantic Ocean—in the form of nor'easters in winter and the rare but occasional hurricane in summer.

HURRICANES

Powerful and incredibly destructive, tropical hurricanes have a special place in weather forecasting. Anthropomorphized by the National Weather Service, every hurricane is given a name, and every summer local weather forecasters carefully track their courses on satellite maps as they blast across the Atlantic Ocean. So why are *tropical* hurricanes covered in *local* weather forecasts? Because there is always the possibility that one of these monsters could take a wrong turn and strike New York City.

Born as cloud clusters off Africa's northwest coast, hurricanes pick up internal speed and energy over the warm waters of the Atlantic Ocean's tropical latitudes, and their track depends on the size of a barometric phenomenon called the Bermuda High. If the Bermuda High covers a large area of the Atlantic, hurricanes may track toward the eastern United States.

In recent years, there have been several close calls. Hurricanes Edouard (1996), Bob (1991), Gloria (1985), Belle (1976), Agnes (1972), Donna (1960), Diane (1955), Hazel (1954), and Carol (1954) all either missed hitting the New York metropolitan region head on or had significantly fizzled by the time they reached this area. The Hurricane of 1938, however, was a different story.

Dubbed the Long Island Express (meteorologists weren't on a first-name basis with hurricanes until 1950), the Hurricane of 1938 caused massive damage and more than 600 fatalities throughout the Northeast—making it the fourth deadliest hurricane in U.S. history. On Long Island, entire beach communities were washed away by 30-foot tidal waves. And though New York City proper was only whipped by the hurricane's tail (the eye of the hurricane passed 50 miles to the east), 3,500 city trees were ripped up by their roots, tombstones were blown down at Woodlawn Cemetery, and 200 rowboats from Central Park's lakes had to be dispatched to Queens to rescue people in flooded areas.

The Hurricane of 1938 was particularly devastating because it struck completely without warning, slamming into Long Island just 9 hours after passing North Carolina's Cape Hatteras. Normally, hurricanes travel rather slowly, at about 15 miles per hour, but when a hurricane moves into the cooler waters north of Cape Hatteras, its forward motion speeds up. In fact, the Long Island Express was the fastest-tracking hurricane on record. Pack-

---

Wild Fact

BLOWING IN THE WIND

Many people believe that skyscrapers are designed to sway in the wind so that they won't snap in two when hit by a 100-mile-per-hour gust. In fact, the opposite is true. Skyscrapers are designed *not* to sway; if they lurched in the breeze, as some badly designed buildings do, office workers on the top floors would feel like they were rolling on the high seas and might even suffer from motion sickness.

While New York City's building code requires that all buildings over 30 feet tall be tough enough to withstand wind speeds of at least 80 miles per hour, each building uses a slightly different method to reduce that "swaying sensation." The 60,000-ton steel frame of the Empire State Building is so rigid that it never moves more than half an inch, even in winds of 110 miles per hour; the World Trade Center has shock absorbers built into its structure that reduce wind vibrations; and the 914-foot-tall Citicorp Center has a "tuned" 820,000-pound weight inside its 63rd floor to counter motion caused by the wind.

Hurricane Edouard approaches the East Coast

ing swirling winds of more than 150 miles per hour, it charged northward at the rate of 60 miles per hour. And though hurricanes often dissipate when they hit land, this one smacked Long Island broadside and continued to cut a swath of destruction from Rhode Island all the way to the White Mountains of New Hampshire.

Today, the National Hurricane Center monitors hurricanes via satellite and predicts their potential fallout. According to the center's assessment, New York City is a high-risk area because of its location, hurricane history, and high population density. In a worst-case scenario, meteorologists predict that at the Statue of Liberty, the storm tide (a combination of the normal high tide and extra water piled on by the hurricane) would be 20 feet, more than three times higher than normal. The entire financial district—in fact, everything below Chambers Street in Manhattan—would experience heavy flooding. And communities like the Rockaways in Queens and Seagate in Brooklyn would be completely under water.

Although some meteorologists believe the paths of hurricanes are so narrow that the statistical chances of New York City sustaining a direct hit are slim, others say it is just a matter of time before we get socked by Hurricane Gotham.

Nor'easters

Almost all of New York City's cataclysmic winter weather events—and plenty of just plain irritating ones—have been caused by nor'easters. Every winter, the Atlantic seaboard is battered by about 30 nor'easters, many of which attack New York City's shores with astronomical force.

Here's what a really powerful nor'easter can do: The day the Great Nor'easter of 1992 rained down on the city, the level of the East River rose above the high-water mark, causing waves to wash over the FDR Drive and into the cars of commuters. Train tunnels under the Hudson River were also flooded, and the venerable Steeplechase Pier off Coney Island was swept away like so many matchsticks. At La Guardia Airport, the National Weather Service clocked wind speeds as high as 90 miles per hour.

In terms of the disarray they can cause, hurricanes and nor'easters have a lot in common. But one key difference is that hurricanes are tropical in origin whereas nor'easters are all-American. Nor'easters begin their lives just off the Atlantic coast (usually near Cape Hatteras) when cold air from Canada dips down into the southern United States and clashes with warm air from the Gulf of Mexico. Under certain conditions, the result of this clash is a whirling cyclone up to 1,000 miles in diameter that—when viewed from a weather satellite—looks like a big fluffy comma. Once formed, these storms travel up the coast from the south; however, their winds, circling counterclockwise, actually come from the northeast—thus the name.

Although hurricanes receive more press and can rouse even the most jaded New Yorker, nor'easters are responsible for the city's most famous and destructive storms,

---

Wild Fact

SPLISH, SPLASH
On October 8, 1903, the biggest rainstorm in New York City's history unleashed close to a foot of water in 24 hours, flooding all of Brooklyn and turning the streets of Lower Manhattan into canals. Although New Yorkers thought they had been hit by an overgrown nor'easter, the freak storm was actually a category-1 hurricane. The results were unprecedented: Commuters alighting at ferry terminals on Wall Street had to take rowboats to dry ground. Horses—the most popular means of transportation at the turn of the twentieth century—were awash from the neck down. And in Brooklyn, salesmen poled from door to door on makeshift rafts, selling food to people trapped by the floodwaters.

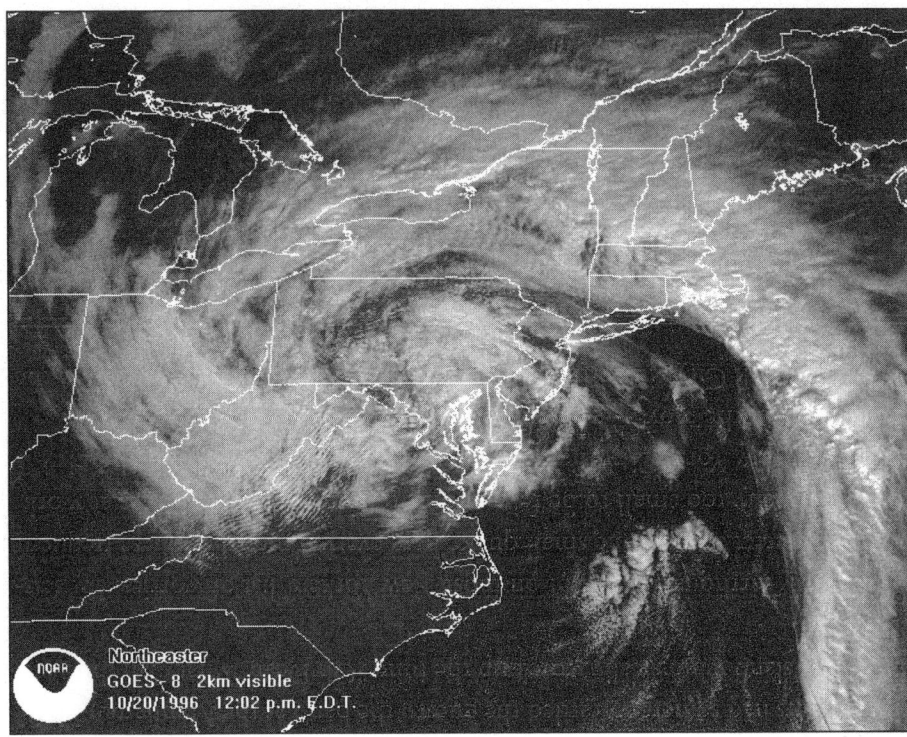

1996 Nor'easter lashes the coast

including the Great Blizzard of 1888, the Snowstorm of 1978, and the Blizzard of 1996. Depending on the temperature, nor'easters are capable of bringing either snow or rain. And both types of precipitation have serious effects.

Typically, nor'easters track slowly up the coast and ram New York City and Long Island with varying levels of ferocity. Because they're so large and travel at such a slow pace, they can last through several high tides. Pounding the city's shorelines over and over again, nor'easters can cause tides up to 5 feet higher than normal and vicious waves that reach 5 to 35 feet in height.

The Nor'easter of 1992 was the most powerful winter storm to hit the New York metropolitan area in 30 years. Because it struck during the highest tides of the month, it caused phenomenal flooding. Areas normally considered to be above the high-tide line found themselves inundated, and seaside communities were completely deluged. At Seagate on Coney Island, the community's seawall collapsed and an entire house was swept into the ocean by repeated hammering. At Broad Channel in Queens, hundreds of parked cars filled to the brim with salt water—and a runaway sailboat plowed into one resident's liv-

Lightning strikes the Empire State Building

ing room. After the storm, New York City and several surrounding communities in Long Island and New Jersey were declared federal disaster areas.

Lightning

According to conventional wisdom, lightning never strikes twice in the same place. Nowhere could this old saw be less true than in New York City. The five boroughs are struck by lightning about 1,400 times a year. And the Empire State Building is one of lightning's most popular targets—its Art Deco spire is zapped nearly 25 times annually.

What makes Gotham and the Empire State Building so attractive? Every year, due to the hot, humid summers, the city is clobbered by about 30 thunderstorms, which bring both torrential rain and the "negative energy" that results in lightning.

Because of friction between rain and ice inside storm clouds, the undersides of thunderheads are charged with negative electrons. When the thunderclouds roll in and cast this negative shadow over the city, positively charged ions attempt to bridge the gap by racing to the surface of the ground and up anything that touches it, from trees to tall buildings. This buildup of positive energy is particularly pronounced at the top of the Empire State Building, where on stormy days, you can literally feel the static in the air.

Since air isn't a very good conductor of electricity, the positively charged skyscraper and the negatively charged clouds remain at a

standoff until the electrical disparity becomes overwhelming. Then, a line of electrons zigzags down from the sky as a stream of ions races up to meet them from the building's pinnacle. This exchange of energy results in a lightning flash that, at 50,000°F, is five times hotter than the surface of the sun. Despite repeated hits, the Empire State Building easily dissipates all this electrical energy, conducting it harmlessly through the building's steel superstructure and into the ground—just like a lightning rod.

When the Empire State Building was first built, its talent for being struck by lightning immediately caught the eye of researchers who were trying to learn more about lightning so that they could prevent it from causing so many power outages. (In the early days of electricity, power companies were constantly plagued by lightning strikes that sent technicians scurrying to restore proper service.) In the early 1930s, General Electric dispatched a scientific team to observe, measure, and photograph lightning at the Empire State Building. In addition to taking over the top floor—where equipment for TV antennas is now housed—the lightning researchers set up a special camera on top of a Fifth Avenue building eight blocks away. Their photographs were among the first to show that lightning does not strike from cloud to ground—like the proverbial bolt from the blue—but results from repeated surges from both above and below that meet in the middle.

They also learned about a related phenomenon: On a particularly "charged" day, one lightning researcher stuck his arm out a window near the top of the Empire State Building. His hand glowed an eery electric blue—what sailors call Saint Elmo's fire—and he experienced a slight sensation as a small amount of current flowed from his hand. Even today, people claim that static-electricity buildup is so strong at the top of the building that when lovers kiss on the observation deck, they sometimes experience an extra "spark."

Despite the advances lightning researchers have made and the effective protection of lightning rods, lightning arrestors, and surge protectors, the powerful zap of lightning can still short-circuit telephones and computers—even the

> ### Wild Fact
> **SUDDEN DEATH**
> On July 10, 1988, thunderclouds rolled over Brooklyn's Prospect Park. As the rain began to fall and hundreds of people raced for shelter, a blinding blue flash lit the sky, accompanied by what sounded like a bomb going off. Afterward, underneath a tall oak on the edge of the park's Long Meadow, 12 people lay prostrate, their clothes smouldering, and one of them, a 38-year-old man, was dead. Today, the oak tree under which they were sheltering still stands; a black scar on its trunk is the only evidence that it was ever struck by lightning.

entire city. In July 1977, Con Edison's chairman had just announced that the power company was easily handling peak demand in the middle of a heat wave when suddenly everything went dark. A series of lightning strikes in Westchester County had cut off six major power lines, causing a chain reaction that resulted in the infamous New York City blackout. During the 25 hours it took Con Edison workers to turn the lights back on, 2,000 stores were looted and more than 3,000 people were arrested.

Earthquakes

On August 10, 1884, New York City was rocked by a strange sensation. A strong tremor caused chandeliers to sway, cracks to form in brick buildings, and a large stone to fall from the steeple of a church in Brooklyn's Park Slope. At first, people thought the rumbling and vibrations were caused by a giant explosion—but tourists visiting from California knew better. It was an earthquake, calculated by today's seismologists to rank a 5 on the Richter scale, and its epicenter was in New York Harbor just off the coast of Coney Island.

The following day the *New York Times* reported the consequences. The Egyptian obelisk in Central Park had trembled—but stood. Diners on Coney Island had leapt from restaurant windows—and landed safely on the sand. Describing the quake on its front page as "muffled thunder in the bowels of the Earth," the *Times* went on to say that, "Men stopped suddenly and listened with fear to the deep grumbling beneath them, and stood transfixed for what seemed at least 5 minutes to the more timid." Actually, the quake lasted only 10 seconds. There was little material damage, and besides speculating about the cause of the quake (one self-proclaimed scientist thought it might have been caused by a meteor), New Yorkers quickly forgot about it. In fact, only a few moments after tremors had so fiercely rattled the guests, the band at the Manhattan Hotel on Coney Island whimsically struck up the tune "Oh Dear, What Can the Matter Be?"

Today earthquakes are not on most New Yorkers' list of worries. Yet seismologists detect at least one small quake here every 2 months. These frequent shakes—usually too small to be felt—point to larger geologic forces at work. Although New York City may not have any active fault lines, the city is nonetheless on the move—geologically speaking.

New York City sits in the middle of a section of Earth's crust called the

North American plate, which is currently traveling southwest at an average rate of just under an inch per year. Most of the stress of travel is released in California and along the Pacific Rim, where the North American plate collides with the Pacific plate. But every now and then, tension builds up en route, and the result is an eastern earthquake.

Unlike quakes in California, where the evidence of faults can be seen on the surface, eastern quakes occur deep underground. In addition, because the East's ancient bedrock is largely unbroken by faults and there is no outlet for stress, the reverberations from a quake's epicenter can dissipate over vast distances. In 1884, shockwaves emanating from New York Harbor were felt in places as far away as Maine and Ohio.

On the basis of historical accounts, seismologists estimate that such magnitude-5 quakes hit the city about once every 100 years, which means we're currently overdue. They further speculate that a magnitude-6 earthquake (the strongest quake thought possible here—though none has ever been recorded) may occur every 800 years. What would happen if New York City underwent such an unexpected shake-up? According to scientists, such a quake would leap to first place as the city's worst disaster in history.

A 1993 study, conducted by seismologists from California, painted an apocalyptic picture of a powerful magnitude-6 earthquake wreaking havoc on tunnels, gas lines, water mains, and older residential buildings. Subway and car tunnels, such as the Holland Tunnel, were labeled especially vulnerable because they often pass from zones of solid bedrock into silt. Such transition zones are like human-made fault lines and could fracture like matchsticks if shockwaves were strong enough. Waterfront neighborhoods built atop landfill, such as Battery Park City on the edge of Manhattan and Howard Beach in Queens, would also be particularly at risk. The wet, loosely packed ground underlying these communities could shake like jello during a magnitude-6 quake and perhaps even liquefy and completely give way. In the same analysis, the city's old brownstones and brick apartments were identified as liabilities; brittle and without structural reinforcement, they are more likely to collapse than to roll with the shocks.

Seismologists and engineers agree that the safest place during such an event would be inside Manhattan's modern high-rises, whose foundations rest on solid bedrock and whose structures are designed to withstand high winds.

Suspension bridges would probably also fare well. During the 1884 earthquake, trolley riders crossing the newly opened Brooklyn Bridge noticed no more shaking than usual.

What is the probability that New York will be hit by a Big Five or even a Big Six? Scientists cannot predict earthquakes very well even in earthquake-prone areas, but eastern quakes are doubly mysterious. Since they begin far underground and happen less frequently, they are difficult to study and, as a consequence, less well understood than quakes occurring along major fault zones. Still, many scientists predict that a large quake is inevitable at some point in the East. Where and when it will strike, however, is anybody's guess.

CHAPTER 2

THE ANCIENT APPLE

PRIMORDIAL MOUNTAINS AND SEAS

New York City is pretty old. Grand Central Station was built in 1913, Central Park was laid out in 1858, and St. Paul's Chapel—Manhattan's oldest surviving building—was erected in 1766, before the American Revolution. But the city's rocky sub-architecture, the bedrock on which New York City stands, is *profoundly* old—older than the Rocky Mountains or the walls of the Grand Canyon. And because of its age, New York City's geology is mind-bogglingly complex—tracing the history of the planet and bearing the imprints of continental collisions, long-dead mountains, and forgotten seas.

Geologically speaking, the city's history goes back hundreds of millions of years and is rooted in the vagaries of continental drift. Though we normally don't think of rocks, mountains, and continents as plastic or mutable, in fact Earth's landforms are constantly changing. Resting on a layer of superhot magma, the surface of Earth consists of about 16 crustal plates that are perpetually traveling around the planet. Colliding plates push up mountain ranges like the Himalayas. Separating plates form enormous troughs where oceans form. And things that we think of as permanent, such as bedrock and boulders, are melted or even vaporized as they're pushed into Earth's belly.

GET MY DRIFT?

460 million years ago

360 million years ago

120 million years ago

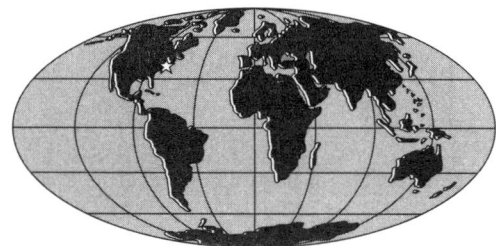

current

☆ = New York City area

© 1997, Mark Stein Studios

At present, New York City rests on the middle of the North American plate, a section of Earth's crust that takes in the North American continent, as well as about half of the Atlantic Ocean's floor. At the rate of about one inch per year, the entire North American plate is moving away from the Eurasian plate. Geologists believe that this slow-motion separation occurs because a line of undersea volcanoes at the center of the Atlantic Ocean (known as the Mid-Atlantic Ridge) is continuously spewing forth newly formed ocean crust and effectively driving the plates apart.

The city's foundation, however, was laid when things were moving in the opposite direction. At least twice in the history of the planet, the continents have merged together, forcing up mountain ranges and closing the oceans that separate them. For New York City, the most significant of these continental mergers began 550 million years ago. At that time, only a sliver of the city's bedrock existed; the entire edge of the old North American continent was flooded by a shallow, tropical sea; and an arc of volcanic islands—like the islands of Japan—was steadily being shoved toward the east coast of North America.

As the continents moved inexorably together (ultimately forming the supercontinent Pangea), the land on which the city now stands began to buckle and bend. Limestone, clay, mud, and ocean crust that lay buried offshore were cooked and recrystallized. Layers of rock were folded over each other—like so much origami—and forced upward into mountains, their peaks reaching as high as the tops of the Alps.

The assembly of this supercontinent

Wild Fact

SCENIC PROPERTY

When Pangea finally broke up 220 million years ago and the continents slowly began drifting apart, the pain of separation caused huge rifts in Earth's interior. Locally—on what's now the western bank of the Hudson River—molten magma jetted horizontally between two layers of red sandstone, and when the magma cooled, it contracted and formed giant, six-sided pillars of a black rock called diabase. Over the millennia, the sandstone on top of the diabase eroded away and these pillars of stone became visible as the New Jersey Palisades.

Today, the Palisades extend 40 miles, from New York Harbor to Haverstraw in Rockland County. At times, they rise as high as 500 feet above the Hudson River, forming an astounding precipice that is visible from northern Manhattan to Storm King Mountain.

WALK THE LINE

Looking at the eastern edge of South America and the western edge of Africa on a map, it appears that they could fit neatly together like two pieces of a jigsaw puzzle. In fact, 320 million years ago, the world's continents *were* joined together. Africa snuggled up against both North and South America, and this "supercontinent" was called Pangea. How do we know about the forces that shaped the world so long ago? Some of the evidence is right here—buried under New York City.

In 1986, 600 feet beneath the bed of the East River in the excavation for a new water supply system, miners found the Holy Grail of New York City geology. Buried in the dark beneath a mountain of solid stone was a 30- to 50-meter-wide band of smashed and fractured rock—what geologists believe is the suture point between the ancient continents of North America and Africa.

Known as Cameron's Line, this eons-old fault has been discovered traveling through western Massachusetts and Connecticut, into New York City down the bed of the Bronx River, underneath Roosevelt Island in the East River, and skirting the shoreline of western Queens. Often disappearing beneath hundreds of feet of undulating and heavily folded layers of bedrock, Cameron's Line marks the point of first contact, the epicenter of the worldwide smashup that pasted most of New England onto the North American continent—not to mention laying the foundations for Manhattan, the eastern Bronx, and Staten Island.

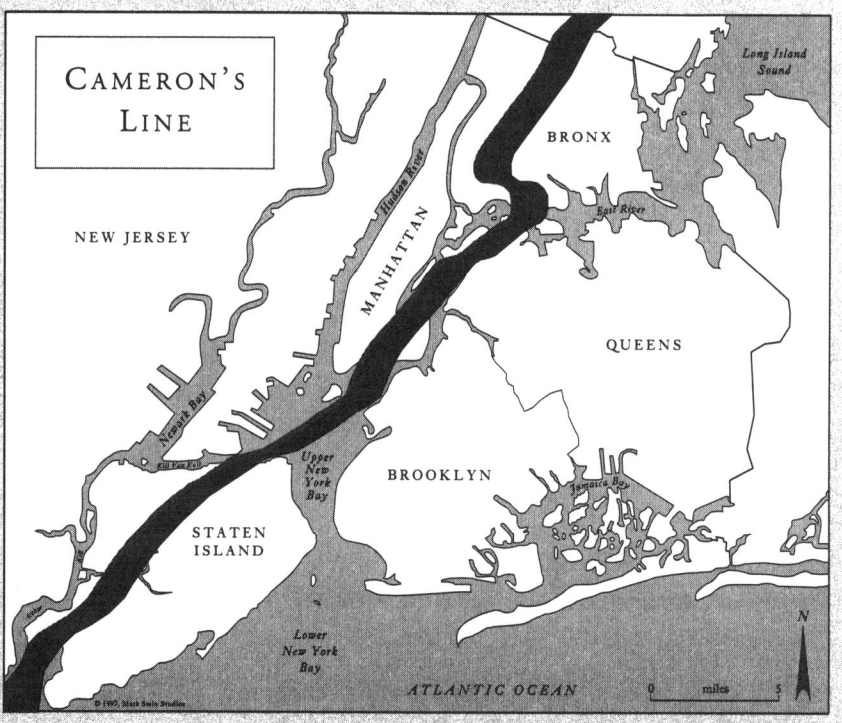

took an almost incomprehensible span of time—230 million years—during which the colliding continents formed and re-formed the landscape. First, the volcanic island arc smashed against the East Coast 450 million years ago; then a micro-continent called Avalon collided with New England 400 million years ago; and finally, northwest Africa itself ground up against the eastern edge of North America 320 million years ago. Each time, new mountain ranges were forced up—the Taconic Mountains, the Appalachians, and the Alleghenies—and what is now the city's bedrock was forged and re-forged, formed and deformed.

When the supercontinent was fully assembled, New York City was part of a mountain range that stretched from Newfoundland to Alabama. For a brief blip in geologic time, the land on which New York City stands soared thousands of feet above sea level, presenting a landscape of barren, rocky peaks.

Time, however, has a habit of moving mountains. About 220 million years ago, the motion of Earth's crustal plates reversed, and the continents started separating again, causing tremendous rifting, earthquakes, and volcanic eruptions; the Atlantic Ocean filled up again; and what's now New York City began drifting from its location in the subequatorial tropics to its current spot in the temperate latitudes of the north.

Through all these eons, the city's summits were slowly worn down—eroded by storms, pounded by waves from advancing seas, and ground down by glaciers during succeeding ice ages. Their legacy, however, remains. Today, the city's bedrock and the occasional mounds of stone that can be seen poking to the surface—in places like Central Park, northern Manhattan, and the Bronx—are, in fact, the well-worn shoulders of the city's ancient mountains.

HOT ROCKS

New York City's geology is maddeningly convoluted—like a three-dimensional puzzle with countless missing pieces. If you could look at a cutaway of subterranean New York—beneath the subway tunnels, gas lines, telephone wires, and water mains—you would see different layers of solid bedrock scrunched around each other like crumpled cloth. Out of this tangled mountain of stone, five different types of bedrock emerge. All five strata are inexpressibly ancient, all five formed as a result of continental collisions, and all five are metamorphic, meaning that they started out as one kind of rock but were cooked, pressurized, and so badly twisted that—without entirely melting—they were forced to take on whole new personalities.

Together, they assemble the base on which New York stands.

Fordham Gneiss

FORDHAM GNEISS

The city's oldest rock, Fordham gneiss (pronounced "nice"), dates back 1.1 billion years to something called the Grenville Orogeny—a continental collision so old that geologists have not dared theorize much about it. All they know is that before any life besides algae and bacteria existed on Earth, an unknown land mass bashed into what is now North America, burying sandstone on the edge of the continent under a mountain of intruding rock. Fifteen miles below the surface, at temperatures of 1,300°F, this sandstone was forged into Fordham gneiss, a banded black-and-white rock of enduring capabilities.

Though most of the primeval rock forged by the Grenville Orogeny is now deeply entombed beneath younger strata in the eastern United States, Fordham gneiss reaches the surface in New York City, where it composes the rocky foundations of the Bronx. Deriving its name from the Bronx's Fordham Heights neighborhood, Fordham gneiss can be seen breaking to the surface in imposing massifs in the Northwest Forest of Van Cortlandt Park, along steep, winding lanes in Riverdale, and emerging from the East River to form the backbone of Roosevelt Island.

MANHATTAN SCHIST

When the world's continents were on a collision course for the second time 450 million years ago, the old continental shelf was squashed like an accordion. Shale, a sedimentary rock made from silt deposited on the ocean floor, was driven and squeezed 9 miles below the surface, where it was superheated to temperatures of 1,100°F. Under this intense heat and pressure, the molecules in the rock reorganized, forming minerals such as quartz, feldspar, hornblende, and biotite (black mica), as

Manhattan Schist

Broadway IRT subway excavation through Inwood marble

well as flecks of silvery muscovite (white mica)—the glittering hallmark of the city's second-oldest bedrock, Manhattan schist.

Today this hard, glittering rock lies buried 100 feet beneath the ground in Lower Manhattan, where it supports the foundation for the twin towers of the World Trade Center. In northern Manhattan it soars to the surface as a ridge of high rock running from West 100th Street through Central, Riverside, Inwood Hill, and Fort Tryon parks on the borough's west side. Manhattan schist also creates the topographic relief for Morningside *Heights*, Hamilton *Heights*, Washington *Heights*, Inwood *Hill*, Sugar *Hill*, and Marcus Garvey Park (formerly known as *Mount* Morris).

Inwood Marble

Like Manhattan schist, Inwood marble is a child of the continental collision that took place 450 million years ago. Once a bed of limestone in the shallow waters off the city's ancient coast, it was cooked during the formation of Pangea and rehabilitated as this sugary, white marble. Though rarely seen on the surface, Inwood marble is the city's most attractive bedrock, and miners blasting underground tunnels beneath Manhattan have reported bursting through oppressively dark layers of Manhattan schist into blinding white chambers of Inwood marble—a stunning scene.

Marble is so elusive on the surface of the city because it is easily eroded. Unlike schist and gneiss, Inwood marble—named for the northern Manhattan neighborhood in which it appears—is a soft rock. In fact, the erosion of large veins of soft marble—now resting at the bottom of the Hudson, Harlem, and East rivers—is responsible for the fact that Manhattan is an island. It also accounts for most of northern Manhattan's variable topography, with Manhattan schist underlying the high ridges and Inwood marble underlying the lowlands of Harlem.

FOSSILS

New York City is not exactly overrun with old bones and fossils. In fact, the city's bedrock is so hard-boiled and metamorphosed that paleontologists have unceremoniously dismissed it as "unfossiliferous." Nonetheless, one soft spot has made up for our unusually recalcitrant rock.

On southwestern Staten Island near Clay Pit Ponds State Park Preserve, hundreds of fossils dating from the Cretaceous period have been discovered in the whitish clay that gives the area its name. Commonly unearthed during construction projects, these 70-million-year-old fossils bear the delicate imprints of leaves from the first flowering plants in the world: ancient magnolia and sassafras trees that are the forebears of every flower we see blooming in spring.

How did these fossils end up here? During the late Cretaceous period (the tail end of the Age of the Dinosaurs), the land along the East Coast was being eroded as rivers carried sand and clay to the shoreline. Leaves from primitive forests were carried along and embedded in the clay, which took perfect imprints. Today, the soft Cretaceous deposits survive—often deeply buried under soil and gravel—in a narrow band cutting across eastern New Jersey, Staten Island, Brooklyn, and Queens. About 300 fossil plant species have been identified in these deposits. And though no dinosaur bones have been uncovered—*yet*—in the five boroughs, just 3 miles away, in Woodbridge, New Jersey, the bones of a pleisiosaurus—a long-necked marine reptile that once swam on the city's coastline—were unearthed in Cretaceous clay.

Staten Island Serpentinite

Normally, when continents collide with ocean basins during continental drift, the heavier ocean crust dives underneath the continent and is recycled into the layer of liquid magma 100 miles below Earth's surface. However, in the case of one New York City rock, Staten Island serpentinite, things didn't work out that way.

When the ancient North American and African continents collided, a few chunks of ocean crust were snapped off by the force of the collision and wedged up *on top* of the continent's edge. Beforehand, these chunks had been metamorphosed by ocean water—heated close to boiling by undersea volcanoes—a process that drew off hard minerals such as magnesium, copper, nickel, and iron. Today, these softened wedges of long-dead ocean basin appear as a discontinuous band of greenish rock known as serpentinite that extends from Alabama all the way to Quebec. In New York City, serpentinite forms the backbone of Staten Island and can be seen looming on either side of the road on the Staten Island Expressway.

Of all the city's rocks, serpentinite is the weirdest. It is composed mainly of lizardite, a rare mineral that gives it its green hue. And unbeknownst to most people, it also contains asbestos. Geologists have found that naturally occurring and potentially cancer-causing asbestos—in the form of fibrous minerals—is abundant in several of Staten Island's outcrops. At one time, these asbestos veins were considered a boon, and in the 1870s a mining operation removed 80 tons of asbestos from the city's serpentinite belt.

Hartland Formation

Probably the most well-known rocks in the city are the outcrops that loom above the lawns in Central Park. These dark mounds are such familiar fixtures of the park's design—wrapping around the Carousel and supporting Belvedere Castle—that it's hard to believe they weren't brought into the park for aesthetic purposes. In fact, these rocky outcrops predate the park by 400 million years and were formed when the first plants and animals were emerging from the sea.

Central Park's famous outcrops are part of the Hartland Formation, the youngest of the city's bedrock types. The Hartland Formation is not a single type of rock, but a group of schists, gneisses, and amphibolites that started out thousands of miles away as seafloor deposits on the rim of the volcanic islands

Hartland Formation in Central Park

that existed during the formation of Pangea. As the old Atlantic Ocean closed, these seafloor deposits were carried along with the island arc and joined to what is now North America, undergoing the same intense metamorphism that characterizes all of New York City's bedrock.

Before the theory of plate tectonics was developed in the late 1960s, the surface bedrock of the eastern Bronx was considered a local mystery and referred to by geologists as being of unknown origin. Meanwhile, the rocks in Central Park were mistakenly labeled as Manhattan schist. Today, both areas have been positively identified as part of the Hartland Formation, and this cooked seabed can be seen jutting to the surface as gneiss in Pelham Bay Park and as schist in Manhattan from Houston Street to 96th Street.

NATURE: THE GREAT ARCHITECT

GEOLOGY AND THE NEW YORK CITY SKYLINE

When archaeologists of the future unearth the city's architecture and skyline of glass-and-metal skyscrapers, New York City will surely be entered into the historical annals as one of the greatest of human achievements—surpassing earlier triumphs such as the Great Pyramids or the Taj Majal. The city's human-created architecture, however, is both limited and shaped by the architecture of nature.

Viewed from New Jersey or Queens, the skyline of Manhattan looks like a glittering steel mountain range with a dip in the middle. Starting at the north end, the office towers of Midtown—of which the Empire State, Citicorp, and Chrysler buildings are the tallest—rise more than 1,200 feet above the East River. Moving south, the "hilltops" become lower, forming a saddle over Greenwich Village, only to rise again as high as 1,350 feet in the downtown financial district, where the twin towers of the World Trade Center define the skyline's highest "peaks."

Why do tall buildings disappear in Greenwich Village? The dip in the skyline closely follows a dip in the bedrock underneath the city. At 34th Street in midtown Manhattan, you would have to dig through a mixture of dirt and gravel 38 feet deep before hitting bedrock; at Chambers Street downtown, the layer of dirt and gravel is about 80 feet deep. In between, however, that layer is much thicker, extending as far as 260 feet below street level in spots. In these areas, it would require too much digging to build the foundations for the soaring, needlelike structures that the city is famous for.

The Empire State Building and the city's other tallest skyscrapers all stand on solid bedrock—Manhattan schist in the financial district and Hartland schist in Midtown (the same rock that pokes to the surface as outcrops in Central Park). Though schist is not considered a particularly hard stone (you can scratch

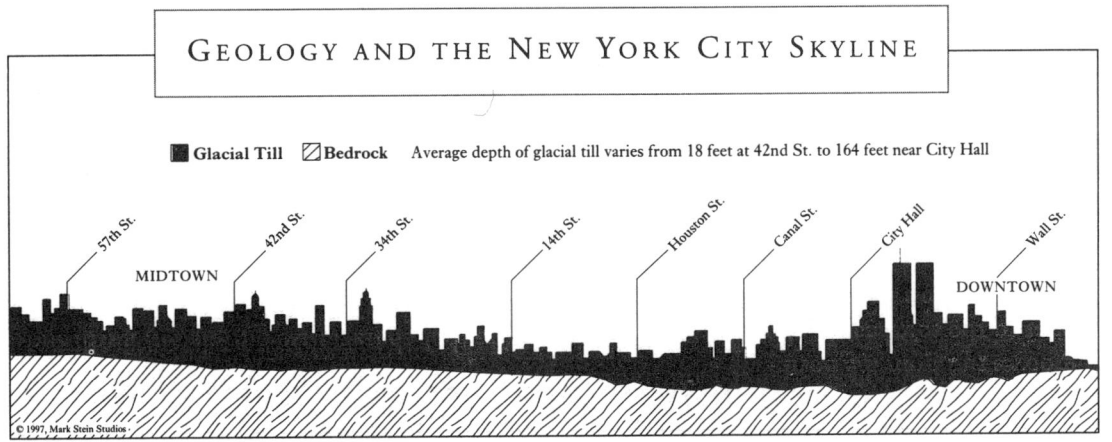

GEOLOGY AND THE NEW YORK CITY SKYLINE

it with a piece of glass), it has tremendous internal strength and can support weights of 160,000 pounds per square foot.

By contrast, the mixture of gravel and broken rock that sits atop the bedrock can support only 4,000 to 12,000 pounds per square foot without giving way. Thus, buildings constructed on this fill-in material have to have their weight spread out and must be designed to be either shorter or squatter in shape.

This squatness of form is particularly apparent in the buildings of the World Financial Center in Battery Park City. Though located downtown, these four hulking glass boxes are built in what used to be part of the Hudson River on landfill taken from the excavation of the neighboring World Trade Center (itself built on bedrock 100 feet below the surface). Whereas the twin towers of the World Trade Center are tall and slender, soaring straight up from Lower Manhattan, the World Financial Center's buildings are chunky—less than half as tall as the twin towers and built on immense bases.

The accessibility of bedrock defines the architectural landscape outside of Manhattan as well. The tallest building in the outer boroughs is the Citicorp Building, which rises 663 feet above an otherwise low-rise landscape in Long Island City. Its foundation rests on the one small section in all of Brooklyn and Queens where bedrock lies close to the surface.

Subterranean Way

During the construction of the transcontinental railroad through the American West, railroad crews built bridges across valleys and used dynamite to blast tunnels through mountains that blocked the railroad's path. Building the New York City subway was not much different. And the work was trickiest during the construction of the 1 subway tracks on Broadway in northern Manhattan. Here, subway engineers faced dramatically varying topography over a relatively short distance—4½ miles from 116th Street in front of Columbia University in Morningside Heights to the northern tip of the island. The solution to avoiding dangerously steep grades and keeping the tracks relatively level was to build a bridge across the valley at 125th Street and to tunnel through solid bedrock in Washington Heights.

A soaring steel viaduct, 52 feet above street level, carries the subway across the plunge of the Manhattanville Valley (a ½-mile-wide "cross-fault" that starts

BURIED TREASURE

Manhattan is internationally famous for its diamond district and rarefied jewelry emporiums, such as Tiffany. Less well known is the fact that the city's own bedrock is unusually rich in mineral crystals and semiprecious gems.

Sometime after the city's bedrock was originally forged, hot, liquid magma jetted into cracks in the rock and slowly solidified there to form veins of light-colored granite that can be seen streaking conspicuously through dark outcrops in Central Park. Today, these coarse-grained bands—known as granite pegmatites—are the city's unofficial mineral mines.

During excavations in Manhattan, thousands of mineral crystals—many of them clear-colored and beautifully faceted—have been rooted out, including hunks of raw silvery mica, elongated black tourmalines, chunks of smoky quartz, gem-quality blue-green aquamarines, and valuable golden beryls. The city's most spectacular mineral find, however, rivals the Hope Diamond in size, if not in value. Unearthed in 1885 on 35th Street near Broadway, the "Subway Garnet" is the size of a cantaloupe and is now in the possession of the American Museum of Natural History. With 20 jewel-like facets, the Subway Garnet weighs in at 9 pounds, 10 ounces, and is valued at about $2,000.

---

at 122nd Street). Then, as the land rises again at 135th Street, the subway disappears into an underground tunnel. From there to about 200th Street, subway builders had to blast through Manhattan's bedrock inch by inch.

This work was perilous—and tremendously exciting. Miners advanced by drilling 8-foot-long holes straight into the bedrock and then packing each hole with explosives. Each blast opened up 8 new feet of subway tunnel and brought down 300 tons of rock. Though other types were encountered along the way, the predominant rock was an uptilted layer of comparatively soft, mica-rich Manhattan schist. Because Manhattan schist is highly foliated—formed in a series of thin sheets—miners said the process of tunneling was like drilling through the pages of a book.

When the miners emerged from the tunnel at the site of the future Dyckman Street station, the land dropped again to form what's known as the Dyckman Street Gap. From there, the 1 train runs as an elevated line—across the bridge over the Harlem River Ship Canal—all the way to its terminus at 242nd Street in the Bronx.

One result of these efforts to keep the subway tracks "on the level" is the

> ### Wild Fact
> #### GROOVY
> Etched into many of the outcrops of bedrock in Central Park are long grooves cutting as deep as 4 inches into the surface of the stone. These furrows record the passage of the ice sheet that pushed into New York City 22,000 years ago. In Central Park, the glacial grooves run from the northwest to the southeast—the same direction the George Washington Bridge and Lincoln Tunnel travel across the Hudson. From these and other clues, geologists believe that the mountain of glacial ice passed through New Jersey before bulldozing New York City.

city's deepest subway station. When passengers get off the **1** train at 191st Street, they are 180 feet underground—beneath 14 stories of solid stone.

THE ICE AGE

Ancient geologic forces created the solid bedrock on which Manhattan's skyline safely rests, but a relatively recent kink in the world's weather is what produced the city's rough outlines. About 28,000 years ago, in one of the many dramatic climate shifts that characterize our planet, Earth suddenly became colder. Instead of melting back each summer, snow near the Arctic ice cap began piling up and ultimately became a mountain range of ice almost 2 miles high. The colossal weight of this icy buildup caused the snowpack at the bottom to solidify, and the ice—rendered plastic—began to flow southward. By the year 20,000 B.C., a 5-

> ### COASTLINE: THE WATERY EDGE
> During the Ice Age, so much of the world's water supply was trapped in icebergs that sea levels were lowered by 330 feet. Thus, much of what is now under water in the vicinity of New York City was then on dry land. Sixteen thousand years ago, mastodons could walk across Long Island Sound from Queens to Connecticut, and they could—and did (paleontologists have recovered their teeth)—walk as far as 12 miles off New York City's shore.
>
> When the ice sheets finally melted, the seas rose and flooded low areas like Long Island Sound, Jamaica Bay, the East River, and the old bed of the Hudson. This explains why 100 miles south of the Statue of Liberty, the seafloor suddenly drops away to form a 3,300-foot-deep trench. Known as the Hudson Canyon, this underwater formation was once the bed of the Hudson River. When sea levels rose, they completely covered the walls of this old gorge.
>
> The post–Ice Age rise in sea level also explains why the present-day Hudson River is flushed by the tides in New York City—the rising Atlantic Ocean has "drowned" or backed up the old riverbed all the way to Albany.

million-square-mile ice sheet covered all of Canada, the Midwest, and New England.

As the ice sheet advanced, it changed the landscape and created many of the nation's most significant landforms. It scratched across the tops of the Adirondack Mountains, leaving gouges in their stony peaks; it carved out the basins of the Great Lakes and New York's Finger Lakes; and it cut the bed of the Hudson River so low that the river is 785 feet deep where it flows past West Point.

When the edge of the ice sheet reached what is now New York City, it was still about 300 feet high—about as tall as the Statue of Liberty. As it advanced across the Bronx and Manhattan, it redefined the city's topography. Carrying rocks and gravel like abrasive sandpaper in its underbelly, the glacier bulldozed away topsoil and polished bedrock. Crossing into the city from New Jersey, it ripped out boulders from the Palisades and dumped them in places like Central Park, where they are now known as erratics. A great leveler, the ice sheet filled in depressions in the landscape—such as the dip in the bedrock between Midtown and downtown—with boulders it had plucked up and ground down to gravel. Then, after all its efforts, the iceberg finally parked itself—right in the middle of New York City.

At its peak, the glacier's leading edge was not exactly on the straight and narrow. It looped and turned from Massachusetts to Montana and left some of its most visible marks on the state of Wisconsin, which is why it is usually referred to as the Wisconsin Ice Sheet. In the New York metro-

> ## Wild Fact
> ### ICE AGE GOLF
> At the same time that the Wisconsin Ice Sheet crept into the United States, the Northern European Ice Sheet was inching its way into Scotland and sculpting the landscape. There, the Ice Age shaped "knob and kettle" topography which—with the perfect combination of hills, water hazards, and sand traps—inspired the invention of golf in the mid-fifteenth century. Such naturally golf-friendly terrain is duplicated in New York, along the terminal moraine that marks the last stop of the Wisconsin Ice Sheet.
>
> Along the length of the moraine—which runs from Staten Island through Brooklyn and Queens out to the tip of Long Island (at Orient Point)—there are no less than 20 golf courses, including Douglaston and Forest Park golf courses in Queens and La Tourette Park Golf Course in Staten Island. Whereas most golf courses have highly artificial topography, these three were landscaped by a natural bulldozer. With an average elevation of 200 feet, Forest Park Golf Course is located right on the ridge of the moraine, and its most challenging section—the "front nine"—is known among golfers for its long rolling hills, stumpy hillocks, and natural water traps.

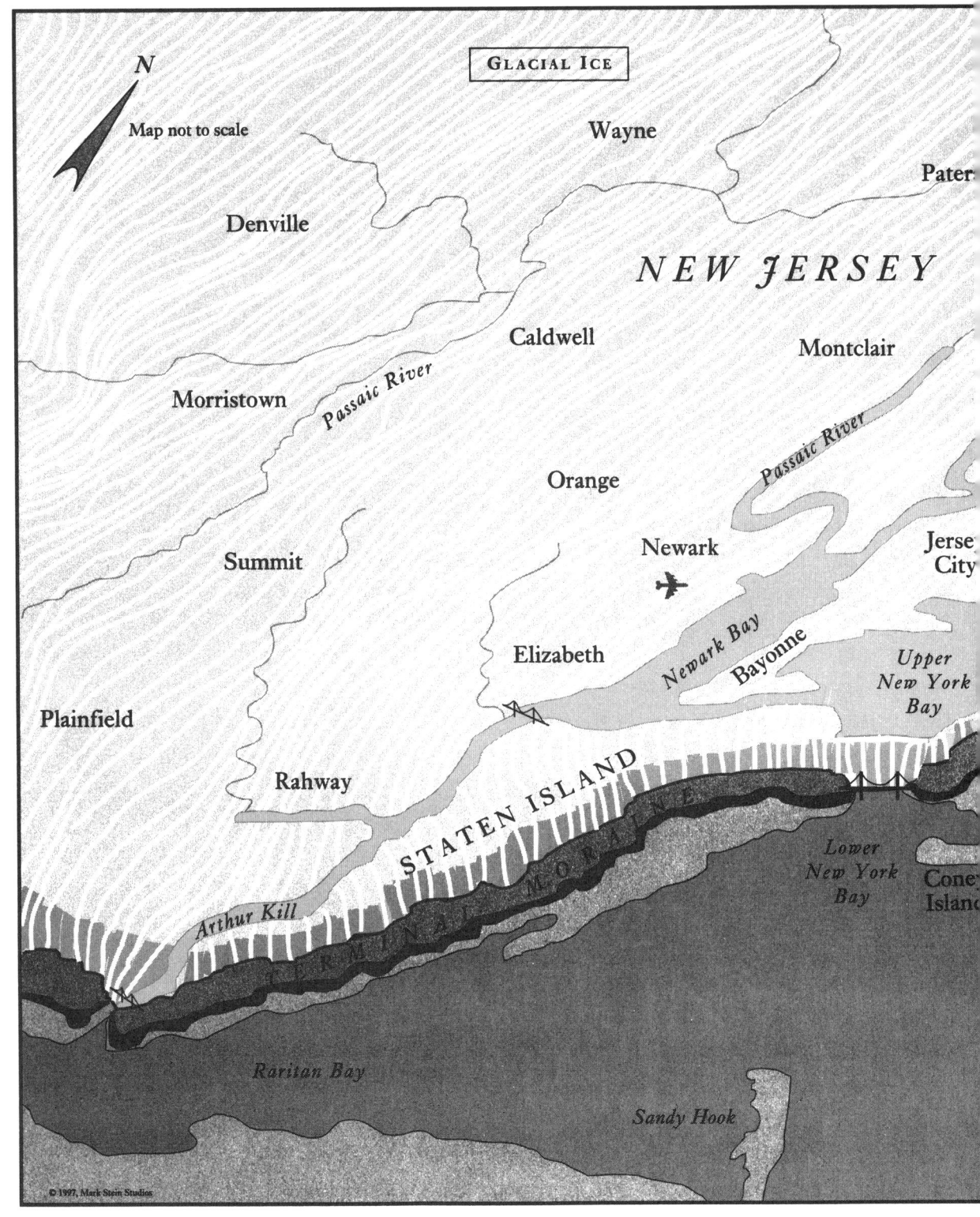

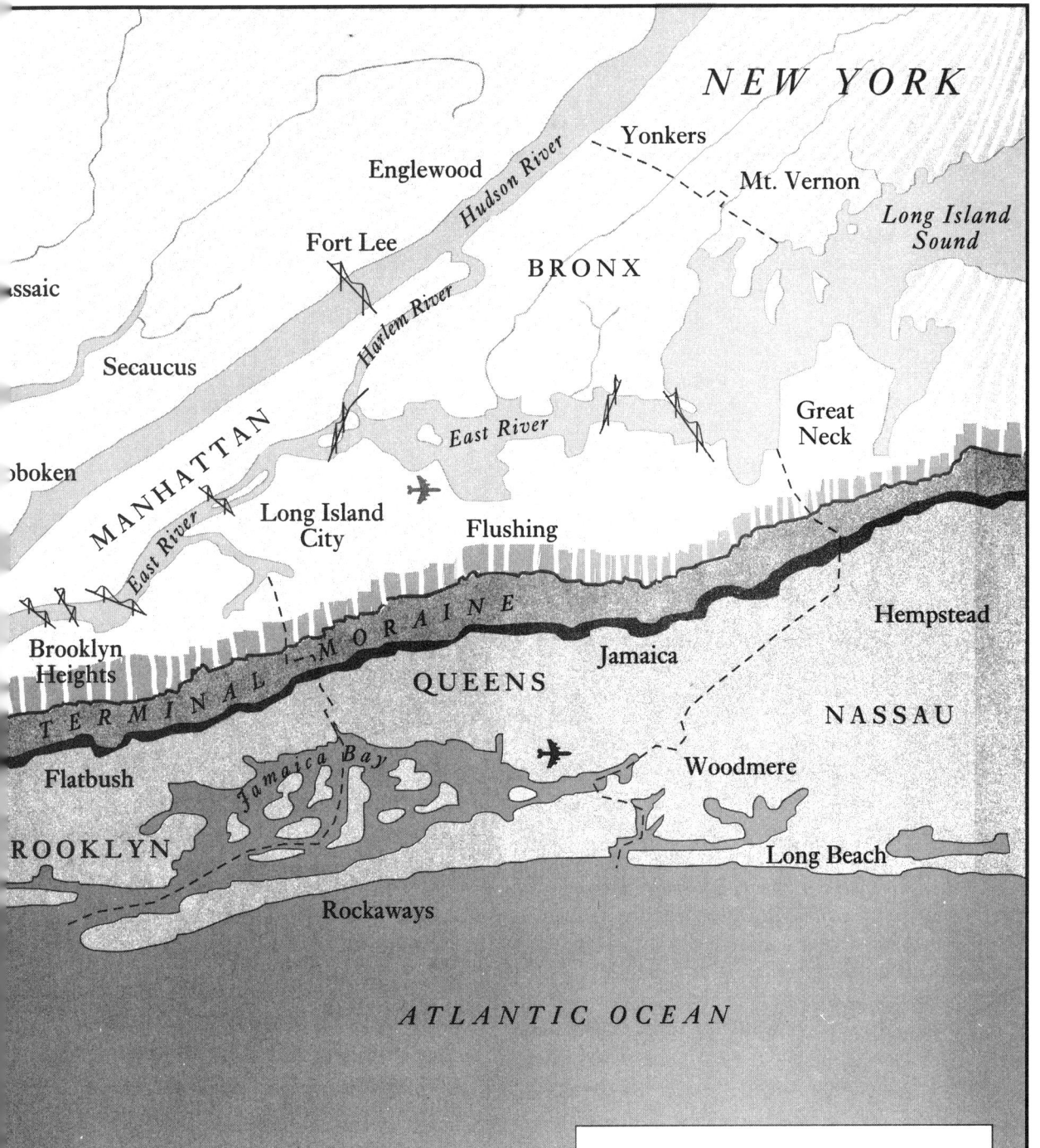

NEW YORK CITY DURING THE LAST ICE AGE

Wild Fact

MANHATTAN MASTODON

Near Broadway and Dyckman Street in northern Manhattan, construction workers excavating a building foundation on March 24, 1925, suddenly heard someone shout, "BONES!" Digging 22 feet below ground, a workman had struck the lower jaw of an American mastodon with his shovel. Along with the jaw, which was preserved in a layer of peat, were 14 mastodon teeth—each weighing 20 pounds.

Elephantlike creatures with 8-foot-long ivory tusks, American mastodons roamed New York City while the Ice Age was beating a slow retreat, about 18,000 years ago. Standing 10 feet tall and weighing 10,000 pounds, mastodons were insulated from the cold by their bulk and dined on spruce and other evergreen trees that sprouted here when the temperature was similar to that of the present-day sub-Arctic.

On the basis of the fossil evidence, paleontologists believe that mastodons, which originally ranged throughout North America and Eurasia, were once as common as modern-day deer. Nonetheless, mastodons and other Ice Age mammals—including the woolly mammoth, the giant sloth, and the saber-toothed tiger—appear to have dropped off the face of Earth about 11,000 years ago. Whether they were unable to adjust to warming temperatures or were hunted to extinction by Ice Age peoples remains an unsolved mystery.

politan area, the edge of the ice sheet drew a straight line through the center of Long Island, Brooklyn, and Queens.

The fact that New York City was one of the glacier's ultimate destinations was a fluke of the world's weather. Ice production in the north and evaporation in the south had simply reached a point of equilibrium, and though the glacier was unable to push farther southward and was melting along its front, it was still technically on the move internally. As long as snow continued to pile up in the Arctic, the ice continued to flow like a conveyor belt, picking up everything from boulders to cobblestones and dumping them at the southern limit. The action of this icy conveyor belt formed a hill along the ice sheet's leading edge that is known to geologists as the terminal moraine. In New York City, this 200- to 500-foot-high heap of Ice Age rubble now runs along the southeast border of Staten Island through the middle of Brooklyn and Queens, and it provides the rocky high ground on which many neighborhoods now perch. Bay *Ridge*, Park *Slope*, Crown *Heights*, *Ridge*wood, and Forest *Hills* all owe their rather elevated positions to this long, narrow hill built by the glacier.

At the same time that the glacier was dumping its load and creating the terminal moraine, it was slowly melting. Imagine standing on Flatbush Avenue, looking north, and seeing rivers of water pouring off a 300-foot-high ice cube. While rocks

NATURAL HIGHS

Life in New York City can be a struggle. Here's how you can still make it to the top:

MANHATTAN. Manhattan Island is best known for high buildings, not high ground. However, around 95th Street on the west side, a ridge of metamorphic rock begins soaring upward, reaching its pinnacle at 183rd Street and Fort Washington Avenue—268 feet above sea level. Now occupied by Bennett Park, this prospect was once the location of Revolutionary War Fort Washington, where on November 16, 1776—just 4 months after the signing of the Declaration of Independence—2,600 American troops were bombarded and forced to surrender to the British redcoats.

BROOKLYN. Although natural vistas are often appropriated by the rich, Brooklyn's highest ground is reserved for the dead. Battle Hill in Greenwood Cemetery is 220 feet above sea level, the highest point in Brooklyn on the terminal moraine. Along with the grave of conductor-composer Leonard Bernstein, Brooklyn's summit is occupied by a bronze statue of the Roman goddess of wisdom, Minerva. Installed in 1920, the statue was designed to complement the Statue of Liberty, which—if it weren't for all the trees—could be seen holding her torch in the harbor below.

THE BRONX. The site of the Bronx's highest peak, the Riverdale community is also home to some of the most sinuous and confusing streets in town. The grid plan doesn't exist here, so if you want to reach the top spot—284 feet above sea level—at Iselin and 250th streets, bring a map.

QUEENS. Fittingly for this highway-dominated borough, the highest point in Queens is on the Grand Central Parkway. Though the moment will pass quickly—perhaps at about 60 miles per hour—Little Neck Hill (266 feet above sea level) is 1,700 feet east of the intersection of the Grand Central and Little Neck parkways.

STATEN ISLAND. At 409.2 feet above sea level, the top of Todt Hill on Staten Island is not just the highest topographic point in the entire city—it also holds the title as the highest point between southern Maine and Florida on the Atlantic coast. As befits its lofty position, Todt Hill is surmounted by the homes of the well-to-do and the Richmond County Country Club. At its very pinnacle—the intersection of Todt Hill and Ocean Terrace roads—is an Eiffel Tower–esque radio tower that allows the New York State Police to transmit over their own band.

and boulders quickly fell out, the meltwaters carried tons and tons of sand, silt, and clay to the south, forming a 5-mile-wide pancake-flat delta that is technically known as the outwash plain. Today, it is better known as *Flat*bush, *Flat*lands, Bensonhurst, Canarsie, Coney Island, and Great Kills Beach.

Were it not for the glacier making a 2,000-year-long pitstop in our area—during which it continuously dumped rock, rubble, gravel, and sand—Brooklyn, Queens, and almost all of Long Island simply would not be here. Throughout the boroughs of Brooklyn and Queens, the bedrock is so far below sea level—as much as 350 feet—that this pile of glacial drift is the only thing keeping them above water.

Chapter 3

STRANGE NEIGHBORHOODS
The City's Ecosystems

New York City is where ecoworlds collide. Here ocean meets land, fresh water mixes with salt, northern and southern climate zones overlap, and because of these convergences we have an incredible variety of ecosystems, many of which—despite almost 400 years of being paved over, filled in, and abused—are still here. Within the 320 square miles that make up the five boroughs are tens of thousands of acres of natural habitat, from woodlands and swamps to salt marshes and sand dunes. Invisible to most New Yorkers, each of these ecosystems is home to a unique collection of plants and animals. Each has its own food chains, and each is a product of delicate adaptations to highly localized landscapes.

Most New Yorkers spend their days in habitats of their own making—on hard streets and byways and inside the steel-and-glass boxes of Manhattan's office towers—places where human beings dominate the landscape. Visiting the city's remaining pockets of wildness can be like entering a parallel universe. When you see wading birds stalking through a salt marsh or a cottontail rab-

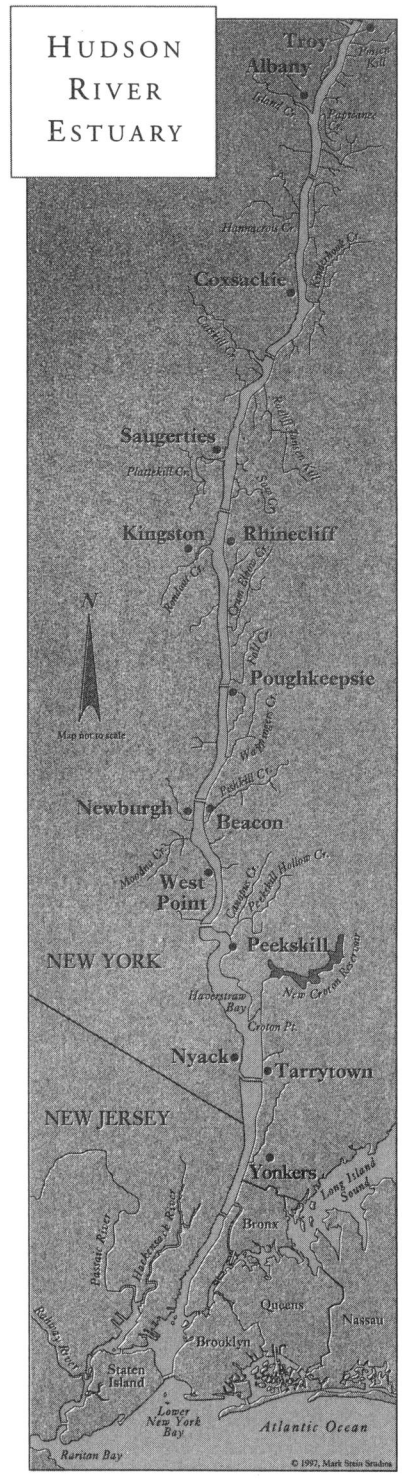

HUDSON RIVER ESTUARY

bit hopping through Prospect Park in Brooklyn, it truly seems as if you have left the city behind.

None of our ecosystems, however, exists in a vacuum. They all continue to be influenced by New York City and its people.

THE HUDSON ESTUARY

Most people think of the Hudson as a river, which it is when it begins trickling down from Lake Tear of the Clouds on the western face of Mount Marcy (elevation 5,344 feet), the highest point in New York State. Traveling 315 miles downstream from its source in the Adirondack Mountains, the Hudson is fed by more than 150 tributary streams and passes by such landmarks as the state capital in Albany, Vassar College, and the U.S. Military Academy at West Point. By the time it runs underneath the George Washington Bridge, however, the Hudson has become a hybrid: half sea and half river. This dual character is what inspired Manhattan's original inhabitants to name the Hudson *Muhheakunnuk* ("the river that flows two ways").

Twice every day, during high tide, 260 billion cubic feet of ocean water flows through the Verrazano Narrows and up the length of Manhattan, making the Hudson run backward all the way to Troy. By contrast, when the tide goes *out*, 75.6 million cubic feet of fresh water pours past the city every hour. This perpetual mixing creates the perfect conditions for an estuary ecosystem.

Technically, the salty swirl of the Hudson Estuary takes in 143,327 underwater acres, including the Hudson River itself, the East River, the Harlem River, Jamaica Bay, and Upper and Lower New York Harbor. In total, the estuary is 10 times larger than Manhattan, making it by far the city's largest and most interconnected ecosystem.

Despite the estuary's significance to the cityscape (more than 60 bridges and 14 car and subway tunnels have been built to span it), most city residents are largely unaware of the life it contains. Almost all of the estuary's biological activity takes place below the surface, and the waters are so naturally dark that it's hard to see what's happening—no matter how hard you look.

A diver's-eye view of the estuary reveals much more. Professional divers plunge into the murky waters almost every day to examine the structures of bridges and piers, to salvage lost cargo, and occasionally to hunt for dead bodies. The water looks dark from above, divers say, because the estuary has a dark, muddy bottom. But under its surface, the water can be remarkably clear. On a good day, at high tide and with a calm wind from the southwest, divers can see as far as 20 feet in front of their masks.

Submerged in New York City, divers have to navigate a landscape that is worthy of a Jacques Cousteau documentary. Striped bass can be seen swimming through the bars of a rusted lion's cage 70 feet underwater at the George Washington Bridge. Long-abandoned piers in the East River have been colonized by eelgrasses that provide shelter for seahorses. Lobsters, their antennae waving in the deep, peek out from the rims of old rubber tires. One diver reported opening the lid of a scuttled toilet bowl only to find a blue crab resting inside, pincers at the ready.

For all these living things, the estuary is a habitat full of pros and cons. On the one hand, the waters are relatively placid and shallow—sheltered from

---

Wild Fact

THE TROUBLE WITH GRIBBLES

A cleaner harbor has a price. In 1995, when a wharf in the East River suddenly collapsed near East 14th Street, city officials suspected sabotage—and they were right. The wharf's pilings had been eaten away by gribbles and shipworms, two wood-boring creatures that were thought to have been driven from the city's waters decades ago by pollution. However, with water quality so much improved in recent years, gribbles and shipworms have returned.

While quarter-inch-long shrimplike gribbles (*Limnoria lignorum*) grind up pier pilings from the outside, shipworms (*Teredo navalis*)—an elongated type of clam that can grow to 2 feet long—perform an inside job, tunneling their way through the wood's interior. Together, this dastardly duo has chewed away the supports for countless piers and wrought over $100 million in damage since 1991. To combat these underwater saboteurs, old piers are now being mummified in plastic wrap and new piers are being built from concrete and recycled plastic, two presumably gribble-proof materials.

both the pounding of ocean waves and the onslaught of river rapids. On the other hand, the changes in salinity caused by the coming and going of the tides confound many creatures. Unless a species has developed a way of compensating for the ebb and flow of salt through its body, it cannot survive in the estuary ecosystem. Despite these difficulties, the Hudson Estuary has become an environmental crossroads that offers shelter to 330 species of birds and 170 different kinds of fish, many of which occur here in surprisingly large numbers:

- When menhaden are born in the harbor in May, schools of these fish become so vast that they can weigh as much as 2 tons. In places like Sheepshead Bay in Brooklyn, the water literally appears to boil with these darting, silvery fish.

- In July and August, the floor of the Hudson Estuary is so thick with side-crawling blue crabs that divers scoop them up by the dozens. Although blue crabs are more commonly associated with the Chesapeake Bay and Maryland crab cakes, biologists estimate that millions of these estuary-adapted creatures live in New York City.

- When brant geese fly in from the Arctic in October to spend the winter on the Hudson Estuary, they come not by twos and threes, but by the thousands. After the tourists go home and the Statue of Liberty closes down for the night, flocks of brant move in to forage along Liberty Island's rocky shoreline.

Even more remarkable is that many of these animals are returning to the estuary after a long absence. Twenty years ago, divers reported seeing little more than the occasional blue mussel and maybe a lethargic-looking underwater snail. Pollution was so bad that most animals were driven out. Today the estuary is becoming healthier, and biologists believe that more plant and animal species live here now than have lived here in 100 years.

SALT MARSHES

Until recently, salt marshes were not the kind of place anyone would want to go for a good time. Flooded by the tide twice a day, salt marshes stand on jello-

ALIVE AND KICKING

Many people laugh at the idea of the term "ecosystem" being applied to the waters around New York City. According to conventional thinking, New York Harbor and the Hudson River are dead—murdered by centuries of nonstop pollution. But the truth is that New York Harbor and the Hudson River have never been down for the count. Despite a long history of environmental insults, New York City's waters are teeming with life—now more than ever, thanks to recent crackdowns on pollution.

Before 1972 (the year the federal Clean Water Act was passed), 450 million gallons of raw sewage were piped straight into the estuary every day. New York City was awash in its own waste. Beaches were closed. Fish fled.

By the mid-1980s, however, the city had cleaned up its act, and the dumping of raw sewage had stopped. Now, every indicator of water quality has improved. Oxygen levels are up; the levels of coliform bacteria, which indicate the presence of sewage, are down; and biodiversity is increasing.

Biologists say that pollution-sensitive creatures such as oysters are making a comeback. So are tiny shrimplike animals known as amphipods, which are a prime source of food for fish in the estuary. The benefits of this burgeoning life can be seen all the way up the food chain. In areas that were contaminated 25 years ago, herons now feed on crabs and minnows, and conditions have improved so much that these stilt-legged wading birds have even established nesting colonies on seven small islands around the harbor.

Of course, it would be naive to believe that New York City's waters are completely pristine. Raw sewage still spills into the estuary—particularly after heavy rains—and environmental hot spots, such as Newtown Creek and the Gowanus Canal, remain unacceptably contaminated. Toxic pollutants, such as PCBs, remain in the sediments at the harbor's bottom, and fish, such as striped bass, still have traces of these pollutants in their systems. Despite these negatives, it would be similarly naive to take a grim view of the estuary's possibilities. No one ever expected that the waters around New York City could bounce back so quickly, and no one can predict what an even cleaner harbor could mean for the estuary's biological future.

---

like mudflats that can suck a person under like quicksand. They also feature a particularly nasty brand of blood-sucking insect, the golden salt-marsh mosquito, which emerges in frightening black swarms every summer. In fact, throughout most of the city's history, salt marshes were considered pestilent pits of disease, and New Yorkers did everything they could to get rid of them.

Over the years, most of the city's original salt marshes were filled in to create new real estate on the edges of the city. Two square miles of Manhattan are built on landfill dumped on what used to be salt marsh, and in the 1960s, the construction of John F. Kennedy Airport swallowed 7 square miles of salt-marsh habitat in the northeast corner of Jamaica Bay.

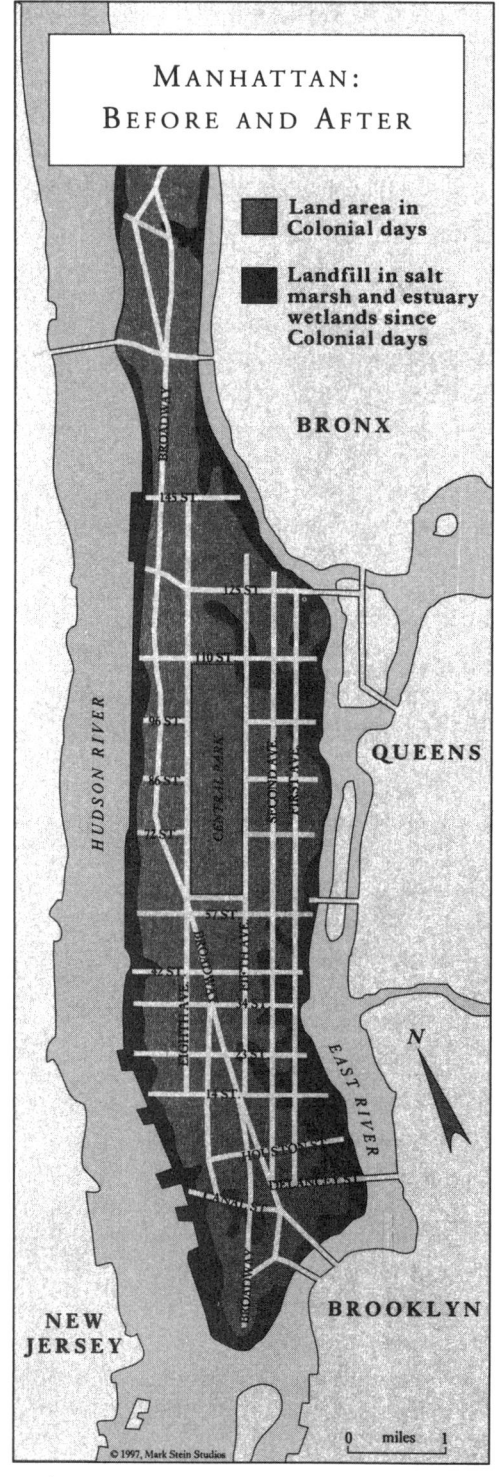

Today, 84 percent of the city's original salt marshes are gone. And those that remain have a new moniker: the "Rain Forests of the Northeast." Why? Because it is now understood by biologists that salt marshes are among the most productive ecosystems on the planet.

Acre for acre, the biological productivity of New York City's salt marshes out-produces the richest farmland in the United States by a factor of six. Only Hawaiian sugarcane fields produce a bigger "crop." And salt marshes are not selfish; about 90 percent of the biomass they produce is let loose into the surrounding estuary, where it becomes the primary source of food for hundreds of different animals.

Today, salt marshes survive in every borough. Even Manhattan boasts a 12-acre salt marsh, on the island's very northern tip in Inwood Hill Park. However, the healthiest salt marshes can be found fringing the shores of Jamaica Bay and Udall's Cove in Queens and Pelham Bay Park in the Bronx. Here, blankets of salt-marsh grass create a scenic landscape suffused with life at every level. Ribbed mussels cling to the grasses' underwater stalks. Fiddler crabs, acutely aware of the tides, emerge at low water to forage for bits of vegetation. Wading birds such as white-plumed great egrets stand motionless—silhouetted against Van Gogh–esque blocks of green grass, blue water, and sky.

Amazingly, this entire web of life depends on a single species: salt-marsh cordgrass, a.k.a. *Spartina alterniflora*. Because the mudflats are flooded by the tides every day, survival in the salt-marsh environment is particularly difficult.

> # CONSERVATION: SAVING A SALT MARSH
>
> On New Year's Day in 1990, a 576,000-gallon Exxon oil spill in the Arthur Kill between Staten Island and New Jersey killed 23 acres of *Spartina alterniflora* at Old Place Creek Marsh on Staten Island, leaving a moonscape of exposed mud and causing the collapse of the salt-marsh ecosystem. Ribbed mussels, fiddler crabs, and herons all vanished. With 84 percent of the city's original salt marshes already destroyed, ecologists from the New York City Parks Department decided that—just 10 miles from Wall Street—Old Place Creek Marsh was too valuable a natural resource to lose without a fight.
>
> Since *Spartina* grasses are what hold a salt marsh together, seeds from surviving *Spartina* plants were propagated in greenhouses and replanted on the oil-slicked mudflats. For the past 5 years, a small crew of salt marsh restoration ecologists has slogged through the marsh in rubber boots—sometimes becoming mired up to their waists in clinging black mud—in order to tend the thousands of seedlings. So far, the results have astounded even the most optimistic biologists.
>
> Because of the high level of oil in the mud, no one was sure if the *Spartina* could survive. But the revival of the emerald-colored grasses that now blanket the restoration site each spring suggests to biologists that New York City *Spartina* is tougher than average, perhaps having evolved into a pollution-resistant strain after enduring for hundreds of years in New York Harbor.
>
> Beneath the Goethals Bridge, 6 acres of *Spartina* grasses have now come back to life at Old Place Creek Marsh. The animals that the grasses once supported appear to be coming back too. So far, ecologists have documented the return of killifish, fiddler crabs, muskrats, and 70 species of birds.

Spartina is the only land plant that has been able to tough it out in this salty environment—literally holding the salt marsh together with its extensive roots. How does *Spartina* survive the daily tidal floods? Rare among plants is *Spartina*'s ability to purge excess salt from its system through glands on its stems and leaves—sometimes leaving salt crystals visible on the reedy stalks.

A little farther inland, where the mudflats are flooded only by the highest tides, a cousin, *Spartina patens,* dominates. Growing in swirling green mats, *Spartina patens* (also called salt hay) was collected by Dutch colonists in Brooklyn and Queens as fodder for their cows, producing some of the richest dairy products this side of Wisconsin. Today, the city's two *Spartina* grasses feed the ecosystem itself. They break down to form the layers of organic mud on which the salt marsh stands. They also form the base of the salt-marsh food chain, producing 20,000 pounds of organic matter per acre every year.

Though, compared to other ecosystems, salt marshes are not rich in their

> ### *Wild Fact*
>
> ### DIEHARD
>
> Killifish (*Fundulus heteroclitus*) are native New Yorkers and are the toughest fish around. Seen swimming like little shadows in some of the city's shallowest and most polluted waterways, including the Arthur Kill and Newtown Creek, killifish were named by the city's early Dutch settlers (*kill* is Dutch for "tidal creek"). Since then, these fish have survived every abuse that's been thrown at them. They can tolerate pollution that is toxic to almost every other kind of fish, as well as extremely low levels of oxygen, unusually high salinity, and even extreme temperature shifts. Although small—rarely growing longer than 5 inches—killifish have a big appetite, removing tons of mosquito larvae from the city's salt marshes every year.

total number of species (most organisms can't withstand the variable salinity), they are renowned for their volume of life, thanks to the plentiful food supply provided by the *Spartina* grasses. Each healthy acre of salt marsh can sustain as many as a million fiddler crabs, hundreds of thousands of ribbed mussels, and a veritable soup of single-celled plants and microscopic animals in tidal channels.

According to estimates, up to 75 percent of all commercial seafood caught in New York State relies on the shelter and nourishment provided by salt marshes. Species such as flounder, fluke, blue crab, bluefish, and whiting are all part of the food chain that begins with *Spartina*. And when salt marshes are destroyed, entire food chains come tumbling down.

FORESTS

Five hundred years ago, much of New York City was covered with a canopy of trees—chestnuts, hemlocks, oaks, and tulips. In these trees were passenger pigeons, red and gray squirrels, woodpeckers, and hundreds of different songbirds. Below them were a decades-thick layer of fallen leaves, rotting branches, and the husks of acorns. Porcupine, deer, and wolves had the run of the place. Then, about 220 years ago, almost all the forests were cut down—the Revolutionary War was in full swing and the occupying British soldiers needed firewood. In the years that followed, any forest lands that remained were cleared for farmland.

Yet, there is one tract of old forest that eluded the saw. On the grounds of the New York Botanical Garden (NYBG) in the Bronx, 40 acres of old-growth forest struggle onward, despite air pollution, heavy metals in the soil, and exotic tree-killing insects. Here, beside two of the city's busiest highways, the Moshulu and Bronx River parkways, there are oak trees that have seen their 300th birthday and that stand 120 feet high. This forest was never cut because its steep terrain was poor farmland and because it was located in a no-man's land that lay between the properties of British loyalists and rebels during the American Revolution. Even in rural areas, the continuing survival of such old-growth tracts is rare.

Until the 1980s, this Bronx forest was called the Hemlock Grove—after the 1,500 evergreen hemlock trees that carpeted its floor with pine-scented needles. Today, the grove has been renamed The NYBG Forest, and the hemlock trees are perishing by the dozens at the hands of an insect from Japan called the hemlock woolly adelgid (*Adelges tsugae*), which appeared in the garden in 1985. In spite of this so-far unstoppable infestation, biologists remain optimistic

---

FOREST ECO-AWARDS

In a *Wild New York* survey, local foresters and botanists were asked to nominate their candidates for the "Healthiest Forest Ecosystem in New York City." To qualify, woodlands had to have lush leafy canopies, healthy soils, regeneration of saplings and understory plants, and predominantly native plant and animal species—all despite the rigors of city living.

FIRST PLACE. When the votes were in, one forest stood above the rest: the woods of the Staten Island Greenbelt. Unlike many of the city's woodlands, which have become fragmented—isolated pockets of green surrounded by highways—the Greenbelt is continuous over 2,500 acres and highly varied. Climbing up and down over hilly terrain, its forest ranges from sweet gum swamps and stream-cut, deciduous woodlands to old stands of oaks and tulip trees perched atop hillsides. Clinching the decision, however, was the Greenbelt's unusually diverse array of native woodland creatures. These include Fowler's toads, red-bellied woodpeckers, box turtles, and black racer snakes.

SECOND PLACE. In the northernmost part of the Bronx, the Northwest Forest in Van Cortlandt Park is a 188-acre cool green woodland with tall black oaks and tulips covering an understory of sassafras, wild grape vines, spicebush, and mapleleaf viburnum. Something good must be happening here, because animals not usually associated with the city—wild turkeys, coyotes, red foxes, and deer—occasionally drop by for a visit, crossing the border from neighboring Westchester County.

THIRD PLACE. Twenty minutes from midtown Manhattan on the "1" subway line is the forest in 196-acre Inwood Hill Park. Its 100-foot-tall tulip trees remind foresters of southern Appalachian forests. Usually at least 10°F degrees cooler than the surrounding city in summertime, this moist, shady grove is visited by about 150 different bird species.

about the city's last stand of virgin forest. Although the hemlocks are dying, the forest isn't. In clearings where the hemlocks have succumbed, wild birch, black cherry, and sassafras trees are coming in to take their place.

Even if all the trees in a forest tract are cut down, it only takes 5 to 10 years for a forest to regenerate itself in some form. Since the American Revolution, a surprising number of New York City's forests have recovered. Altogether, the city has about 8 square miles of forest land, a precious 2.5 percent of the total land area in the five boroughs. These wooded pockets range from The Clove in Manhattan's Inwood Hill Park to the fern-filled swamp forests of Cunningham Park in Queens to the oak barrens at Clay Pits Pond State Park Preserve on Staten Island.

Despite the existence of such woodland tracts, conditions for a self-sustaining forest ecosystem are less than ideal here, and the city's forests are increasingly stressed. Because New York City is at the crossroads of international trade, its forests often fall prey to invasive, exotic species. In the Hemlock Grove it was the woolly adelgid. In the rest of the city it has been deceptively attractive exotic vines: porcelain berry and oriental bittersweet—two vines from Asia that were originally introduced as garden plants. When these vines escape into the wild, they literally shroud tracts of woodland, pulling down trees with their weight and growing so thickly that no other plants can compete. In many areas, the city's woodlands have also suffered from human crowding. With so many people visiting urban forests, off-trail walking and mountain biking have caused the soil to become so compacted that water and nutrients cannot reach the trees' roots.

Conditions have become so bad that some New York City woodlands have been described as "the living dead." The trees grow more than 70 feet high, and they look healthy and flower in the spring—but they are not reproducing. If you look at the forest floor in many parks, you see bare ground and no saplings to keep the forest going.

Lately, there has been a movement to bring New York City's embattled forests back to life. Since 1990, the Urban Forest and Education Program of the City Parks Foundation has hand-cleared 600 acres of vine-choked forest land and planted 120,000 tree saplings. These plantings have included white pines, pitch pines, hemlocks, red cedars, red oaks, white oaks, black oaks, blackjack oaks, chestnut oaks, pin oaks, tulip trees, sweet gums, sugar maples, green ashes, hackberries, and dogwoods—all native New York City species grown in greenhouses from seeds found in the city's public parks.

In some woodlands, the work of the forest restoration crew has caused a significant turnaround. For example, the woods at Blue Heron Park on Staten Island were once a dumping ground for garbage and stolen cars. Starting in 1991, the restoration crew and neighborhood residents began cleaning up the woods; they cleared dozens of acres of invasive vines, removed hundreds of pounds of trash, and dragged out 85 abandoned cars. As a result, the forest is reviving. The park's older trees, 70-foot-tall sweet gums, now thrive in the park's moist soils, and a hardy new generation of black locusts and cherries can be seen sprouting up in areas that were once thick with trash.

from top: Bay Scallop, Northern Quahog (right), Eastern Oyster (left), Atlantic Razor Clam, Atlantic Surf Clam

BEACHES

Every summer, 12 million people sunbathe by the boardwalk, eat Nathan's hot dogs, and splash in the waves at Coney Island, New York City's most popular beach. Yet, for all their seeming familiarity, Coney Island and the rest of the city's beaches are among its least-known ecosystems.

A close-up look at a typical city beach reveals much more than seagulls, turbid sandy water, and the occasional jellyfish. In fact, an extremely close look exposes an alien landscape inhabited by strange creatures of which most beachgoers are completely unaware.

When you walk into the wet sand and feel the chill of the lapping surf, you are entering one of the toughest environments on the planet. Inundated by waves able to exert as much as 6,000 pounds of pressure per square foot, and baked in the sun (reaching temperatures of 110°F), the beach is like a waterlogged desert. Yet, hundreds of animals are adapted to life in the sand below.

If you were to dig 2 feet beneath the sand's surface, you would encounter an alien scene. Beneath the surf at Coney Island and all of the city's other beaches are predatory 2-inch-long worms covered with armadillolike scales; sand-burrowing amphipods (also known as bugs of the seas); and 1-inch, almost translu-

Wild Fact

SHARKS

The New York Aquarium's poster fish is a snaggle-toothed creature known as a sand tiger shark (*Odontaspis taurus*). On any given day, you can see seven of these 9-foot-long, 400-pound creatures patrolling the aquarium's 90,000-gallon shark tank. What exotic waters do these fearsome-looking fish come from? All seven were captured just ¼ mile offshore—right in front of the Coney Island boardwalk.

The preferred habitat of sand tiger sharks is inshore waters, where they are so common that they are frequently caught incidentally in the nets of commercial fishermen out for smaller fry such as butterfish and Spanish mackerel. In fact, sand tiger sharks are so easy to come by in New York City that the aquarium sends locally caught juveniles to aquariums in Japan, in exchange for more exotic species.

Despite their rows of long tricuspid teeth, sand tiger sharks are not considered particularly dangerous to human swimmers. Usually, these sharks cruise the bottom and prefer a diet of menhaden, weakfish, herring, and squid.

cent mole crabs that harvest the sand for tiny organisms. Marine biologists estimate that on any cubic meter of wet sand on which a bather stands, there are 500 to 1,000 individual creatures—all small, but visible to the human eye. Floating in the water around that same bather's legs is these creatures' food—microscopic plants and animals, phytoplankton and zooplankton, that exist by the tens of thousands per cubic meter.

A little farther out, in the area where swimmers venture, the diversity of life is even more palpable. About five times a year, the Pan Aqua Diving School in Manhattan receives a special permit to scuba dive off the beach at Coney Island. Just 50 feet offshore in 20-foot-deep water, divers find hundreds of red-spotted lady crabs scuttling along the bottom, hundreds of red orange sea stars clinging to submerged rock jetties, and countless hermit crabs occupying various types of borrowed shells. Many of these creatures are collected as specimens and transferred to the New York Aquarium on the other side of the boardwalk, where they often end up as exhibits in the aquarium's touch tank.

Back on dry sand, a variety of shells provide further proof of the busy world just offshore. The shells of quahogs, razor clams, bay scallops, and moon snails are among the most common on the city's beaches. But the most abundant are the shells of surf clams—white saucers that can grow as large as 6 inches across. Found washed up on the beach, surf clams often end up as ashtrays or sand shovels. While alive, however, they live buried in the sand in waters 15 to 300 feet offshore, where they filter the ocean water for nutrients.

Moon Snail

Whereas beachgoers usually define the seashore by its scenery—waves, wind, sun, and sand—ecologists see it as a series of interlocking zones, each having different life forms. Surf clams live in the "subtidal zone," the area that is always covered with water, and they wash up as shells in the "wrack zone," the area where debris is deposited by the highest tides. Mole crabs live in the "intertidal zone," where waves roll in and out. And little gray barnacles live off slim pickings in the "splash zone" on rock jetties that occasionally are hit by ocean spray and carry food in the form of microscopic plankton.

One zone, however, is missing from the city's more popular beaches. Where the boardwalk, the Wonder Wheel, and the Cyclone at Coney Island now stand, there were once sand dunes covered with beach grass, bayberry bushes, and seaside goldenrod. Protecting the inland areas from storm surges,

ALL WASHED UP

The strangest stuff washes up on New York City's beaches. In 1988, it was illegally dumped medical waste in the form of syringes. In the late 1940s, it was torpedoes left behind by Nazi U-boats lurking just a few miles offshore. Whatever gets dumped in the harbor ultimately comes back to haunt us.

During one all-day beach cleanup organized by the American Littoral Society in 1995, volunteers picked up 21,545 pounds of trash from 9.7 miles of city waterfront. Among their findings were 4,539 plastic bags and wrappers, 3,692 plastic straws, and 3,352 cigarette butts. They also found a set of false teeth and a waterlogged toupee.

What is the source of all this trash? According to city reports, most beach flotsam starts out as litter on New York City sidewalks. Every month during the height of the beach season, 415,000 "floatable items" like empty Fritos bags, Snickers wrappers, and Coke bottles wash down street sewers into the Hudson and East rivers. From there, it's just a short swim to Coney Island.

the dunes were able to withstand wind, waves, and salt spray—but not the desire for seaside amusement.

Today, sand dunes can still be explored at some of New York City's wilder beaches, such as Fort Tilden and the Breezy Point Tip in the Rockaways, Plumb Beach in Brooklyn, and Great Kills Park on Staten Island. These areas, all under the protection of the National Parks Service, are fascinating landscapes and the only places in the city where you can see the beach ecosystem as it was originally designed.

FRESH WATER

Ponds and lakes are one of the best-loved types of scenery. Gazing across a sheet of calm, sun-dappled water can be intensely satisfying. Some psychologists believe this sense of emotional well-being in response to lakes and ponds may be an inborn trait, an evolutionary by-product of our ancestors' need to be near a source of fresh drinking water.

European bitterling

A RIVER RUNS THROUGH IT

Many bodies of water bear the title of river in New York City without, ecologically speaking, living up to their names. The East "River" is actually a saltwater strait that connects Long Island Sound with New York Harbor. The Hudson "River" is more salty than fresh as it rocks up and down on the whim of the tides. Meanwhile, the Harlem "River" is nothing more than a tidal inlet.

Only one river within the city limits has earned its title. Running 20 miles from its headwaters in Westchester County through the Bronx Zoo and the New York Botanical Garden on its way to emptying in the East River, the steep-banked Bronx River is the only wild, freshwater river in New York City. Although you won't see much fly fishing there, the Bronx River is home to both brown trout and largemouth bass—two of the most sought-after fighting fish ever to grace the cover of *Field and Stream*. All told, the Bronx River shelters a motley crew of 17 fish species, from transplanted goldfish and carp to native freshwater fish with names like redfin pickerel, golden shiner, white sucker, and tesselated darter. Also lurking within its waters are American eels and an unusual little fish called the European bitterling, an escapee from the aquarium trade that has lived in the river since the 1920s.

Whatever the attraction, fresh water draws people like a magnet. The track around the 106-acre Central Park Reservoir is one of the most popular spots for runners in the world. The restaurant at the Boathouse overlooking the Central Park Lake is jam-packed every summer afternoon with hundreds of diners watching ducks paddling by their tables. And at the otherwise genteel Brooklyn Botanic Garden, the Japanese Pond is often besieged with visitors vying to feed the carp and turtles.

Although some natural ponds still exist, most of the city's bodies of fresh water were artificially created. Frederick Law Olmsted and Calvert Vaux, who designed many of New York City's parks, were huge fans of "sheets of water," and they typically deepened naturally low areas so that they would fill with water and provide attractive scenes. Fed by pipes, these ersatz water bodies now support a surprising amount of biological activity.

> ### Wild Fact
> ## POND-ERING BIODIVERSITY
> In 1996, city parks officials determined that a 2-acre, 4-foot-deep watering hole next to the Great Lawn in Central Park—called Turtle Pond—had to be temporarily drained. As a result, the pond's wildlife was evicted, giving biologists a peek at species normally hidden below the surface. Though small and artificially created, Turtle Pond passed the test when it came to biodiversity—and lived up to its reptilian name. Among the animals pulled from the pond and relocated to the Central Park Lake, 4 blocks south, were no fewer than 10,000 fish, thousands of crayfish, 2 full-grown bullfrogs, and 33 healthy turtles.
>
> Among the turtles, five different species were represented: 17 red-eared sliders; 2 painted turtles; 2 musk turtles (also known as stinkpots, because they release a foul odor); 2 cooters; and 10 snapping turtles, the largest of which was the size of a bulldog and weighed 44 pounds.

All of the city's artificial lakes have been stocked at one time or another with fish—usually carp, sunfish, and bass—and the degree to which these animals have thrived is sometimes remarkable. Seven-pound largemouth bass and foot-long pickerel have been caught at Central Park's Turtle Pond, and 12-pound carp have been landed in Prospect Park Lake.

Even in the middle of the city, water attracts wildlife. Although it sometimes seems as if ducks, geese, and swans have been placed in city lakes for scenic purposes, they are actually here on their own terms. Waterfowl raise ducklings, goslings, and cygnets by the hundreds in New York City. Pairs of mallards can often be seen plowing through lily pads with as many as eight ducklings paddling behind. And these young families don't survive on handouts from warmhearted bird lovers. They make it on their own, living off underwa-

> ### *Wild Fact*
>
> ## SILENT STREAM
>
> Two hundred years ago, dozens of creeks flowed across Manhattan; a canal cut across the island at what is now Canal Street; and Manhattan's largest natural body of fresh water, the 60-foot-deep Collect Pond, was located where the New York County Courthouse now stands, north of City Hall. But when it came time for the city to expand beyond the Wall Street area, early real estate developers didn't take a gentle approach; they just filled in unwanted waterways with sand and gravel and paved them over.
>
> Today, water still runs ghostlike through many of its old channels—even when they are 6 feet under. One of the best places to find evidence of this phenomenon is at 2 Fifth Avenue, an apartment house in Greenwich Village, where just outside the front entrance you can see the waters of otherwise buried Minetta Brook bubbling up through a glass fountain. Before it was laid to this unquiet rest, Minetta Brook meandered from Union Square through Greenwich Village to the Hudson River and was reputedly a popular spot for trout fishing.

ter plants and the green duckweed that grows naturally on the surface of the city's lakes.

Ultimately, wildlife doesn't care whether a pond is natural or artificial, or even whether it is intended for their use. In 1991, freshwater jellyfish suddenly appeared in the Conservatory Water in Central Park, where model boat races are held every Saturday. No one knows exactly how these translucent, dime-sized creatures made it to this concrete-lined pool, but with a population of more than 5,000, they now vastly outnumber the armada of tiny yachts.

Similarly, the Central Park Reservoir—until recently an emergency backup system for the city's water supply—has always been a popular spot for migratory waterfowl such as canvasback ducks, mergansers, and even loons. Although this delighted bird-watchers, it dismayed city officials, who were concerned about maintaining the purity of the water. Over the years, they tried warding off the birds by lowering the water level and adding chlorine. Finally, in 1993, after years of trying to persuade the avian visitors *not* to come, the city gave up, declaring the reservoir obsolete as a source of drinking water and leaving it in the hands of its de facto owners.

Although the majority of the city's lakes and ponds were constructed, quite a few are natural, particularly in Queens and on Staten Island, where the Wisconsin Ice Sheet created bowl-like depressions in the land, known as kettles. Rainwater and runoff fill these low-lying areas, creating shallow bodies of water that are rich in plant and animal life. Located especially in woodlands such as Cunningham Park in Queens and Blue Heron Park on Staten Island, these "kettle ponds" are quieter and more secluded than the wide-open lakes in the city's parks. Typically ringed by wetland-loving trees such as sweet gums and red maples, their waters are still and dark under the cloak of foliage. Often the only ripples are caused by frogs, the signature species of these small ecosystems.

Natural kettles provide such vital habitat for wildlife in the city that even these freshwater wetlands are now being made artificially. At the Jamaica Bay Wildlife Refuge, which is run by the National Parks Service, an artificial kettle known as Big John's Pond was dug out with a bulldozer in 1982. Biologists then successfully stocked the pond with a type of native tree frog called the spring peeper, a species that can be found existing naturally in the kettles of Alley Pond and Cunningham parks in Queens. The Parks Service constructed a similar pond at Floyd Bennett Field in Brooklyn. Both of these spots have become scenic oases, filled with reeds, water plants, and unstocked animals such as dragonflies and egrets.

GRASSLANDS

From the steppes of Asia to the pampas of Argentina, grasslands cover 25 percent of the world's land area. Yet unlike forests and seashores, which have been studied and protected for decades in this country, North American grasslands have only recently come into vogue with conservationists and researchers. Usually associated with the American buffalo and the Great Plains, North American grasslands can also be found in New York City—although they are few and far between.

Historically, there were several large grasslands in the metropolitan area. Harlem was described as a meadow filled with flowers by early Dutch settlers. The Hempstead Plains on Long Island was, at 60,000 acres, the largest natural grassland east of Ohio. And early maps from the colonial period show patches of land in Brooklyn marked "prairie."

Today, however, the city's wide-open spaces have been reduced to a handful: a 10-acre grassland in Van Cortlandt Park on Vault Hill; a 25-acre meadow in Pelham Bay Park;

Wild Fact

TAKEOFF

The upland sandpiper (*Bartramia longicauda*), a "shore bird" that never goes near the beach, flies 2,000 miles from Argentina every spring to nest in North America's grasslands. Notoriously picky about where it sets up house, this rare bird will nest only in completely treeless and shrubless terrain. The mowed areas around John F. Kennedy Airport offer the perfect habitat, and dozens of upland sandpipers nest among the runways every year, making the airport one of the most important breeding areas for these birds in the Northeast.

> ### Wild Fact
>
> **AIRPORT OWLS**
> The typical habitat of the largest of all owls, the snowy owl (*Nyctea scandiaca*), is the frozen tundra of Greenland and Baffin Island. There, the owl's all-white plumage provides the perfect camouflage against a snow-covered terrain. Why, then, are these 2-foot-tall birds found to be frequent flyers at John F. Kennedy Airport, where sightings are reported alongside the runways almost every winter?
>
> Like all other Arctic birds, snowy owls fly south for the winter. Since the grasses at JFK are mowed short, the airport's treeless winter landscape reminds the owls of their home turf. As for food, the airport's grasslands conceal a healthy supply of rats, mice, meadow voles, and rabbits. These New York City critters act as stand-ins for the snowy's usual prey: lemmings and snowshoe hares.

1,200 acres of prairielike turf in and around the runways at John F. Kennedy Airport; and a 140-acre tract of waist-high grasses at Floyd Bennett Field, a former airport at the southern end of Flatbush Avenue.

To a casual observer, the flat, sun-baked grassland at Brooklyn's Floyd Bennett Field looks to be little more than a seriously overgrown lawn. In fact, it is a grassland biopreserve created and managed by the New York City Audubon Society in conjunction with the National Parks Service. From 1985 through 1990, a small cadre of volunteers spent their weekends clearing what had become an impenetrable thicket surrounding the runways at the old airfield. Using chainsaws and axes, the volunteers chopped down woody plants and pulled roots out with their bare hands. The purpose of this grueling effort was to create a refuge for grassland-adapted birds that had been left virtually homeless in the Northeast because of habitat destruction.

Though grasslands are subtle landscapes—difficult to appreciate and easy to overlook—they are the most biodiverse of all the city's ecosystems. Local biologists have determined that Floyd Bennett Field and New York City's other small grasslands support hundreds of different plant species. Among the most prominent of these plants is a grass called little bluestem (*Andropogon scoparius*)—the same bunchgrass that once fed armies of American buffalo in the short-grass prairies of the Midwest. Similar to lawn grass, little bluestem grows a network of thick underground root mats that help keep non-grassland plants—such as the dreaded tree—from taking over.

At Floyd Bennett Field, little bluestem now grows up to 3 feet tall, and this Brooklyn grassland is home to a unique array of animals, all adapted to living in environments without trees, cover, or shade. Grassland birds like savannah and grasshopper sparrows make their nests on the ground at Floyd Bennett Field and raise their young behind the low screen of grasses. Also typical are burrowing animals such as meadow voles (also called field mice), which operate like

THE RAREST OF THE RARE

An idiosyncratic grassland dominated by heavy-metal–loving plants, the "serpentine barrens" exist only on Staten Island, where green serpentinite bedrock breaks up to form a thin layer of dusty—and poisonous—topsoil. The serpentinite rock contains heavy metals, such as chromium and magnesium, which leach into the ground and interfere with the metabolic processes of most of New York City's native species. A few tough customers, however, have evolved to live in these toxic conditions, and together, these plants create the serpentine barrens ecosystem. They include little bluestem, Indian nut grass, goatsbeard, goldenrod, purple milkweed, green milkweed, birdfoot violets, bayberry bushes, and quaking aspens—as well as nonnative plants such as mugwort and Japanese knotweed.

Although they are considered rare ecosystems, there is actually a "new" serpentine barrens on Staten Island. In the 1960s, on what is now called Moses Mountain in the Staten Island Greenbelt, huge chunks of serpentinite bedrock were dumped into a pile during excavation for the Staten Island Expressway. Now, 30 years later, the soft serpentinite rock has weathered to form a thin topsoil and the "mountain" has been colonized by heavy-metal lovers.

Little Bluestem

miniature prairie dogs, excavating miles of tunnels through the base of the grass stems.

In the eastern United States, which is naturally dominated by forest, grasslands are usually transitional ecosystems—the first plant communities to take over in areas that have been burned, flooded, or cleared. Grasses and wildflowers grow in these transition zones until trees and shrubs take hold again. For a grassland to remain a grassland in this region, something or *someone* has to keep it from reverting to a woodland. In the case of Floyd Bennett Field, it is volunteers from the Audubon Society and rangers from the National Parks Service.

At Floyd Bennett Field, they have actively maintained this rare habitat by chopping down invasive saplings and even setting controlled fires to prevent shrubs and other woody plants from gaining a toehold. At JFK Airport, where the areas around the runways must be kept free of obstructions, giant tractor mowers maintain the grassland habitat so successfully that the airport attracts short-eared owls, upland sandpipers, and many other ground-nesting birds. In other prairie pockets around the city, such as Vault Hill, it is fires started by careless barbecuers and arsonists that maintain the ecosystem.

Chapter 4

CITY ANIMALS

Before the Dutch settled New Amsterdam, the New York City area was surrounded by marshes and covered with thick forests that were filled with native animals, including beaver, deer, wolves, black bears, and timber rattlesnakes. Although these larger animals couldn't make it in the Big Apple, several smaller animals stuck it out. Squirrels, ducks, snapping turtles, and bluefish have all managed to survive—sometimes with surprising success—and alongside these native New Yorkers are many newcomers. Pigeons, sparrows, rats, and cockroaches are just a few of the nonnative creatures that piggybacked into the city with the Old World settlers.

Today, an estimated 330 different species of birds, 30 mammals, 32 reptiles and amphibians, and more than 200 kinds of fish inhabit the city's skies, trees, buildings, parks, and waterways. Yet this only accounts for animals with backbones. If invertebrates—insects, arachnids, mollusks, crustaceans, and other spineless creatures—are added to the list, human beings may be sharing New York City with as many as 10,000 different members of the animal kingdom.

PEREGRINE FALCONS

New York City is not exactly famous for its rare birds. Golden eagles don't stop by too often, and the northern spotted owl never does. However, one bird that is prominent on the federal list of endangered species is more successful here than almost anywhere else. Since 1983, peregrine falcons (*Falco pere-*

grinus)—powerful birds of prey that are adapted to living on mountain crags—have made their nests in places like the George Washington Bridge and the Bank of New York—seemingly oblivious to the deafening accompaniment of passing traffic or the crowds of office workers below.

What are these birds doing here? Originally, peregrine falcons ranged across all of North America, from Alaska to Georgia. But in the 1950s and '60s, they were wiped off the map by the pesticide DDT. Because the adults ate small birds that had fed on DDT-doused insects, the peregrines' eggshells became so thin and fragile that the eggs broke before they had a chance to hatch. By the time DDT was banned in 1972, no peregrine falcons were left east of the Mississippi River.

After the Endangered Species Act was passed in 1973, wildlife biologists undertook an intensive effort to bring the falcons back from the brink. Hundreds of peregrines were bred in captivity and about 150 hand-raised birds were released throughout New York State during the 1970s and '80s. The hope was that the young falcons would reestablish their historic nesting sites along the Hudson River Palisades and in the Adirondack Mountains. No one was sure if the young falcons would make it on their own, and no one expected that the first places they would choose to set up house would be in Brooklyn and the Bronx—on the Verrazano-Narrows and Throgs Neck bridges.

Today, peregrine falcons nest on at least 11 sites within the five boroughs, including the Manhattan tower of the Brooklyn Bridge and an old gun turret on the Marine Parkway Bridge at the end of Flatbush Avenue. They have even moved into the heart of Manhattan. One Park Avenue pair lives on a window ledge at the Metropolitan Life Building at East 45th Street, while an Upper West Side couple nests in the bell tower of Riverside Church.

Just as the bridges, buildings, and churches that the peregrines have chosen as nest sites are considered triumphs of modern architecture and engineering, the falcons that inhabit them are themselves miracles of natural design. About 1½ feet tall, with blue gray wings, these falcons have sharp, curved beaks and yellow, razor-sharp talons. With narrow, tapered wings, they are one of the fastest birds in the world and have been clocked at speeds exceeding 60 miles per hour during level flight. Fierce and effective predators, they execute aerial hits on other birds, dive-bombing them at 150 miles per hour and killing their prey instantly in midair.

Although the urban aeries that the birds have chosen might seem less ideal than a windswept cliff, these human-made structures almost exactly duplicate the peregrines' idea of good real estate. They are remote, exclusive, have great views, are best approached by air—and are near lots of fast food.

In wilderness areas, each pair of peregrine falcons requires a territory with a 5- to 10-mile radius between nests. In the city, they sometimes set up house less than a mile apart. Scientists believe that the high density of pigeons on the city's streets and bridges is what enables so many of these highly territorial falcons to live so close together. In Manhattan, the peregrines have even adapted their hunting strategies to accommodate the skyscraper-dominated topography. Instead of dive-bombing their prey, the falcons curve and weave between buildings to catch pigeons on the wing.

Although peregrine falcons tried to nest in the city before their DDT-induced decline, they were usually chased away. This time around, however, the city is giving the birds the royal treatment. When a peregrine pair starts a nest, wildlife biologists from the city's Department of Environmental Protection place a wooden nesting box filled with rounded gravel on the site, thereby preventing the avian parents from laying their eggs on the surface of a ledge, where they would be liable to roll off. The eggs are laid in early spring and are incubated by both parents for 32 to 33 days; during this period the falcons are left completely to themselves. After the falcon chicks are born, biologists return to weigh the chicks, inspect them for parasites, and place numbered bands around their legs so that they can be tracked. While all this attention is being paid to the chicks, the overprotective peregrine parents dive-bomb the biologists repeatedly, often drawing blood with their outstretched talons.

Wild Fact

CELEBRITY HAWKS

The most successful hawks in the wild, red-tailed hawks (*Buteo jamaicensis*) were never considered particularly urban birds. Now, however, they are commonly seen soaring on thermals as high as 400 feet above city parks, scanning the ground for rats, squirrels, and other lunch items with their binocular vision. Like the peregrine falcons, these stocky broad-winged birds—named for their cinnamon-colored tails—have recently begun nesting in unlikely spots, such as the Quaker Cemetery in Prospect Park and the area around the Delacorte Theater in Central Park. Their most talked-about love nest, however, was built on the 12th-floor ledge of a fashionable Fifth Avenue and East 74th Street apartment building, right above a limestone frieze of two cherubs. There, in the spring of 1995, a pair of red-tails raised three baby hawks—an unusual occurrence, since these birds typically nest in trees. Perhaps the hawks, which returned again the following spring, were first lured to the building by fame: Actress Mary Tyler Moore lives five floors below, and Woody Allen owns the penthouse next door.

Wild Fact

NIGHT OF THE HUNTER

From the tiny, 7-inch-tall saw-whet owl to the great horned owl, which has a wingspan of more than 4 feet, eight species of owls reside or pass through the five boroughs, including screech owls, snowy owls, barred owls, long-eared owls, and short-eared owls. The most urban of these is the barn owl (*Tyto alba*). This species, whose heart-shaped face resembles that of a monkey, typically nests in old warehouses, abandoned buildings, and the steeples of churches. One of nature's most effective predators, the barn owl can locate and capture its prey in total darkness with the help of its acute sense of hearing.

Because of their known rodent-killing prowess, barn owls were recruited by the city government in 1989. Wooden nesting boxes were installed in trees in Central Park in an effort to lure the owls to control the park's rat population. The owls never had a chance to do the job, however, because their nesting boxes were vandalized. At the Jamaica Bay Wildlife Refuge, a barn owl nesting-box program has been more effective. Scattered around the tiny islands that dot Jamaica Bay are 13 nesting boxes, all of which are occupied by *Tyto alba*. There is no doubt that the refuge's rodent population has been affected. In 1986, after just one season of use by a barn owl pair, a nesting box was cleaned of 38 pounds of remains, including the bones of 546 house mice, 234 Norway rats, and 1,947 meadow voles.

Like any youngsters, peregrine chicks face a wide assortment of hazards in the big city. Growing up on bridges and the tops of office buildings, their perilous first flights often land them on heavily trafficked roadways or send them crashing into skyscraper windows. In one case, a falcon chick plummeted into Eastchester Bay below its nest on the Throgs Neck Bridge, and tried to do the butterfly stroke back to shore. Its life was saved by a bird lover who jumped in the water and towed it to dry land. Similarly, at New York Hospital, where a pair of falcons has a nest, a young bird fell 30 stories down a smokestack; it survived after being dusted off by the hospital's maintenance crew.

Despite the trials and tribulations of life in the big city, New York now has one of the largest concentrations of peregrine falcons in the world—and some of the most successful and productive families. Since 1983, 145 falcon chicks have successfully fledged from New York City nests, and chicks banded by biologists here have been spotted all over the country. One former New York bird has set up house in Baltimore. Another falcon, born on Wall Street, is now raising a family in Sheboygan, Wisconsin.

EGRETS— WE HAVE A FEW

THE HARBOR HERONS

Something strange is happening on the city's tiniest islands. Every spring, hundreds of long-legged wading birds congregate in the East River, underneath the Verrazano-Narrows Bridge, and alongside Fresh Kills Landfill on Staten Island. If it weren't for the smokestacks, high-tension power lines, and passing oil tankers, the scene would look like something out of the Florida Everglades.

Are these birds confused? Apparently not. Since these flyers first began

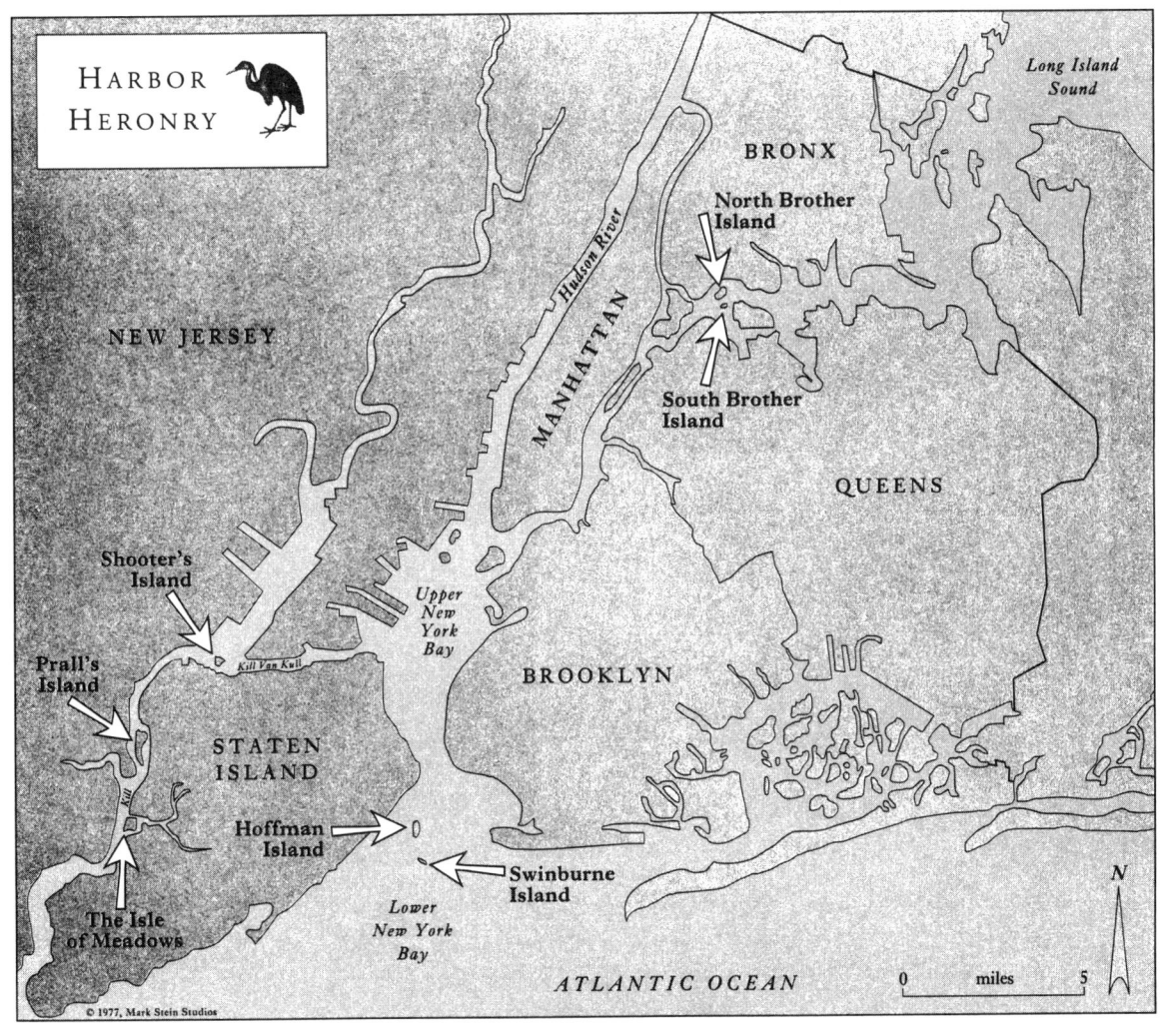

FASHION VICTIMS

The fact that elegant wading birds have taken over abandoned islands in New York Harbor is hard to believe, but what makes the birds' appearance even more impressive is that they were once on the brink of extinction.

During the mid- to late 1800s, it became the rage for fashionable women to wear hats decorated with the feathers of herons, egrets, gulls, and other beautifully plumed birds. The foot-long, pure-white feathers of the great egret were among the most prized. Although hatmakers claimed they obtained the decorative feathers without hurting the birds, they actually bought them from plume hunters who shot the birds en masse in their rookeries. With about 5 million birds killed a year, the result of this bizarre fashion trend was that by 1900, wading birds were close to extinction all along the Atlantic seaboard.

To stop the slaughter, an unusual coalition of ornithologists, sportsmen, and society women organized the first Audubon societies. Members gave lectures about the cruelty of the hatmaking trade, lobbied Congress to pass laws prohibiting plume hunting, and hired their own game wardens to protect the surviving rookeries. As a result of these conservation efforts, herons and egrets year by year have slowly regained their nesting grounds, and their triumphant arrival in New York Harbor is heralded as one of the greatest comebacks in the history of the environmental movement.

nesting on Shooter's Island in the Kill Van Kull shipping channel in 1974, more and more herons and egrets have been coming every year, and an increasing number of the Big Apple's forgotten islands have become avian sanctuaries. In all, eight species of wading birds—including great egrets, glossy ibises, and green-backed herons—now nest in New York Harbor, and thousands of chicks are raised here every year.

When the herons first came house hunting in the 1970s, most of the city's small islands—including Liberty, Ellis, Governors, and Riker's—were already claimed. But several lesser-known outposts had been left to grow wild, and where people saw floating vacant lots, the birds saw real estate.

On 51-acre Shooter's Island off Staten Island, hundreds of great egrets and snowy egrets now arrive each spring to build platter-sized nests on the island's low-growing cherry trees. The males and females share the task of sitting on the eggs and feeding the chicks, and both make flying forays into nearby salt marshes to bring back tasty killifish and fiddler crabs. Once a thriving shipyard, Shooters is now surrounded by the skeletons of old wooden piers and barges, and in recent years, cormorants—black seabirds—have also arrived to nest among the ruins.

All the way across town, just west of the penitentiary on Riker's Island, North and South Brother islands have also been taken over by the birds. Now, in the shadow of prison guard towers, about 1,000 black-crowned night-herons and 200 snowy egrets raise their chicks every year.

Altogether, on island rookeries throughout New York Harbor—on Shooter's, North and South Brother, Pralls, the Isle of Meadows, Hoffman, and Swinburne islands—more than 4,000 wading birds are nesting. These birds have chosen their sites so well that most New Yorkers will never see a heron's nest. In addition to being almost totally inaccessible (the harbor acts like an enormous moat), the islands are near sparsely populated, industrial areas where, despite passing boats, the birds can keep a relatively low profile.

Great blue heron

Although the rookeries are well concealed, the herons themselves are easy to find—particularly the great egrets. During the summer, they fly to surrounding areas, their long white necks curved in a trademark S and their wide, 4½-foot-long wings cutting across the sky like billowing sails. They can also be seen walking on stiltlike legs in the shallows of ponds and lakes in city parks, along the shoreline at Jamaica Bay, and in the salt marshes beneath the Whitestone Bridge and along the Hutchinson River Parkway.

PIGEONS: BIRDS WITH A PAST

The bird most associated with New York City, the bird we see waddling around our city parks and streets—the pigeon (*Columba livia*)—has a far more interesting past than most people would expect. Also called rock doves, pigeons were first brought to this country from Europe, probably during the 1600s, and their original status here was that of a barnyard animal, raised purely for the table.

Over the years, however, these captive pigeons struck out on their own, transforming themselves from potential dinner entrees into birds that roamed freely throughout the urban terrain. Despite this newfound freedom, pigeons never really severed their ties with people. Today, New York City's pigeons survive primarily on a diet of bread and birdseed left out by pigeon lovers. Perched

> *Wild Fact*
>
> ## ANNALS OF BIRD-WATCHING
>
> **Exotic birds, blown thousands of miles off course, sometimes show up in New York City. In the autumns of both 1992 and 1993, an orange-legged seabird—the spotted redshank (*Tringa erythropus*)—usually found in Siberia, turned up in a salt marsh near Avenue X in Brooklyn's Marine Park. Within 24 hours of the first sighting, a veritable stampede of bird-watchers had arrived to stare at this unlikely Russian immigrant.**
>
> **News of such avian visitors is spread through the "New York Rare Bird Alert," a telephone hotline that offers detailed information and daily highlights about unusual birds passing through the city. For the latest scoop, call 212-979-3070.**

atop the heads of bronze statues and flocking around park benches, pigeons wait around for handouts and can even recognize the people who regularly feed them.

The fact that pigeons thrive in such close association with people is not surprising, given their early history. Originally, pigeons came from northwest Africa and the Mediterranean, where they nested in the wild (and still can be found living today) on cliff sides. About 10,000 years ago, people living in North Africa figured out that they could entice some of the wild birds into their villages by building housing for them. Called dovecotes, the first pigeon coops were 10-foot-high, column-shaped birdhouses made of clay and mud—with holes built into them for each rock dove family. Adult pigeons came and went, but the young birds—squab—usually ended up on the dinner table.

Today, pigeons have traded in the dovecotes for building ledges and the girded undersides of bridges and overpasses. In these well-hidden nooks and crannies pigeon families live, and rarely seen baby pigeons are reared. These families are extremely close. The mother and father care for their young together, feeding them "pigeon milk," a curd-like protein-rich substance produced in the crops of both parents. The reason that no one ever sees baby pigeons is that they grow up remarkably fast, reaching close-to-adult size after only a week of pigeon milk feedings.

Despite this nominal independence, some pigeons maintain intimate ties with New Yorkers. Every now and then, you might spot flocks of pigeons flying in tight formation, banking and turning in unison above the rooftops. These are coop pigeons, raised by people who continue the tradition of keeping "lofts" of pigeons that compete in long-distance races. New York City was once one of the nation's pigeon-racing capitals. Pigeon lofts, or coops, were found in almost every neighborhood during the 1930s, '40s, and '50s. On any given racing day, 500 different pigeon owners would compete in long-distance races, driving their birds to release sites as far as 500 miles away. Once let go, the pigeons would fly home at speeds between 45 and 75 miles per hour, using their homing abilities to find their lofts.

During World War II, five pairs of birds from every loft in the city were drafted into the U.S. Army to breed homing pigeons, and this project became an important part of the war effort. In cases where no other means of communication were possible, fast-flying, homing pigeons could carry messages to their home bases. Some of the offspring of New York City's pigeons even went on to become war heroes, but others never adjusted to military life. In 1942, the *New York Times* reported that Red McWilliams Star, a champion racing pigeon, had gone AWOL from his military post at Fort Monmouth, New Jersey, flying back to his neighborhood coop on 52nd Street in Brooklyn. The *Times* reported, "Army Intelligence is vague on Red's motives. He may have just been homesick. . . . for days he ignored his mates in the cote and looked only in one direction—toward Brooklyn."

Today, only about 50 of the city's pigeon lofts remain, but at these lofts, thousands of dollars are spent caring for the birds. Even more is spent to purchase new pigeons, some costing as much as $3,000. Most loft birds, which are bred for speed and endurance, look similar to street pigeons; they have bluish gray feathers, two dark wing bands, and an iridescent sheen around their plump necks. The main difference is that loft birds have larger, more powerful chests—they're "pumped up" for faster flying. Coop pigeons have been clocked doing about 80 miles per hour, while street pigeons can fly only about 45 miles per hour (which still makes *Columba livia* one of the fastest birds in the wild). Some loft birds, called fancy flyers, are bred to have unusual color patterns like white, reddish brown, and silver. A pigeon on the street that has such colors is probably a loft escapee or the recent offspring of an escapee. Birds that have "flown the coop" commonly join the ranks of street pigeons, and their offspring usually revert to their native blue gray coloration after three or four generations.

Despite their impressive past, city pigeons are known troublemakers. They destroy statuary and architecture with their acid-rich droppings, which eat through limestone and discolor brass. Their droppings have even been blamed for causing the death of a human being. In 1982, when a cable on the Brooklyn Bridge snapped—killing a tourist visiting from Japan—the accident was attributed to the corrosive effect of pigeon droppings, which had worn the cable down to a thread.

Pigeon or rock dove

In some cases, an enormous amount of energy is spent keeping pigeons from fouling New York City's buildings and monuments. Following a $9-million renovation of Bryant Park in midtown Manhattan in 1994, flocks of pigeons were discovered to be soiling the just-cleaned statuary and eating freshly planted flowers. To stop this vandalism, the pigeons were put on the "pill," a type of avian contraception called Ornitrol that was laced into kernels of corn. The effort worked, reducing the population from about 150 to less than 20, at a total cost of $2,400 per year. However, the least expensive and most effective check on the city's pigeons is the peregrine falcon population. It has been estimated that these predatory birds remove 200 pigeons from city streets each week.

D-DAY FOR GOTHAM'S RAREST BIRD

A broad expanse of sand strewn with the shells of clams and sea snails, the Breezy Point Tip in the Rockaways is one of New York City's last pristine beaches. On spring days, however, the calm rhythm of the surf is broken—from dawn to dusk—by the whistle and crack of explosives. Positioned behind the dunes, gun-toting biologists are waging a war to save New York City's most embattled species.

A tiny sand-colored shorebird, the piping plover (*Charadrius melodus*) has been on the federal list of endangered and threatened species since 1986. Yet, every spring about a dozen pairs of these people-shy birds still fly into Breezy Point to lay eggs and raise their chicks. For reasons that mystify biologists, the ¾-mile-long beachhead at Breezy Point—with a view of the Manhattan skyline—currently boasts one of the highest concentrations of nesting piping plovers anywhere in the Northeast.

Because they are on the endangered species list, the plovers have been under federal protection since 1988. To safeguard the plover families, the National Parks Service virtually locks down the beach at the Breezy Point Tip—part of Gateway National Recreation Area—each spring and summer. A team of rangers and volunteers patrols seven days a week, shooing away sunbathers and anglers, setting up cagelike shelters over plover nests to keep predators out, and peppering the sky with noise-making, aerial explosives to drive off marauding herring gulls.

FLOCKS OF SEAGULLS

While the piping plovers cling to survival, another group of shore birds is taking over. Biologists estimate that there are as many as 1 million seagulls in New York City—up from almost none 100 years ago.

Though most people don't notice the difference, there are actually four species of seagulls common in New York City: the herring gull, the great black-backed gull, the laughing gull, and the ring-billed gull. Among these, the herring gull (*Larus argentatus*), with its white body, slate-colored wings, yellow beak, and high-pitched cries, is far and away the most familiar. The herring gull can be seen all along the city's hundreds of miles of shoreline—sailing, diving, and hovering above lapping waves and pier pilings. Not particularly finicky about what it eats, the herring gull has experienced an enormous human-abetted range expansion throughout North America, thanks to easy pickings at local garbage dumps. Of all the herring gulls that live along the eastern seaboard, *one-third* are believed to live in the New York City area. And they don't come here for the culture. At Staten Island's Fresh Kills Landfill—the largest garbage dump in the entire world—herring gulls can be seen swarming like locusts over the mountain of trash.

Though the herring gull is the most common of the city's seagulls, the laughing gull (*Larus atricilla*) is the species that is causing trouble across town. Named laughing gulls because their calls sound like hysterical cackling, these black-capped birds were once driven completely from the state of New York by sportsmen and plume hunters. In 1979, however, about 15 pairs of laughing gulls began nesting at Jocos Marsh, a wetland in Jamaica Bay that borders John F. Kennedy Airport. By 1991, the number of nests had grown from 15 to more than 7,000, and airport officials became increasingly concerned about the number of collisions between birds and airplanes, in particular because they recalled a 1975 incident at JFK when a DC-10 was brought down by a flock of great black-backed gulls. Though no people were injured, the plane was destroyed. Meanwhile, the current situation has done nothing to relieve concerns: Between 1986 and 1995, airport officials reported the deaths of 1,129 laughing gulls in collisions with aircraft.

JFK workers have used noise cannons, pictures of owls, and recordings of "distressed gulls"—all without success—to try to convince the laughing gulls not to enter JFK's airspace. Finally, in 1991, sharpshooters were brought in to bring down any gulls that dared near the runways. More than 30,000 gulls were blasted out of the skies in the program's first four years, prompting protests from animal rights and environmental groups. Today, the protests continue—and the airport is trying a new tactic. Trained hawks and falcons are being brought in to attack the gulls when they approach the forbidden zone.

Great black-backed gull

Ironically, the herring gulls—once a rare species themselves because of overhunting—have become one of the biggest threats to the plovers' survival here. Able to thrive in a variety of situations (particularly among people and near garbage dumps), herring gulls have successfully adapted to urban life and dramatically increased their population, establishing a colony of about 1,000 birds behind the Breezy Point dunes and laying siege to the plovers' territory.

Meanwhile, the plovers' survival strategies have actually worked against them. In early spring, New York City's plovers fly in from their wintering grounds in Florida and South America and proceed to lay three to four sand-colored eggs right on the beach. Although this technique helps camouflage the eggs from animal predators, it does not work very well when thousands of human sun worshippers are mobbing the shore. Moreover, when the eggs hatch, around Memorial Day, the plover families must make numerous daily trips to the water's edge to feed, stamping their tiny feet to force insects and marine worms to the surface. Unfortunately, when these painfully shy birds see people or gulls on the beach, they protectively corral their chicks back to the dunes—sometimes causing the protein-needy youngsters to starve while they are in hiding.

Piping plovers were placed on the endangered species list because their lifestyle brought them in direct conflict with an increasing number of beach-goers. Decades ago, these plovers nested on local beaches by the hundreds, but they began to disappear when beach development and recreation mushroomed after World War II. The destruction of natural dunes and beach ecosystems has eliminated most of their prime nesting habitat. All told, biologists estimate that there are only 1,100 pairs of piping plovers remaining on the Atlantic coast from Newfoundland to North Carolina—most of them concentrated in small government-protected seashores such as the Breezy Point Tip.

Although the plovers must endure being attacked by other birds, being squashed by off-road vehicles, and even having their nests vandalized by people (who risk a $25,000 federal fine for harassing an endangered species), they maintain an uneasy peace with crowded conditions in New York City. "New York City plovers are tougher," observes Mary Hake, a National Parks Service biologist who worked in the plover protection program for eight years. "They're up against pressure from the natural world—from high tides, feral cats, and gulls—and pressure from the human world. Helicopters, jet skis, and even the

Concorde are zooming by all the time, yet they still use these beaches. You have to have respect for these little birds."

With the protection of the National Parks Service, New York City's piping plovers have managed to raise 118 chicks at the Breezy Point Tip since 1988—not a major success story and not without some bitterly disappointing years, but enough to help keep the species going.

WARBLER MANIA

Every weekend in April and May, thousands of bird-watchers crowd into the wooded areas of Central Park in search of bright red, yellow, and blue songbirds called warblers. Hundreds of these tiny birds stop in New York City on their way from Mexico, the Caribbean, and South and Central America. Surrounded by admirers, they rest a few days, eat a few insects, and soon are on their way again to nesting sites farther north. For them, the city is just one of many welcome pitstops on what could be a 1,000-mile-long migration. For people, however, the warblers' arrival in New York City is as enthusiastically anticipated as the return of the swallows to Capistrano. Often, the warbler-watchers outnumber the birds.

Forty-one species of warblers, many of which are hard to tell apart from a distance, have been spotted in Central Park alone. Frequently, the birds are not actually seen but are identified by their songs, which sound more buzzy than tuneful. For warbler connoisseurs who master these distinctions, expeditions to visit these brightly colored birds have become both a rite of spring and an obsession.

Each week brings a new wave of warbler species. Central Park's bird-watchers say you can even set your calendar by the birds. In mid- to late April, yellow-rumped warblers coming from the American South stop over by the hundreds. In early May, American redstarts—black warblers with vivid orange patches on their wings, tails, and bodies—

Wild Fact

THEY'RE PLAYING OUR SONG

Almost every songbird is known for its unique species-specific call, warbling, twittering, or chirping to attract mates or threaten interlopers. Mockingbirds (*Mimus polyglottos*), however, do not write their own songs. One of nature's most talented mimics, they imitate other birds, stringing together the calls of bluejays, robins, and crows like a medley of greatest hits. One study found that male mockingbirds could learn and imitate as many as 36 different birdsongs. In New York City, mockingbirds have been known to add city sounds to their repertoires, doing near-perfect impressions of police sirens and even car alarms.

TIPS FOR FLEDGLINGS

With more than 320 resident and regularly migrating species, New York City offers some of the best bird-watching in the country, and city bird-watchers have an advantage over their rural counterparts: Because many of our birds have grown used to having people around, avian aficionados have a chance to see their quarry up close and personal. All you need are a sharp pair of eyes, a cheap pair of binoculars, and a field guide to North American birds.

David Burg, former president of the New York City Audubon Society, suggests that beginning birders head for the Ramble in *Central Park* to hone their skills. "In the Ramble, many birds act almost as if they were tame," he says. "This is a great place to get to know woodland birds like warblers. They don't maintain their distance or fly away, because they haven't necessarily learned to see people as a threat." For waterbirds, Burg recommends the *Jamaica Bay Wildlife Refuge* in Queens. Surrounded by green marshland, it's the best spot to see a wide variety of ducks, long-legged waders, and sandpipers—they sometimes fly right overhead on the refuge's trails.

More advanced birders may want to try farther-flung sites within the city to observe particular species and their habitats. For example, at the *Breezy Point Tip,* a federally protected beach in the *Rockaways,* you can visit a springtime nesting colony of common terns, rare white seabirds with orange bills. Or try *Floyd Bennett Field,* a decommissioned airport in Brooklyn that is now part of the Gateway National Recreation Area, to observe grassland birds such as kestrels (sparrow hawks) and savannah sparrows.

The New York City Audubon Society (212-691-7483) is the mecca for local birders. With about 10,000 members, it is the biggest Audubon chapter in the country. Its members lead birding expeditions throughout the five boroughs, going to spots like *Inwood Hill Park* to look for migrating songbirds and to Crooke's Point on the Staten Island shore to spy on rare seabirds. Classes for beginning birders are held at the society's headquarters in Manhattan, where novices are taught, among other things, to tell rose-breasted grosbeaks from common grackles.

fly in from Central and South America. In late May, black-throated blue warblers arrive from as far south as Bolivia.

One reason that warblers are so special is that they are increasingly rare. Over the past 20 years, warblers and other songbirds have been slowly vanishing. According to data from the North American Breeding Bird Census, three-fourths of all Eastern songbird species are seen less and less with each passing year. As forests are cut down in their wintering grounds south of the border and in their nesting grounds here, migrating songbirds have fewer and fewer places that they can call home. They have also suffered along their migration routes, where they have fewer and fewer places to stop and feed, thus making the continued preservation of sites like Central Park surprisingly critical.

LOCAL HEROES— SQUIRRELS

In the *Audubon Society Field Guide to North American Mammals,* the habitat of the gray squirrel is described as "hardwood or mixed forests, with nut trees." Obviously, New York City's squirrels have not consulted this publication. In fact, these bushy-tailed rodents are such a common sight that most city residents take them completely for granted. In Manhattan, the squirrel population density is thickest in pocket parks, such as Union Square, Madison Square, Tompkins Square, and Washington Square, where gray squirrels can be seen perched atop benches, prancing across lawns, and spread-eagle on the sides of wire-mesh trash cans.

Manhattan's plump, glossy-coated squirrels (*Sciurus carolinensis*)—which come in gray- and, less commonly, black-furred varieties—are descendants of the wild squirrels that lived in this region's forests before New York City was founded. Today, however, there are far more squirrels than when European settlers first arrived. In a natural forest habitat, each squirrel has a territory of about 1 acre, which it fiercely defends against interlopers (some squirrel-on-squirrel attacks result in death or dismemberment). Yet in Manhattan's pocket parks, more than 20 squirrels have been known to live on a single acre in apparent harmony.

The source of squirrels' complacency toward high-density living is easy access to food. City-slicker squirrels successfully mine the city's trees for acorns and seeds, and they mine the city's residents, too. These cute operators have so endeared themselves to people that some squirrel lovers befriend individual animals and return to the same spot every day to give them their favorite snacks. Thus, while squirrels in nearby forests spend their lives dodging predators and foraging for a limited food supply, New York City's squirrels are dining on unshelled peanuts, pecans, and filberts purchased from gourmet markets like Balducci's.

Despite their reliance on handouts, city squirrels maintain certain wild affinities. Most significantly, they need to be around trees—something that the city's parks provide them in abundance. Female squirrels raise their families, usually three or four babies, in nests constructed out of leaves in the crooks of tree limbs, and both female and male squirrels use trees for resting. Looking at a tree from the third story of a building often affords a view of normally frenetic squirrels loafing high in the branches. Squirrels also forage in trees and can be seen scampering up and down pin oaks for acorns and Norway maples for seeds. Thrifty souls, squirrels bury any unshelled nuts that they don't immediately eat and dig them up again in the winter.

Aside from their dependence on trees and a certain sense of frugality, city squirrels behave differently than their wild counterparts. In the country, squirrels are active only at dusk and dawn—the times when they're safest from predators like owls and hawks. New York City squirrels, however, have adopted a slightly different schedule and are most active during daylight hours when they are most likely to get freebies from squirrel lovers.

In rural areas where they are hunted, gray squirrels are known to be extremely wary of people. In a 1974 issue of the *New Yorker*, however, Eugene Kinkead proposed that the city's squirrels could not be accused of similar craftiness. Kinkead reported that in 1901, after Central Park's squirrel population had reached a peak of over 1,000, park officials decided that the population needed to be culled. Within a week, hired guns had blasted about 300 squirrels—presumably from close range. Since then the unwary squirrels have bounced back. Central Park's squirrel population has not only rebounded but far surpassed its original numbers. In the early 1980s, more than 13,800 squirrels were estimated to live within the park's 843 acres.

Wild Fact

SQUIRREL PARK

Surrounded by architectural gems like the Flatiron Building, Madison Square Park is one of the city's most urbane green spots—a holdover from Old New York. But such gentility didn't stop the 6-acre park (on Manhattan's East 23rd Street) from becoming the site of a neighborhood fracas. In the early 1990s, a turf war broke out between barking dogs and "stressed-out" squirrels—or, to be more accurate, between dog owners and squirrel fanatics, each of whom claimed the park's central lawn for their favorite mammal. The dogs, it seemed, were chasing the squirrels as part of their daily exercise and, as a result, the squirrels were becoming nervous and losing weight.

After two years of confrontation (during which two priests were brought in to bless the park's animals), a truce was declared, and each faction was given its own territory. The canines were relegated to a fenced-off, wood chip–carpeted dog run, and the squirrels were presented with a "hotel" at the eastern end of the park. There, a dead royal paulownia tree, with its limbs cut off and holes bored into the trunk, now serves as rent-free housing for the city's most popular rodent.

RAT NATION

They go by many names—sewer rat, brown rat, water rat, wharf rat, and most recently, "Super Rat." But they all refer to the same species, the Norway rat (*Rattus norvegicus*), a gray-furred, beady-eyed rodent that is the object of fear and hatred wherever it dwells.

Nothing freezes the blood of a New Yorker quite as much as meeting a rat scuttling out of a dumpster or maneuvering through the underbrush on the edge of a park. But such encounters—though memorable—only hint at the enormity of the rat's true presence here. Estimates of the city's rat population traditionally allow one rat for every person. That's 7.3 million rats. However, many experts believe that their numbers actually far exceed the human population.

Norway rats thrive in every borough. They live in old, abandoned, and neglected apartment buildings in East Harlem and the East Village; they occupy vacant lots in the Bronx and old wharves on Staten Island; and they prosper in the basements of high-rise buildings on Park Avenue. But it is *how* they live that makes the "Rat Nation" largely invisible to us. Grouped in colonies of anywhere from 20 to 150 members, Norway rats live in areas normally inaccessible to humans. They excavate elaborate underground homes, a foot below the surface, in abandoned lots and subway tunnels, and they travel inside the walls of buildings. Their favorite haunt, however, is the city's sewer system, where the amenities include running water, easy access to the street, and all the privacy they need. Biologists estimate that there may be 500 rats for every mile of New York City sewer line.

Rats enter the human world usually when they are scavenging for food. During their 1- to 2-year life span, most rats never stray more than 100 feet from their home turf, and a typical food foray can be just a matter of yards—from a midtown Manhattan sewer grate to a food-filled garbage bag outside a two-star restaurant. Rats also raid storage sites in basements and warehouses, accessing these areas by squeezing their supple bodies through holes as small as nickels. Where there are no holes, the rats create their own, gnawing through walls with their sharp teeth, which can grow as much as 5 inches a year.

Rats live off of any food in their reach; indeed, part of their success comes from the fact that they are not finicky eaters. Like humans, rats are omnivorous,

> ### Wild Fact
>
> **REALITY BITES**
>
> New York City's rats can conjure nightmarish visions worthy of *Willard* and *Ben*, two horror films that depict rats swarming over their victims and biting them to death. But when it comes to real-life attacks on human beings, rats don't live up to their Hollywood billing. According to the city's Department of Health, out of an average 13,000 animal bites reported every year, only about 150 are inflicted by *Rattus norvegicus*. By comparison, people are bitten 10,000 times by dogs, 1,500 times by cats, and 1,400 times by other human beings.

eating from all four food groups—meat, vegetable, cereal, and dairy. They also don't mind sloppy seconds. In fact, they eat anything from pet food left outside for stray cats to last night's Chinese takeout. On rare occasions, they have even crawled into children's beds to snatch cookies.

Our loathing of rats has tended to exaggerate their size to the level of urban legend. People traumatized by rat sightings on the street commonly make claims such as, "It was as big as a cat, I tell you!" Despite the heartfelt nature of such reports, all adult rats weigh in at about 1 pound and measure about 12 inches in length—with little variation.

By contrast, stories about the Norway rat's feats of physical prowess are based on fact. With sharp incisors and jaws that can exert more than 20,000 pounds of pressure per square inch, Norway rats can chew through lead pipes, concrete, and even bricks. They can swim half a mile and tread water for 3 days. They can jump 3 feet in the air and climb straight up brick walls. They can use their naked, scaly tails—which are half again as long as their bodies—as balancing rods while navigating exposed plumbing and pipes.

Even more impressive is their rate of reproduction. An adult female Norway rat can bear five litters every year, each containing 7 to 11 pups. Thus, in a single lifetime, one rat can produce 150 progeny.

The name "Norway rat" is a misnomer, for *Rattus norvegicus* comes originally from central Asia, where it lived in the wild on the cold, dry steppes, adapting to its harsh environment by digging extensive underground burrows. This rat was not recorded in Europe until the mid-1700s, and it was not documented in Norway until 1762. How these rats initially expanded their range is still debated. They may have traveled to Europe in wagons that accompanied migrants fleeing famine-stricken areas, or they may have made the journey on their own. In 1727, huge armies of rats were reported swimming across the Volga River in Russia—headed west. However they made their first move, Norway rats quickly spread throughout the world, traveling in the holds of sailing ships and ultimately colonizing six continents.

Norway rats are said to have first arrived in North America on the boats of Hessian troops during the American Revolution. And ever since their arrival on these shores, New Yorkers have been trying to eliminate them. At Manhattan's Bellevue Hospital, arsenic, strychnine, and even terrier dogs were used to kill thousands of rats during the 1850s. In spite of these efforts, a baby who had died on the heavily infested "female ward" was partially devoured by rats in 1860. Later, in 1931, thousands of toxic sandwiches (made with toast dipped in digitalis) were planted in known rat hangouts at the Central Park Zoo—because rats were stealing meat from the zoo's lions and terrorizing the hippopotamus.

Countless efforts to eradicate the Rat Nation have continued ever since. During the 1960s, when President Lyndon B. Johnson declared a national "War on Poverty," New York Governor Nelson Rockefeller simultaneously declared a "Total War on Rats." Millions of dollars were spent spreading anticoagulant poison throughout the worst rat-infested neighborhoods in the city. But after a couple of years, the enemy came back with a secret weapon, the "Super Rat." The Super Rat was immune to the anticoagulant poison and passed this immunity on to its offspring. Exterminators were then forced to change their strategy—switching their poisons every month to prevent the creation of more poison-resistant rats. To make things worse, rats have acquired another trait. Through their long association with people, rats have—as a survival mechanism—become "neophobic"; that is, they fear anything new, and even turn up their noses at fresh cheese and other goodies if they appear in unfamiliar spots. As a result, rats are wary of eating anything that is put out as bait. Today, exterminators actually have to coddle their prey, sometimes plying the rats with non-poisoned delicacies for days before sneaking in the deadly stuff.

These days, there is no more talk of a full-scale war against the rat world. City officials limit their battles to small, winnable skirmishes. Recent engagements have included the tunnels of Grand Central Station and the streets around Brooklyn's Borough Hall. Thousands of rats perished at both locations, but these victories can be seen as only a momentary blip. If this is war, the rats are winning.

Rattus norvegicus

Wild Fact

LOST LUGGAGE

Coyotes are not the only varmints to have migrated here from the American West. Black-tailed jackrabbits—rangy, long-eared critters that can leap 20 feet and are native to Texas—have made a home for themselves alongside the jumbo jets at John F. Kennedy Airport. How did they get here? According to airport workers, a crateful arrived 40 years ago and was supposed to be shipped to a game farm, where the rabbits would be stalked by hunters. Instead, the jackrabbits broke loose and discovered that the grassy areas alongside the runways were similar to their native desert flatlands. The escaped jackrabbits and their descendants have been living at JFK ever since—and new litters of baby jackrabbits are born at the airport every spring.

COYOTES: "NEW YORK CITY OR BUST"

In the winter of 1995, the discovery of coyotes running wild in New York City caused a media sensation. First, two coyotes were found dead—victims of hit-and-run accidents—in the Bronx. Then, a few days later, a sickly coyote, nicknamed Wiley, was reported in Woodlawn Cemetery, where a kindly couple, who thought it was a weird-looking stray dog, had been feeding it leftover spaghetti and meatballs. Following Wiley's discovery, the local *paparazzi* started staging stakeouts to photograph the animal, and when the Parks Department finally held a press conference about the "coyote situation," so many TV camera crews descended on the cemetery that Wiley decided to go permanently incognito.

A mammologist with the Bronx Zoo, Ed Spevak, also known as Dr. Coyote because of a stint he served in Texas, was the first to identify the bodies of the runover coyotes. Though coyotes (*Canis latrans*)—which, like the wolf, are a truly wild species of canine—are more commonly seen in the West, Spevak wasn't at all surprised to see them turning up in New York City. Ever since the early twentieth century, these bushy-tailed and pointy-nosed canines have been extending their home base, moving farther and farther east with every opportunity. "It was only a matter of time," says Spevak. "We knew coyotes were in Westchester, and there's nothing separating Westchester from the Bronx."

Coyotes are incredibly adaptable animals, making them ideal candidates for city life. They're the fastest canines in the wild, able to reach speeds of 25 miles per hour at a trot and 40 miles per hour in short bursts. They're not finicky, eating everything from rats and squirrels to grass and table scraps. And though shy of people, they make the most of their situation: In Los Angeles, they're vilified for occasionally making a snack out of house cats, and in New Jersey they have recently begun occupying small wooded lots, right next to suburban homes.

The road to New York City, however, has been a long one. Before 1900, coyotes lived only west of the Mississippi River. Then, they followed the trail of sheep farmers and openings blazed by the elimination of their enemy, the wolf. First, coyotes loped into the Midwest, then into Ontario, and finally into the Adirondacks in the 1920s. Since then, they have infiltrated almost all of New York State, where—despite early attempts to eradicate them by placing bounties on their heads—they are currently greeted by wildlife biologists as a welcome mammal, now that all the state's native wolves are gone. Today, coyotes are walking right into New York City. All they have to do is take the Old Croton Aqueduct Trail, which leads straight from Westchester County into Van Cortlandt Park.

Since the original three coyotes arrived, several others have been spotted in the Bronx—unfortunately, usually dead on the highway. These sightings have prompted proposals to put up "Coyote X-ing" signs on the Major Deegan Expressway.

REPTILES AND AMPHIBIANS

In 1929, the American Museum of Natural History conducted a census of reptiles and amphibians in New York City to determine how many kinds of snakes, turtles, frogs, toads, and salamanders were living within the five boroughs. The census found that some animals that had once lived here, such as the poisonous timber rattlesnake, had been driven out. However, many less-conspicuous reptiles and amphibians remained, and in total 44 species were counted.

During the 1990s, the New York City Parks Department conducted its own reptile and amphibian census to find out which species the city had lost during the intervening 6 decades. Biologists and volunteers searched the city's parks, working in the middle of the night, when these animals are most active. Using headlamps on their nocturnal expeditions, searchers looked and listened (many frogs and toads were identified by their mating calls). Altogether, they rooted out 32 species—12 fewer than their predecessors had in 1929. Among the 12 species that were missing were the wood turtle and the northern

MARINE MAMMALS

Most marine mammals, such as whales, dolphins, and seals, are confined to the city's aquariums and zoos. However, wild sea creatures sometimes do come calling in New York City's waterways:

- Perhaps the most renowned visit was paid by "Chessie," a 1,200-pound, rare Florida manatee. First sighted far from home in Chesapeake Bay, Chessie—who looks like a walrus minus the tusks but is more closely related to elephants—astounded wildlife biologists by continuing his journey northward, swimming by Manhattan through the East River and past Riker's Island on August 7, 1995. One of only 1,800 manatees left in the United States, Chessie ultimately traveled 2,000 miles round-trip from his home in Florida's Banana River to Point Judith, Rhode Island. On his return home, he passed through New York City again, where he was spotted in Staten Island's Kill Van Kull.

- Less carefree was the journey of Whilhemina, the pilot whale that contracted pneumonia and was spotted swimming in the waters off Orchard Beach in the Bronx. Rescued by volunteers from the Okeanos Ocean Research Foundation, the 1,300-pound, 12-foot-long whale was taken to Coney Island's Aquarium for Wildlife Conservation, where for 8 months she was nursed back to health. To be released back into the Atlantic on April 9, 1994, Whilhemina had to be lifted from her tank at the aquarium by crane, driven in a flatbed truck filled with ice to Canarsie, and taken by Coast Guard cutter to ocean waters 60 miles offshore. A few days after being set free, Whilhemina was spotted by a fishing boat, swimming off the New Jersey shore.

- The one marine mammal that can be called a frequent guest of New York City is the harbor seal. Though they usually prefer to lounge on Long Island's secluded beaches and offshore islands, harbor seals—which reach 5 feet in length and weigh up to 300 pounds—are seen more and more along the city's coastline. In winter they sometimes "haul out," or flop themselves up onto dry docks, in Brooklyn and Queens. They have also been seen sunning themselves on rocks in the East River underneath the Williamsburg Bridge. In the past decade, the number of harbor seals spending the winter on Long Island's watery perimeter has increased tenfold—from 400 to 4,000—and marine biologists believe that the local tribe is thriving because of laws that give seals and other marine mammals federal protection.

cricket frog. Among the lucky 32 survivors were red-spotted newts, garter snakes, and painted turtles. The researchers also found that some boroughs had fared worse than others. In Brooklyn and Manhattan, only tough "superspecies" like the snapping turtle and the bullfrog persisted in large numbers. Queens, the Bronx, and Staten Island, on the other hand, had pockets of habitat where an array of rarer species, like the spotted salamander and the northern water snake, could still make their homes.

Black racer snake

Reptiles and amphibians have suffered losses in the city for a variety of reasons. Many of the areas where they once lived—ponds, streams, and swamps—simply were filled in, and unlike birds, these animals couldn't flee when their homes were being destroyed. The building of highways also fragmented areas of suitable habitat, and turtles, frogs, and salamanders often wound up getting hit by cars as they traveled back and forth between land and water during their life cycles.

One reptilian species for which the situation has improved, however, is the diamondback terrapin (*Malaclemys terrapin*). An aquatic turtle that lives in local estuaries and salt marshes, the diamondback terrapin was once almost eaten out of existence. A popular delicacy all along the Atlantic seaboard, terrapin flesh was the main ingredient in turtle soup, a dish that was all the rage at New York dinner parties during the latter half of the nineteenth century. By the 1940s, the terrapin's numbers had declined precipitously. When the terrapin soup fad faded away, however, diamondbacks began to return. Now these salt marsh–loving terrapins are once again thriving in the brackish waters around New York City.

Attempts are currently being made to reintroduce other reptiles into areas where their habitats have been restored. On hundreds of acres of protected land within the Gateway National Recreation Area in Brooklyn and Queens, black racer snakes, hognose snakes, painted turtles, and eastern box turtles are all being turned loose—and many of these creatures are doing well in their new homes. The eastern box turtle, a species of land turtle that was reintroduced at Floyd Bennett Field in Brooklyn, has now begun breeding. The Fowler's toad, a 5-inch-long warty toad that was reintroduced onto federal land on the Breezy Point Tip, has also been multiplying. In the spring of 1993, a Rockaways home-

THE SNAPPING TURTLE: URBAN SURVIVOR

Although the story of alligators living in New York City's sewers is pure urban legend, another fierce reptile, the snapping turtle (*Chelydra serpentina*), does inhabit the five boroughs. Able to grow to a weight of 40 pounds, the snapping turtle has a deserved reputation for being pugnacious, and it is the city's most successful native reptile. A member of the Testudines, an order of animals that has persisted through 200 million years of Earth's history, the snapping turtle has—perhaps even more impressively—survived the last 4 centuries in New York City.

Nearly every body of water, no matter how small, contains at least one snapping turtle. Dubbed "ecologically tolerant" by biologists, these turtles live both in freshwater ponds, like the lake in Prospect Park, and in the salty waters of estuaries, like Jamaica Bay. Snapping turtles have also been found living in some of the city's most contaminated waterways, including the notorious Newtown Creek in Queens and ponds within the Fresh Kills Landfill on Staten Island.

Aside from this tolerance for brackish, dirty water and a limited supply of oxygen, snapping turtles derive their success from their ability to live unobtrusively—a tough act for a creature whose shell is 2 feet across and whose serrated tail has a dinosaurlike appearance. Snapping turtles manage to keep a low profile by spending most of their time submerged. Although they may snatch an occasional duckling or gosling, snapping turtles more commonly eat dead fish, expired frogs, aquatic vegetation, and even sandwiches dropped into the water. This nonpicky attitude toward food has earned them the nickname "pond janitors."

Like many other animals that thrive in the city, snapping turtles are prodigious breeders. Female snapping turtles lay an unusually large number of eggs, as many as 70 per clutch, a strategy that increases their hatchlings' chances of survival. However, it is while laying eggs in late spring that females are also most vulnerable. To lay their eggs, snapping turtles must leave the safety of the pond and risk being hit by cars while they look for an appropriately sandy egg-laying spot. It is during these perilous land expeditions that these turtles are most likely to show their nasty streaks. To defend themselves, snapping turtles are more than happy to earn their names, and their bite can separate a person from a finger.

Eastern box turtle

owner thought he was being visited by one of the seven plagues when thousands of baby toads besieged his backyard. The story received great play on local newscasts, but it turned out the Fowler's toads were just having a good year.

A peregrine falcon comes in for a landing on a ledge above its 59th floor nest on Manhattan's Metropolitan Life building, next to Grand Central Station. Despite the peregrine falcon's status as a federally endangered species, a dozen pairs now nest on New York City's buildings and bridges. *Photograph by Michael Feller*

The foundations of the city are surprisingly ancient. Most of the New York City's bedrock lies buried beneath buildings, streets, and thick layers of soil—however, New York's basement layer sometimes makes it to the surface. This outcrop of schist, a type of metamorphic rock, near 63rd Street in Central Park was formed 400 million years ago. However, the grooves in its surface were carved just 22,000 years ago by the Wisconsin Ice Sheet as it traveled across Manhattan. The outcrop in the forest at the Bronx's Van Cortlandt Park (*right*) is more than twice as old. Its gray-and-white bands are characteristic of the city's oldest type of bedrock, 1.1-billion-year-old Fordham gneiss. *Photographs by Michael Falco*

Existing on New York's watery edges and flushed daily by the tides, salt marshes are one of the city's most significant ecosystems, providing critical wildlife habitat for a wide variety of birds, commercial fish such as striped bass and bluefish, crab, and shellfish. Although only about one-sixth of the city's original wetlands have survived the onslaught of development, salt marshes can still be found throughout the city.

This aerial view of Jocos Marsh, next to John F. Kennedy Airport in Jamaica Bay's northeast corner, is dominated by tidal channels and green salt marsh cord grasses (*Spartina alterniflora* and *Spartina patens*), the keystone species of the salt marsh ecosystem. Two great egrets (*inset right*) perch atop an abandoned boat in Four Sparrow Marsh at the southern end of Brooklyn's Flatbush Avenue. Manhattan's last surviving salt marsh (*inset above*) can be found at the island's northern tip in Inwood Hill Park beside the Harlem River Ship Canal. A diamondback terrapin (*inset top right*) lays its eggs on the edge of a salt marsh at the Jamaica Bay Wildlife Refuge, and a male fiddler crab (*inset middle right*) emerges from its tiny burrow in the mud flats during low tide. *Joco Marsh Aerial: Photograph by Don Riepe; Egrets: Photograph by Michael Feller; Terrapin: Photograph by Don Riepe; Inwood Marsh: Photograph by Michael Feller; Fiddler Crab: Photograph by Don Riepe*

At the city's sandy seashores in Brooklyn, Queens, and Staten Island, beach ecosystems are home to a diverse array of plant and animal life.

After a storm, the shells of surf clams are piled at the high tide line at Rockaway Beach. Prickly pear cactus (*inset, top*) blooms in sandy soil along New York City's shores. Smooth sumac, a tough shrub-like tree, (*inset, bottom*) also thrives in sandy areas; dark green in summer, its leaves turn crimson in fall.

A rare sight, the sand-colored eggs (*inset, middle*) of the piping plover, a federally endangered shorebird, are laid on the beach at the Breezy Point Tip every spring. *Photographs by Don Riepe.*

At Brooklyn's Floyd Bennett Field, an abandoned airport that is now part of the Gateway National Recreation Area, the flatlands around the old runways have been turned into a grassland wildlife preserve, where hawks and other birds of prey, such as the snowy owl *(inset, far right)*, can be seen hunting for field mice. Managed jointly by the New York City Audubon Society and the National Parks Service, the grasslands are sometimes intentionally set afire *(inset, below)*. These "prescribed burns," preserve the grassland habitat, prevent non-grassland plants from taking over, and clear the way for a diverse array of sun-loving wildflowers *(inset, above)*. Photographs by Don Riepe.

The city's 5,000 acres of forest, from the Ramble in Central Park to the sprawling Staten Island Greenbelt, are secluded havens for both wildlife and urban naturalists. At Alley Pond Park in Queens, the autumn leaves of sweet gums, red maples, and cherry trees color the surface of kettle ponds in the park's upland forest.

Three long-eared owls *(top)* occupy a winter roost on Hunter Island at Pelham Bay Park in the Bronx. Jack-in-the-Pulpit *(right)* grows in the city's damp woodlands, and spotted salamanders *(above)* manage to survive in and around the kettle ponds in Alley Pond Park by spending most of their lives underground. *Photographs by Michael Feller.*

Besides *Homo sapiens*, numerous species of animals get their first glimpse of the world in New York City. At the Jamaica Bay Wildlife Refuge, nesting boxes put up by biologists for barn owls (*top right*) have attracted several families. Bunnies, the babies of wild Eastern cottontail rabbits (*above*), are also reared at the refuge. Born high above the fray on a nesting platform erected at the Gateway National Recreation Area, a pair of ospreys (*bottom right*), a once-federally threatened species of hawk, prepare to leave home after just eight weeks of life. Two great egret chicks (*bottom left*) await the return of their parents to their nest on South Brother Island in the middle of the East River; thousands of such wading birds are born on tiny islands around the city each spring. *Barn Owls: Photograph by Don Riepe; Bunnies: Photograph by Don Riepe; Osprey and Chicks: Photograph by Don Riepe; Baby Egrets: Photograph by Michael Feller.*

Biorhythms: Shown here at Jamaica Bay, horseshoe crabs (*right*) congregate along the city's shorelines in late spring to mate and lay eggs. Taking advantage of this annual ritual, a tagging study performed by the National Parks Service is determining the summer and winter ranges of these ancient creatures.

During spring and fall, birds migrating along the Atlantic Flyway can be seen in flocks along the city's shores. Sanderlings (*left*) feed on the beaches of the Rockaways after journeying from their breeding grounds in the Arctic. Several kinds of insects migrate too, most notably monarch butterflies, which can be seen sipping nectar from seaside goldenrod (*below*) while on their migration flight to Mexico.

Perhaps the city's most curious natural phenomenon, the periodical cicada (*bottom*) spends most of its life buried underground and only emerges in its 17th year when it makes its grand entrance en masse—accompanied by an enormous racket. Now confined to the borough of Staten Island, this insect is scheduled to make its next appearance in the year 2013. *Horseshoe Crabs, Sanderlings and Monarch butterfly: Photographs by Don Riepe; Cicada: Photograph by Michael Feller*

At the Hunter Island Marine Zoology and Geology Sanctuary at Pelham Bay Park in the Bronx. (*top*), an erratic boulder defines the landscape. Despite receiving 16 million visitors annually, Central Park (*above*) remains one of the city's wild places. *Photographs by Michael Feller.*

Freshwater wetlands and near-pristine scenery greet visitors at Blue Heron Park on Staten Island. *Photograph by Michael Feller.*

The moon and the A-train loom over the East Pond at the Jamaica Bay Wildlife Refuge.

Photographs by Don Riepe

COCKROACHES: THE GUESTS THAT WOULDN'T LEAVE

Cockroaches (pronounced "cock-a-roach" in New York–ese) are the city's most common animals. Exterminators, who are on intimate terms with cockroaches, say that if there is one rat for every New Yorker, there are at least 100 roaches for every rat, putting the city's cockroach population well into the billions.

Despite cockroaches' strong attachment to city life, they are not native New Yorkers or even originally from North America. Among the New World's earliest settlers, cockroaches are known to have immigrated along with the colonists on wooden ships, perhaps as early as the Mayflower. Although their origins have been traced to tropical Africa, New York City's most common roach species have never been found anywhere in the wild. Apparently, they have adapted well to their new lifestyles, preferring the cozy comforts of drainpipes and crumb-strewn kitchens to the unpredictability of scavenging in the great outdoors.

Cockroaches need warm, humid environments to survive, and that makes them feel right at home in New York City, where heating and plumbing systems create a kind of artificial tropical habitat. If the city's buildings can be thought of as a vast zoo designed for this exotic animal, then the apartment tenants and homeowners are the zookeepers, providing daily feedings of food crumbs, book bindings, shed human skin, and even hair follicles as fodder. Entomologists say that if people suddenly abandoned the Big Apple and turned off the heat as they left, cockroaches would probably die off. However, these adaptable little pests are such tough survivors that no one is willing to bet that they wouldn't make it here on their own.

Within the five boroughs, four species of cockroaches live in close association with people. German cockroaches (*Blatella germanica*) are the small, light brown roaches that vanish in a flash after the kitchen lights are turned on. Growing to just over half an inch long, they stake out damp, warm places, such as under the kitchen sink, and can disappear into a crack only a sixteenth of an inch wide. American cockroaches (*Perpiplaneta americana*), or "water bugs," are much larger, growing up to 3 inches long. These slow-moving, red-tinted giants with long, waving antennae hang out in humid boiler rooms and occasionally drop by bathrooms and kitchens on steamy summer nights. One species

Wild Fact

THE ROACH: A CITY SALUTE

New York City's roaches have inspired literary outpourings of various kinds. The most famous was New York *Sun Dial* columnist Don Marquis's "archy and mehitabel"—in which archy was a cockroach that supposedly wrote the column by jumping on the keys of an old typewriter. Since he couldn't use the shift key, the cockroach's columns were printed entirely in lower case letters, a la e. e. cummings. One such poem read:

> *i do not see why men*
> *should be so proud*
> *insects have the more*
> *ancient lineage*
> *according to the scientists*
> *insects were insects*
> *when man was only*
> *a burbling whatisit*

Perhaps the most histrionic defense of the roach was written by Mayor Fiorello La Guardia's deputy, Henry H. Curran, who called cockroaches the "seagulls of the sink" and wrote the following in an open letter to the press in 1938:

> *Alas, poor roach. Is there no little place in your heart for this industrious and peaceable member of the world's family of living things? . . . Industry, courage, thought, philosophy—they are the gifts which come, night by night in the kitchen sink, from the roach as he rises hand in hand with mankind on the long, long climb from savagery to civilization.*

that has become more numerous in the last 30 years is the brown-banded cockroach (*Supella longipalpa*), which often seeks refuge in computer terminals and clock radios. Winding up the public enemy list are the 1-inch-long, all-black Oriental cockroaches (*Blatta orientalis*), which live outdoors in dumps, where they are kept cozy by the heat generated by decomposing garbage.

Of these four species, German cockroaches are the most common, accounting for about 95 percent of the city's roaches. These are the cockroaches that New Yorkers spend so much time battling—with boric acid, roach motels, cans of insecticide, and plastic roach baits. Over the years, cockroaches have proved formidable opponents. They are light-phobic (they come out only in the dark) and touch-philic (they feel—and are—safest when they are being touched on all sides, such as in a tiny crack where they can't be reached by a boot heel or rolled-up newspaper). They are also maddeningly quick. Although they have wings and can fly, they usually don't bother, since they can run 50 body lengths per second. (If humans could move that fast, they would reach speeds of 200 miles per hour.)

One reason that New Yorkers try to cleanse their homes of cockroaches is that they think these insects are creepy and gross, but medical researchers have discovered an even better reason. A 1996 study sponsored by the National Institute of

Allergy and Infectious Diseases found that the German cockroach was the number-one cause of asthma among children in America's inner cities. Although roaches carry no diseases per se, the proteins in their tiny droppings, shed skins, and carcasses can cause a powerful allergic reaction—especially after prolonged exposure. In heavily infested homes, children inhale this roach dust all the time and frequently develop chronic asthma, which is characterized by wheezing and labored breathing. Even research scientists who work with cockroaches in laboratories sometimes complain about such symptoms.

From top to bottom: German, American, Brown-banded, and Oriental Cockroaches

Until recently, cockroaches have proved impervious to almost every pesticide thrown at them. Because they live long (up to 3 years) and are amazing breeders (a single female cockroach produces as many as 35 offspring every 3 weeks), they can easily evolve into pesticide-resistant strains. But the arrival of Combat, a designer pesticide that first hit the shelves in the 1980s, has knocked cockroaches for a loop. Early advertisements for Combat showed distressed New Yorkers sharing horror stories about roaches walking across their toothbrushes. But a single 12-pack of Combat Superbait used in combination with Combat roach-killing gel can reputedly zap as many as 80,000 roaches. By 1995, New Yorkers were buying $9.8 million in Combat products a year (second only to Los Angeles), with no sign—yet—that the cockroaches were achieving any immunity to the poison.

Nonetheless, such products target only small-scale, self-contained infestations. One reason that cockroaches have always been tough to exterminate is that they move around a lot—and not just from apartment to apartment. German cockroaches have been recorded in sailing ships, airplanes, and buses. In fact, in the summer of 1987, both the driver and passengers on a New York City bus abandoned ship, fleeing in disgust when cockroaches started streaming out of the seats.

Despite efforts to eliminate them, cockroaches in all likelihood are here to stay. In terms of evolutionary history, they are ancient and highly perfected beings. Not only did cockroaches outlast the dinosaurs, they emerged eons before the first dinosaur. Fossils of roachlike creatures have been found that date back at least 330 million years, to the Carboniferous era, when Earth's climate was particularly tropical. In fact, cockroaches are so common in the fossil record from that era that scientists have nicknamed the Carboniferous the "Era of the Cockroach." With so many cockroaches around today, however, we may have to reclaim this title for the twentieth century.

FISH AND OTHER UNDERWATER CREATURES

New York City is a watery town—surrounded by the Atlantic Ocean, the Hudson River, several bays, tidal creeks, and the Long Island Sound. As one nineteenth-century issue of *Harper's Magazine* put it, "Venice itself is hardly more completely a city of the waters." Residing in these submarine zip codes are thousands of varieties of fish, mollusks, and crustaceans—creatures that can spend their entire lives under water.

While people congregate in offices and apartment buildings, the city's underwater denizens have their own ready-made hangouts. Bluefish loiter next to underwater rock outcrops in New York Harbor, lying in wait for smaller fish that are carried by the tides. Communities of hard-shell clams carpet parts of Jamaica Bay, often obscuring areas of the bay's sandy bottom. Shipwrecks just offshore are so thick with blackfish that anglers and divers call them fish hotels.

Whereas people are trapped on bridges and in tunnels as they move from borough to borough, the city's submarine residents have more freedom. Striped bass commonly travel from the Long Island Sound to the Hudson River via the East River. American eels, one of the most common species in the city's waters, swim 1,000 miles to the Sargasso Sea—without passport or plane ticket—to lay their eggs. When the eggs hatch, the young eels make the return trip, ending up in places like the Bronx River and Spuyten Duyvil Creek north of Manhattan. For further evidence of New York City's link to this underwater world and its inhabitants, take the Circle Line cruise around Manhattan. Anglers can be seen poised with bait and rods all along the city's shore.

Historic Shellfisheries

New Yorkers have always had a taste for seafood. The Native Americans, who were living in the five boroughs when the Dutch settlers first arrived, lived close to the shoreline. To them, Long Island was *Paumonok,* meaning "island of shells," and they were known to dine abundantly on shellfish, eating hard-shell clams (called *quahogs* in the Munsee language), oysters, scallops, and blue mussels.

When the Dutch showed up in 1626, they quickly joined the feast. They called what is now Ellis Island Oyster Island, and Liberty Island was Great Oyster Island. As New York grew, oysters and hard-shell clams became one of the city's biggest exports, and different New York neighborhoods became world-renowned for their delicious *frutti de mare*. Throughout the nineteenth century, Little Neck Bay on the north shore of Queens was plied by clam boats for the plump quahogs that lived on its shallow, muddy bottom. Staten Island's Prince's Bay became famous for its fat, succulent oysters; in the best years, 500,000 bushels were sent to market.

Although New York shellfish was shipped all over the country and even to London, most of it was devoured right here in the storefront oyster saloons that riddled downtown Manhattan. At these bars, oyster fanciers gobbled down millions of dollars a year of the locally harvested bivalves, consuming them raw with lemon and mustard and washing them down with locally brewed beer. Ultimately, however, the feast was doomed to end.

The city's shellfishing industry slammed to a halt when several cases of typhoid fever were traced to oysters taken from New York Harbor in 1916. The

Wild Fact

SHELLING OUT

Found on the city's sandy beaches, hard-shell clams *(Mercenaria mercenaria)* are one of New York's most common shellfish, and they are easily identified by their creamy white shell linings, usually splotched with purple. In precolonial days, the Native Americans on Manhattan Island fashioned both the white and purple parts into beads—*wampumpeag*, later called simply wampum—that they used like money to trade with the Iroquois tribes upstate. When the Dutch and English settlers arrived in the early 1600s, they quickly adopted wampum as a medium of exchange. Three purple beads were worth six white beads, and both amounts were worth an English penny.

Purple wampum was made by breaking off the purple parts of clam shells and polishing them into one-third-inch-long cylindrical beads. A hole was bored through the shell parts with a sharp stone and the beads were strung on animal sinews. But you couldn't just go down to the seashore and mint your own wampum; quality of workmanship was integral to its value.

Ultimately, wampum became so crucial to the commerce of the colony that the Dutch had to pass anticounterfeiting laws. In 1641 a New Amsterdam ordinance responded to the sudden appearance of "bad" wampum in town, noting that "nasty rough things imported from other places" were being circulated and that well-polished, Manhattan wampum was on the wane. To save the local economy, the Dutch governor decreed that anyone trying to pass bad wampum as the real thing had to pay a fine of 10 guilders to the town's poor.

> ## *Wild Fact*
>
> ### BLUE CRAB
>
> Every spring is soft-shell crab season at the city's finest restaurants, where this easy-to-eat delicacy is available sautéed in butter and lemon or breaded and fried on a bun. Often this dish is labeled as Maryland or Chesapeake Bay crab, but that doesn't mean it's really from out of town. Every year, 800,000 blue crabs (*Callinectes sapidus*) are taken from New York Harbor and Jamaica Bay and sold in fish stores up and down the Atlantic seaboard; some are even shipped to Baltimore, the blue-crab capital of the country.
>
> Besides being fished commercially, blue crabs are caught by recreational anglers in New York City. Every summer, crabbers can be seen tossing crab cages—usually baited with chicken pieces—into the waters below Steeplechase Pier at Coney Island and Canarsie Pier on Jamaica Bay. Although blue crabs are considered safe to eat (as long as you limit your intake to no more than six per week), the yellow liver, or tomalley, of locally caught crabs should be removed after cooking.

relentless use of the harbor as an open sewer and garbage dump had taken its toll, and the oyster beds had to be condemned by the city's Board of Health. An important chapter in New York's culinary and natural history had come to a close.

Today, clams still thrive beneath the surf on almost every beach in New York City. On Staten Island's southern shore, the beaches are still littered with shells from oysters living in the old beds in Prince's Bay. Despite these signs of life, most of the city's shellfisheries remain off-limits. Because mollusks eat by filtering food from seawater—as much as a quart an hour—their fleshy bodies, more than any other type of seafood, become the repositories for bacteria and toxic chemicals in the water surrounding them. Nonetheless, the city's waters have become cleaner in recent years, and—in a small way—the shellfishing industry has returned. Today, clam boats take as many as 11 million hard-shell clams from Staten Island's Raritan Bay each year and transport them to clam beds in Eastern Long Island. After filtering clean water for a month, these expatriate clams are considered safe to sell to the public.

In fact, clams are becoming so popular these days that officers from the city's Department of Environmental Protection have to watch out for clam rustlers. In 1996, three men in scuba gear were arrested for allegedly poaching 12 bushels of clams from Jamaica Bay. Though the bay's clams are not considered fit for human consumption, such illicit clams can be sold for large amounts of cash on the black market.

URBAN ANGLING

Many anglers have discovered the great secret of city fishing, and surveys have shown that more than 80,000 New Yorkers fish from the city's shores each year.

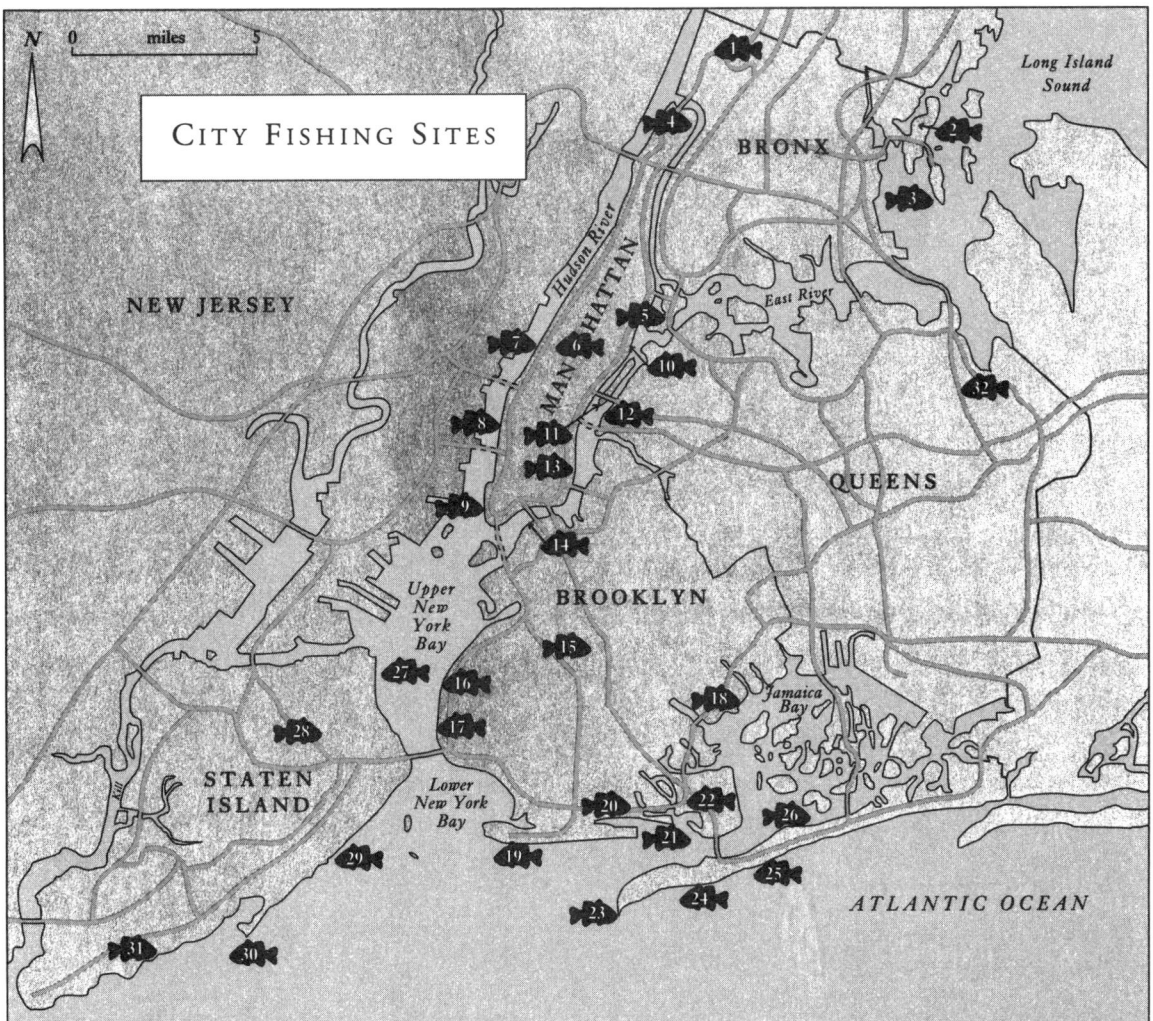

City Fishing Sites

1. Van Cortlandt Park, The Bronx: Van Cortlandt Lake and Swamp
2. Pelham Bay Park, The Bronx: The Lagoon, Twin and Hunter Islands
3. City Island, The Bronx: Party boat fishing and boat rentals for Long Island Sound
4. Inwood Hill Park, Manhattan
5. Ward's Island Nature Area
6. Central Park, Manhattan: Harlem Meer and Central Park Lake
7. Riverside Park, Manhattan
8. Pier 62, Chelsea Waterside Park at 23rd Street, Manhattan
9. Battery Park City, Manhattan
10. Carl Schurz Park, Manhattan
11. Roosevelt Island, Southern Tip
12. 44th Drive Pier, Queens
13. East River Park, Manhattan
14. Fulton Ferry Park Pier, Brooklyn
15. Prospect Park, Brooklyn: Prospect Park Lake
16. 69th Street Pier, Brooklyn
17. Shore Parkway, Brooklyn
18. *The Canarsie Pier (Rockaway Parkway), Brooklyn
19. Steeplechase Pier (West 17th Street), Brooklyn
20. Sheepshead Bay, Brooklyn: Party boat fishing on Emmons Avenue and fishing from the Manhattan Beach Foot Bridge
21. *Plumb Beach, Brooklyn
22. *Floyd Bennett Field, Brooklyn
23. *Breezy Point Tip, The Rockaways
24. *Fort Tilden, The Rockaways
25. *Jacob Riis Park, The Rockaways
26. Rockaway Sea Wall (Beach Channel Drive), The Rockaways
27. Robbin's Reef, New York Harbor (Accessible by boat only)
28. Clove Lakes Park, Staten Island
29. Midland Beach, Staten Island
30. *Great Kills Park and Crooke's Point, Staten Island
31. Wolfe's Pond Park and Acme Pond, Staten Island
32. Alley Pond Park, Queens: Oakland Lake

* Part of the Gateway National Recreation Area

© 1997, Mark Stein Studios

In summer and fall, surf casters line the seawall in the Rockaways in pursuit of bluefish and striped bass. Private motorboats cruise Jamaica Bay in October and November, their captains obsessively searching for winter flounder. And almost every day, "party boats" leave from Brooklyn's Sheepshead Bay, taking as many as 30 deep-sea fishermen out to fish-filled wrecks beyond the Verrazano Narrows. Anglers have even been spotted parked next to the East River, fishing from the backseats of their cars.

The best times of year for fishing are late summer and fall, when an enormous number of species are in town—including bluefish, weakfish, porgies, fluke, and even albacore. Striped bass, considered by many anglers to be the king of northeastern sport fish, are in city waters in amazingly large numbers. Marine biologists estimate that 1 to 2 million stripers enter the harbor every year, many of them sizable. Twenty-pound stripers are common, and the unofficial record for a striped bass caught in New York City was a 50-inch-long, 43-pound giant (estimated to be 20 years old) that was landed in Staten Island's Raritan Bay in 1991.

Although the abundance of fish is not a problem, getting to the fish can be. The majority of New York City's 578 miles of coastline are off-limits to the public, owned by commercial concerns or the Port Authority. Every waterfront spot that is legal (or not aggressively defended against trespassing) is quickly rooted out by savvy urban anglers. People fish high atop bridge roadways, their bait dangling 50 feet down. Anglers risk their necks on dilapidated piers and rock jetties slippery with algae. For urban anglers, the appeal of casting into city waters for a wild fish, with one of the world's greatest views as a backdrop, is addictive. As one longtime Hudson River fisherman, Christopher Letts, an educator for the Hudson River Foundation, put it, "When you're out in the middle of the river with a view of the city skyline, and hear the traffic and sirens from Manhattan, it's magic pulling a silvery fish from the dark waters of the river. It's wilderness in the middle of the city."

Beginners who want to take on a wild fish can get into the act simply by purchasing a rod and reel preloaded with fishing line. Sinkers and bait can be found at tackle stores in fishing-friendly places ranging from City Island in the Bronx to Cross Bay Boulevard in Queens. The rest involves finding the right fishing hole, which can be anywhere from the easily accessible Battery Park City Esplanade along the Hudson River to Robbins Reef (reachable by boat only) in the middle of the harbor, near the Statue of Liberty. Those without their own

THE URBAN ANGLER'S LEXICON

BLUES (a.k.a. bluefish, *Pomatomus saltatrix*). Bluefish are the city's most popular game fish. Weighing up to 30 pounds and equipped with sharp, conspicuous teeth, bluefish voraciously attack schools of smaller fish, often slaughtering more than they actually eat. Although bluefish are feared by swimmers, their arrival in New York Harbor in summer is heralded by anglers who admire their fighting spirit. Hooked blues are known to put up a battle and often break fishing lines. Anglers have to be especially careful when removing fishhooks from blues, because these carnivores have been known to bite people's fingers off. Usually served grilled or broiled, bluefish have a strong, gamy taste.

BUNKER. "Bunker" is local lingo for the Atlantic menhaden (*Brevoortia tyrannus*), a silvery herring that is among the most common fish found in New York City waters. Every spring, 12- to 18-inch-long bunker run into the harbor in enormous schools that, as a unit, may weigh several tons. Bunker are often accompanied—and eaten—by schools of hungry bluefish and striped bass.

BUNKER CHUNKS. Bunker are not generally considered good eating, but carnivorous fish think differently. Bits of bunker meat, called bunker chunks, are often used as bait by anglers hoping to catch stripers and blues.

FLUKE (a.k.a. flatties, summer flounder, *Paralichthys dentatus*). Fluke are flatfish that hide on the sandy bottoms of the city's bays, rivers, and inlets from May to October. Camouflaged in the sand, with just their eyes peering above the surface, fluke aggressively ambush smaller fish as they pass by. Delicious, with firm, sweet white flesh, fluke can be caught by gently skipping baited fishing line along the bottom of the city's waterways.

SNAPPERS. Snappers are baby bluefish, usually less than 7 to 10 inches long, that show up during late summer in shallow bays and tidal creeks around New York City. Easily caught from piers and bridges, these small fry are among the best targets for young and first-time anglers.

STRIPERS (a.k.a. striped bass, *Morone saxatilis*). Streamlined silver fish with purplish brown racing stripes, stripers reach weights of 50 pounds and are one of New York's most coveted game fish. Known to live as long as 50 years, stripers have a certain mystique and are not easily caught. Striped-bass anglers will fish at any time of day, in any kind of weather, to match wits with them. Because of overfishing in past decades, there are strict limits on the number and size of stripers that can be kept. Most anglers simply catch them for the pleasure of the hunt, and then release them.

equipment or the desire to seek out their own secret spots can go fishing in boats that depart twice each day from Emmons Avenue in Sheepshead Bay. And fly casters unable to escape to Beaverkill for the weekend have been known to take their hip waders into the Central Park Pond beneath the Plaza Hotel to fish for bass.

All this fishing raises the inevitable question: Can you eat what you catch? The waters around New York City have become much cleaner in recent years, and most city anglers admit that they do eat the fish. However, depending on the type of fish and where it is caught, this may not be such a good idea. In general, the New York State Department of Health advises anglers to eat no more than one meal a week of fish caught in city waters, and women of childbearing age and children under the age of 15 are advised *not to eat any* fish taken from local waters. That said, these restrictions are aimed primarily at fish caught in the Hudson, East, and Harlem rivers, and the harbor. Fish caught in the Atlantic Ocean off the Rockaways, in Jamaica Bay, in Long Island Sound, and from party boats are considered safe to eat—as long as they are washed and cleaned in fresh water. (To be doubly safe, anglers are also advised to remove the skin and dark, fatty parts of the meat before cooking, and to restrict eating striped bass and bluefish to once a month.) For the latest health updates, call the state Health Department's Environmental Health Information Line at 1-800-458-1158.

In addition to health regulations, the number and size of fish that anglers can keep are limited by the New York State Department of Environmental Conservation. In particular, strict regulations protect striped bass, which are recovering from overfishing. Currently, anglers may keep only one striped bass per day, and it must be at least 18 inches long. For detailed regulations, call the Recreational Fishing Information Line at 1-800-REGS-DEC.

Because most of New York City's waters are marine—meaning that they are affected by the tides—anglers do not need a license to fish here. (According to federal law, oceans and estuaries are open to anyone.) However, if you are fishing within Gateway National Recreation Area, parking permits are often required for anglers' lots (call 718-318-4300 for more information). For fishing in fresh water—such as the lakes in Central Park and Prospect Park, where all fishing is on a "catch and release" basis—a state fishing license (obtainable at many sporting-goods stores) is required if you're older than 16.

CHAPTER 5

PUTTING DOWN ROOTS
The City's Plants

Chronicling all of the thousands of plant species that grow in New York City seems like an impossible task, but the Brooklyn Botanic Garden currently has a project to do just that. Called the New York Metropolitan Flora Project, this botanical mission, which is scheduled to be completed in the year 2015, aims to identify and catalogue all the trees, shrubs, vines, flowers, grasses, and ferns that grow within a 50-mile radius of Times Square.

Volunteer plant detectives are now searching in obvious botanical hot spots like the Staten Island Greenbelt as well as in seemingly unlikely locales, such as the abandoned industrial land along Brooklyn's waterfront. What the project has found so far is that in terms of plants, this region is a melting pot, with about 2,850 species, including a wide mixture of both native and nonnative plants.

In Forest Park in Queens, for example, there are an estimated 71 different trees, 57 shrubs, 168 herbaceous (flowering) plants, 27 grasses, and 6 types of ferns. Native red oaks and tulip trees thrive alongside long-established exotics, such as the European beech tree and timothy grass. Forest Park also has examples of newly arrived immigrants, such as the Amur honeysuckle, a native

> ### Wild Fact
>
> ### WEST SIDE WEEDS
>
> One urban botanist, Naomi Dicker, conducted an inventory of "unplanted plants" (what most people think of as weeds) on the West Side of Manhattan between 41st and 59th streets. Growing within the cracks of concrete, in vacant lots, and along the edges of parking lots, she found nonnative species like mugwort and Asiatic dayflowers as well as a fair number of native plants. Popping up through the tiniest cracks in the sidewalk were two native grasses, combed love grass and fall panic grass. Seaside goldenrod, a native wildflower, was also recorded. All told, 100 weeds were tallied in the cache area, and Dicker estimates that about 300 such plants are living secret lives on the island of Manhattan.

of Russia; garden escapees, namely day lilies (originally from Eurasia); and even *Cannabis sativa* (marijuana). And that's just one 538-acre park.

Each of the city's parks and ecosystems has a unique set of native and introduced plants. On beaches in the Rockaways, native plants like poison ivy, staghorn sumac, and bayberry bushes share space on sandy dunes with Russian olive trees and multiflora rose, an Asian variety of rosebush. Even the city's freshwater ponds can support dozens of plant species, from cattails and duckweed to native and nonnative water lilies.

Although more than 1,000 native plants still exist in the city, nonnative species are clearly taking over. Just 400 years after New York was settled by Europeans—an evolutionary eye blink—the region now has more exotic plants than native ones. The arrival, expansion, and retreat of these introduced species—some from clear across the world—makes the tallying of the city's plant species a never-ending task.

Mugwort (*Artemisia vulgaris*), an herb used in Japanese cooking, is one of these newcomers. With pointed leaves and small green flowers, this Asian import has turned out to be a particularly scrappy urban plant, often creating lemon-scented banks of greenery along the edges of parking lots and roads. Because mugwort is an exotic plant that evolved in a completely different environment, it can take advantage of situations that native plants cannot—even growing abundantly in recently demolished building sites, where it is nourished by the high lime content of the concrete dust.

Native plants, by contrast, thrive in pockets of natural habitat, and in recent years botanists have unearthed many interesting native plant stories within the city. In one case, a grove of wild papaw trees was discovered growing in Tottenville, a neighborhood on Staten Island. The usual range of papaws, the only "tropical" fruit trees that grow in North America, is the Deep South, but somehow a completely wild grove produces banana-shaped fruits in New York City's southernmost borough.

Even on the streets—where nothing is expected to grow—botanists have discovered surprising biodiversity. A botanical survey of a ½-acre lot in downtown Manhattan, detailed in a 1993 issue of the *New York Times Magazine*, found more than 60 kinds of plants—including black cherry and mulberry trees, Canada thistle, hops, sorrel, and wild strawberry—growing amid trash and rubble.

THE CITY'S TREES

According to the official count, New York City has about 2.5 million trees, 2 million in parks and half a million lining the streets on 33,278 city blocks. These woody plants transform the city, and without them, New York would be little more than a vast parking lot. New York City's trees represent hundreds of different species, ranging from the exotic cherries that bloom every spring on Park Avenue to the billowing elms on the Mall in Central Park to the stands of native oaks and tulips that form the backbone of working forests in places like Van Cortlandt Park in the Bronx and Manhattan's Inwood Hill.

Anyone who has walked down a treeless street in the middle of a scorching summer day intuitively knows the value of New York City's trees, but their importance to the city can also be quantified. Under a canopy of more than 24,000 green-leafed trees, Central Park in summer is anywhere from 5 to 20°F cooler than nearby midtown Manhattan. All you have to do is walk across Fifth Avenue into the park's shade to feel the difference. There are other benefits as well. According to studies of urban trees conducted by the U.S. Forest Service, each tree planted in New York City—by absorbing toxic gases and intercepting airborne particles—may remove as much as a quarter pound of pollution from the air every year. With 2.5 million trees, that means that hundreds of tons of carbon monoxide, sulfur

> *Wild Fact*
>
> **COLD-BLOODED KILLERS**
>
> On January 25, 1996, a hit-and-run driver mowed down and killed 30 young trees in the Alley Pond Park woodland in Queens. The victims included oaks, maples, birches, pines, and cherries. Although the perpetrator was never apprehended, the outcry over this wanton slaughter was so great that neighbors planted 4,000 new saplings the following spring. In response to an increasing number of such "premeditated" tree killings, the city council passed a tough new arborcide law—what Parks Commissioner Henry Stern hailed as the "Magna Carta for Trees." This legislation stipulates a penalty of up to 1 year in jail and a $15,000 fine for executing even one city-owned tree.

dioxide, nitrogen dioxide, ozone, and particulate matter are kept from entering our lungs annually.

Each year, an average of 10,000 new street trees are planted throughout the five boroughs, at a cost of $310 to $425 per tree. Once planted, however, the life of a sapling is fraught with perils; recent studies have found that a young tree planted in Manhattan has only a 50 percent chance of surviving beyond its fifth birthday.

What makes life on the street so tough? Planted to make our lives more bearable, street trees face innumerable challenges. Salt used to de-ice streets in winter leaches into sidewalk plots and can literally suck water from a tree's roots. The soil in sidewalk plots often turns concrete-hard, preventing water and nutrients from getting to the roots. Poor drainage can "drown" a tree, by cutting off its oxygen. And trees, like people, fare badly in the city's brutal summers, suffering dehydration that results in leaf die-off and stunted growth. To add insult to injury, street trees are frequently hit by cars that jump the curb, or are "pruned" by passing trucks.

Nonetheless, hundreds of thousands of trees flourish on New York City's streets, and they're not here by accident. These species—most of them imports, hybrids, or cultivars—were chosen because they can handle urban hazards. Pin oaks, ginkgos, and Japanese zelkovas are all up-and-coming, but the four most prevalent street trees currently are:

HONEY LOCUST (*Gleditsia triacanthos*). The most common street tree in Manhattan, the wispy-looking honey locust, with small, delicate leaves and long, brown fruit pods in fall, is a lot tougher than it appears. Tolerant of drought, hard-packed soils, leachate from construction sites, and rock salt, honey locusts dominate the scene on some of the city's meanest streets. Growing in the wild, thorn-like spikes, more than five inches long, stud the bark of honey locust trees, but these dangerous barbs are bred out of street trees.

LONDON PLANE (*Platanus x acerifolia*). Number one in Brooklyn, London planes tower as high as 70 feet above the tops of brownstones and streetlights. Unlike most trees, London planes shed their outer bark every summer, dropping sheets of gray peelings and giving their massive gray-and-tan trunks a distinctive mottled pattern. Designed for urban living, the London plane can tolerate extremes of temperature and drought. London planes were considered highly elegant trees by the city's early park designers, who planted bosks of them in many of Manhattan's most formal parks, such as Bryant Park and Union Square. Because of the enduring popularity of this tree, the official insignia of the New York City Department of Parks and Recreation is the silhouette of a London plane leaf.

NORWAY MAPLE (*Acer platanoides*). Beating the London plane tree for the top spot in the Bronx, on Staten Island, and in Queens, this European import is one of the city's most resilient trees, able to tolerate extremes of temperature and over-watering that would easily kill its more sensitive American cousin, the sugar maple. The leaves of Norway maples have the classic five-lobed mapleleaf shape, and the trees drop wing-shaped seedpods that children like to peel apart and stick on their noses. Though kids like them, urban foresters loathe Norway maples because they have a habit of escaping into native woodlands and outcompeting other tree species. Despite the Norway maple's success in the concrete jungle, planting new ones is now banned in New York City.

BRADFORD CALLERY PEAR (*Pyrus calleryana*). The second-most common street tree in Manhattan, the Bradford pear puts forth exquisite clusters of small white flowers in the spring, and its leaves turn purple and scarlet in the fall. Originally planted by horticulturists because it was pretty and highly tolerant of pollution, it is now the tree most commonly requested for planting. Despite its grassroots popularity, the Bradford pear is on the Parks Department's list of "bad" trees because its low-growing branches and poor branching habits have made it an easy target for passing trucks and buses.

Altogether, about 35 species of trees are deemed tough enough to make it on the street. Dozens of others, however, thrive in the city's parks, where different conditions prevail. Central Park has 110 species, ranging from imported Japanese maples to Siberian elms. But once you get into real woodlands—in the Staten Island Greenbelt, Cunningham Park and Alley Pond Park in Queens, and even Manhattan's Inwood Hill Park—the city's native trees assert them-

Wild Fact

COLD-BLOODED KILLERS II

Though New York City has an "arborcide" law which makes it illegal for civilians to kill city-owned trees, this law does not prevent the city from selling forested land to private developers, who can then kill as many trees as they want. Nor does the law prevent the city from killing its own trees, as long as there is not too much opposition.

In 1994, the city's Economic Development Corporation bulldozed four rare, sweet bay magnolia trees (*Magnolia virginiana*) that were part of a relict swamp forest in Staten Island's northwest corner. More than 100 years old, these trees had come into bloom with white saucerlike flowers every June since before the turn of the twentieth century. Though 20 of these Victorian-era magnolia trees survived after the bulldozing, the EDC had planned to sacrifice them all to build a corporate office park. Today, a coalition of local botanists is negotiating to preserve the remaining trees and their swamp habitat.

---

selves. Like the street trees, which are adapted to handle the urban ecosystem, the city's native trees have evolved to meet different conditions in the woods. Black oaks, the most common trees growing wild in the city, prefer dry, well-drained slopes. Beeches, with smooth silver bark and leaves that turn copper in fall, prefer moist, rich soil. Sweet gums, which produce telltale spiky fruit balls and star-shaped leaves, prefer wet, swampy spots—something the city's parks offer in abundance.

In fact, some native trees seem to be uniquely adapted to city life. Just one of at least eight different acorn-producing species of oak trees that grow naturally in New York City, the red oak (*Quercus rubra*) has always been a part of the forest scene in the Northeast. But it is particularly successful in the city's woodlands because it tolerates pollution, salt, and most diseases. In addition to reaching heights of 75 feet in the "wilds" of New York City, these native New Yorkers are now recognized for their toughness and increasingly are being planted as a street tree.

right: Red oak
below: Tulip tree leaf and flower

Similarly, tulip trees (*Liriodendron tulipifera*)—which are usually more closely identified with more southern forests, such as in the Appalachians—thrive here. Foresters believe that tulip trees have taken off because they can withstand small forest fires—an asset, since the city's woodlands are constantly plagued by arson. Thought to be one of the most beautiful trees growing in the East, tulip trees have long straight trunks (they can grow as tall as 120 feet), distinctive wing-shaped leaves that turn yellow in fall, and tulip-shaped orange yellow flowers that bloom in June. One of the city's largest stands of tulip trees is in the forest in Manhattan's Inwood Hill Park.

With so many different species of trees adapted to life here, city residents may ask, "Why don't we have more?" Only half of all the available plots for trees along city streets are occupied, and some streets have no trees at all. Critics blame this poor showing on both the stresses of city living and the lack of care given to street trees after they are planted. In New York City, trees are not pruned or tended by city workers unless collapsing branches or some other imminent calamity pose a hazard to people or property. By contrast, in Chicago young street trees are regularly pruned; the result is that Chicago's sapling mortality rate is one-tenth that of New York City. This statistic isn't surprising when

GINKGO: THE FOSSIL TREE

New Yorkers may be surprised to know that one of the city's most common street trees, the ginkgo *(Ginkgo biloba)*, is a living fossil, the last-surviving member of a large family of trees that had its day 100 million years ago and then went extinct—almost. The distinctive fan-shaped leaves of the ginkgo were first known to scientists as fossils, but then in the 1700s, one last stand of living ginkgos was found in a remote valley in central China, where individual specimens had been cultivated for centuries by Buddhist monks.

The ginkgo is so radically different from any other tree in the world—it shares characteristics with both deciduous and coniferous trees—that it is referred to as a taxonomic oddity. Furthermore, after the relict ginkgos were found alive in China and taken as specimen trees to Japan, western Europe, and the United States, it was discovered that they were free from both insect and fungal infestations. Botanists theorized that these survivors from the Age of the Dinosaurs outlived the pests that had once attacked them. It was also found that ginkgos were ideally suited to life in the city, able to withstand compacted roots, high tempertures, and smog.

Now among the most common street trees in New York City, ginkgos have one small drawback: During the fall, when thousands of fleshy seeds fall from the female ginkgo trees to the ground, the seeds' outer layers rot, breaking down into foul-smelling butyric acid. The upside, at least for some people, is that properly prepared ginkgo seeds are edible. In Central Park and the New York Botanical Garden, people collect them by the sackful. In East Asian cultures, these seeds are thought to improve short-term memory and longevity. Among alternative medicine practitioners in our country, however, the fountain of youth is thought to reside in the ginkgo's leaves. In fact, extracts made from ginkgo leaves are among the most popular products sold in the city's health food stores.

Ailanthus leaves, (right)

you consider that every year Chicago spends $4.31 per capita on street trees, compared to New York City's measly $1.23.

A Tree Grows in Brooklyn— and Everywhere Else

Able to grow under the most unlikely conditions, the ailanthus (*Ailanthus altissima*) is New York City's toughest tree. Its skinny trunk can be seen emerging from subway grates and cracks in the sidewalk, and its fanlike branches are the most common source of shade in the city's vacant lots. Although some people call the ailanthus a weed, others call it the tree that grows in Brooklyn. In the best-selling 1943 novel *A Tree Grows in Brooklyn,* author Betty Smith wrote this about the ailanthus:

> It had pointed leaves that grew long green switches which radiated from the bough and made a tree which looked like a lot of opened green umbrellas. Some people called it the Tree of Heaven. No matter where its seed fell, it made a tree which struggled to reach the sky. It grew in boarded-up lots and out of neglected rubbish heaps and it was the only tree that grew out of cement. It grew lushly, but only in the tenements districts. . . . That was the kind of tree it was. It liked poor people.

What the ailanthus tree *really* likes is poor soil. Its seeds can germinate in virtually any patch of dirt, no matter how dry, hard, or nutrient-poor. Its saplings grow fast, as much as 12 feet in a year. Moreover, the ailanthus tree is notoriously hard to kill: Cut one down, and another sapling sprouts from the dead stump.

The ailanthus tree originated in central China, a region with blazing-hot summers, where trees have to cope with droughtlike conditions. It was first imported into the United States as an ornamental tree in 1784, and the first plantings in New York City were recorded in the early 1800s, when the ailanthus quickly caught on as the city's most popular street tree. "Pre-evolved" in its desertlike homeland to flourish under the worst conditions, the ailanthus could withstand smoke, soot, and every other urban insult. It was also considered attractive, with lush, tropical-looking leaves, yellow-green flowers in spring, and red fruit in late summer.

But the city's residents quickly noticed that the ailanthus had a couple of drawbacks—namely, that the flowers of the male trees reeked with an offensive odor in springtime and that the ailanthus, which produces as many as 325,000 seeds per year, would not stay in one place. In the late 1800s, New York City banned the planting of ailanthus trees, but by then it was too late. Fugitive ailanthus trees had already escaped from the gardens, street plots, and parks they were meant to adorn. A century later, the ailanthus is still one of New York City's most common "unplanted" trees, with an estimated 500,000 prospering in back alleys, on sun-baked vacant lots, and along rubble-strewn roadsides.

Recently, however, botanists and foresters have reported that a large number of adult ailanthus trees are dying. Their demise is being caused by a new fungal disease that makes their bark fall off and their leaves wilt. While the blight has yet to stop these prolific organisms from reproducing, it does prove that even the city's toughest tree is not completely immune to the forces of evolution.

THE AMERICAN ELM: THE CITY'S MOST PAMPERED TREE

American elms (*Ulmus americana*) were once the most popularly planted trees in the United States. Considered perfect street trees because of their high-arching limbs, sturdy buttressed trunks, and butter yellow fall foliage, elms were planted on streets all across New England and small-town America. But this graceful shade tree's success story came to a crashing halt in the 1930s, when Dutch elm disease, caused by a killer fungus, left millions of dead, leafless trees standing like skeletons on once-shady thoroughfares across the country.

American elm leaf

Today, American elms are a rare sight, yet two large collections of these trees survive in Manhattan—one on the Mall in Central Park (from East 66th to East 72nd streets), and the other along Riverside Drive from West 80th to West 119th, next to Riverside Park. Among the most pampered trees in the city, Manhattan's elms each receive regular limb-by-limb inspections. A tree doctor visits them annually and, when necessary, orders the amputation of infected branches. In 1992, an "Elm-posium" was held to examine new ways of preventing the spread of the disease. And tens of thousands of dollars are raised annually in both public and private funds to provide the elms with pruning and care. Though a few of Manhattan's elms succumb each year to the disease, the extra attention seems to be paying off. On the Mall, 150 of Central Park's original American elms are still standing in four elegant rows. And on Riverside Drive, 400 of the city's century-old elms are still growing, making this the most significant remaining stand in North America.

FLOWERS

When New York City was New Amsterdam, the sweet scent of wildflowers on Manhattan Island sometimes so stunned Dutch settlers that they would stop in their tracks in confusion. Later, in the 1800s, city residents would go on wildflower walks to view blossoms and take in the pleasant scents.

Today, New Yorkers are still flower-crazy. The combined admissions at the Brooklyn Botanic Garden and New York Botanical Garden total 1.4 million visitors annually. Flower-addicted city residents do their own gardening too, teasing flowers from tiny window boxes and pots placed on fire escapes, paying landscape designers thousands of dollars to lay out miniature roof gardens, and turning hundreds of abandoned lots into bloom-filled community oases.

Along with the crocuses, tulips, and rosebushes that grow in these horticultural hot spots, there are *wild*flowers out there. They blossom in the city's more natural areas, and they have colonized the built-up city, pushing up between cracks in the sidewalks and filling vacant lots.

With so many public and private gar-

Wild Fact

WILD PLANT WALKS

The Torrey Botanical Society, a club made up of both academically trained and amateur botanists, has been "botanizing," or searching for and identifying plants, in New York City since the 1860s. Created by John Torrey, an eminent nineteenth-century botanist, this local botanical society, formally incoporated in 1873, is the oldest of its kind in North America. Today, Torrey members lead between 20 and 30 plant walks throughout the metropolitan region each year, taking nonmembers to destinations including Clay Pit Ponds State Park Preserve on Staten Island to look at the remnant pine-and-oak barrens ecosystem, and the Upper West Side in Manhattan to identify the plants growing in sidewalk cracks. A complete listing of the Torrey Botanical Society's tours is released every March and can be obtained by writing to The Torrey Field Committee, Dr. Patrick Cooney, 221 Mt. Hope Boulevard, Hastings-on-Hudson, NY 10706.

dens, some flowers have escaped over the years from their tended plots and taken off on their own. These garden renegades are often from faraway places and were brought here as ornamental plants by horticulturists fascinated with the exotic. Japanese honeysuckle (*Lonicera japonica*), a vine with sweet-smelling white-and-yellow tube-shaped blossoms, was first brought to the city during the early 1800s. This Asian ornamental became an escapee, because birds began eating its black berries and thus dispersed its seeds throughout the city. Once a seed finds a new spot to grow, the honeysuckle vine grows quickly, as much as 30 feet in one year, sending out runners that form new plants. Tangled hedges of Japanese honeysuckle—looking like misshapen topiaries—can be seen growing along the grassy embankments of highways like the Belt Parkway in Brooklyn and the Grand Central Parkway in Queens.

Whereas Japanese honeysuckle was intentionally imported for gardens, other nonnative flowers were introduced accidentally, their seeds hitchhiking along with immigrants from Europe. Some of these species have grown in this region for so long, it seems unbelievable that they were not always here. White clover, the oxeye daisy, and Queen Anne's lace all were brought to the United States from Europe. Even the common dandelion (*Taraxacum officinale*), which is now one of the city's most common plants, came to this country with the colonists. Like many other plant species that are referred to as weeds, dandelions are well adapted to surviving in poor soil and sun-drenched areas. Their stems are covered with hairlike filaments that help keep the plant from becoming dehydrated. Despite the vast numbers of these well-adapted plants, it is technically illegal to pick dandelions or any other plant in the city's parks. In 1986, "Wildman" Steve Brill, a naturalist and edible-plant buff who leads foraging tours throughout the five boroughs, was arrested by undercover cops for taking a bite out of a dandelion in Central Park.

Although hardy exotics like the dandelion dominate the city's most urban areas, native wildflowers are also hanging on. Growing in the shaded, damp soil

> ## *Wild Fact*
> ### BLOSSOMING
> The blossoms that New Yorkers seem to love the most are those of cherry trees. Imported from Japan, more than 40 varieties of these ornamental trees put forth springtime pink and white blossoms in the city. One of the most impressive types is the weeping Higan cherry tree, whose drooping branches are saturated with small, pale pink flowers. Higan and dozens of other varieties can be seen at the Brooklyn Botanic Garden, known for having the best collection of cherry trees in New York City. Other great cherry blossom spots are on the Reservoir Path near 90th Street in Central Park, and the Memorial Cherry Grove between 92nd and 95th streets on Riverside Park's lower promenade.

of forests, the city's native woodland wildflowers are quick to bloom (usually during spring) and delicately beautiful. Found off the beaten trail in places like Inwood Hill and Van Cortlandt parks, they are the hidden jewels of the city's flower world. Pinxter flower (*Rhododendron nudiflorum*), a native azalea with small pink flowers, and Dutchman's breeches (*Dicentra cucullaria*), whose white-and-yellow flowers look like tiny breeches or pantaloons, are two of the more common ones. A rarer variety is bloodroot (*Sanguinaria canadensis*), a white poppy that has an orange-yellow center. This plant grows in only a few sites in New York City, but nowhere more abundantly than in "Bloodroot Valley" in the Staten Island Greenbelt. There, in a stream-cut woodland, botanists have counted hundreds of these spring-blossoming flowers growing on about 2 acres of land. The red root sap of bloodroot plants was used by Native Americans as a dye and as a remedy for sore throats and is now being used in holistic medicine as a topical treatment for moles and warts.

Bloodroot and a handful of other native wildflowers growing in New York City have been listed by the State Department of Environmental Conservation as "vulnerable," meaning that they are "in danger of becoming endangered" from the double threats of habitat loss and plant poaching. An orchid called the pink lady's-slipper (*Cypripedium acaule*) is a perfect example. This plant, which grows to a height of over a foot, takes up to 15 years to show its pink-and-red slipper-shaped flowers and to reproduce. This slow growth, combined with the fact that they are often victims of orchid poaching, has caused the pink lady's-slipper to decline in New York State. Although more common on Long Island, this orchid is believed to exist in only one population in New York City: four single specimens growing in Cunningham Park in Queens.

Pink lady's-slipper

The birdfoot violet (*Viola pedata*) is another flower that has suffered from habitat loss. Once common in grasslands throughout the East Coast, its numbers have shrunk as grasslands have disappeared. Called birdfoot because its leaves are shaped like little bird claws, the plant is known for its beautiful violet-and-purple blossoms. The one area where it grows in New York City is in a habitat that mimics a grassland: A healthy patch grows at La Tourette Golf Course on Staten Island—a less than ideal location since the fans of these flowers constantly worry that they will be crushed by stray golf carts.

In places where both are given habitat to grow, native and nonnative wildflowers mix in abundance. Areas within the Gateway National Recreation Area, where shoreline and beach habitat have been restored, are among the best blossom-viewing spots in the city. At the Jamaica Bay Wildlife Refuge alone, rangers have documented more than 150 wildflower varieties growing in the park's sandy soil. Flowers such as seaside goldenrod (*Solidago sempervirens*) and salt-marsh asters (*Aster tenuifolius*) occur naturally, but many wildflowers were introduced years ago by the park's staff to provide habitat and food for the refuge's birds. Among these plantings are the salt-spray rose (*Rosa rugosa*), which has showy lavender blossoms, and the prickly-pear cactus (*Opuntia humifusa*), which often surprises visitors with its thorny pads and plush, yellow blooms.

Prickly-pear cactus and flower

THE NEW YORK UNDERWORLD: MUSHROOMS AND FUNGI

The Fifth Kingdom is alive and well in New York City. About 500 mushrooms and other members of the fungal world make their home here, from the stinky squid, an orange-tentacled foul-smelling mushroom that pops up in places like Union Square Park in Manhattan, to the destroying angel, a deadly poisonous mushroom that grows in the woodlands of Forest Park in Queens. Hidden for most of their lives underground or within living and dead wood, mushrooms produce "fruit" only when they are ready to reproduce (each mushroom releases millions of spores). Even then they are scarcely noticed by most New Yorkers.

Since mushrooms, unlike plants, do not photosynthesize, they need to spend only a few days each year in the open air. The rest of the time they obtain nourishment by decomposing dead organic matter such as mulch, attacking or parasitizing living organisms, and engaging in a symbiotic relationship with plants, particularly trees, in which they facilitate the uptake of mineral nutrients by the trees' roots in exchange for carbohydrates produced by the tree. As long as there is plenty of rain (spores require moisture to continue their life cycles), mushrooms will thrive, ultimately producing a diverse and intriguing array of edible, poisonous, and even hallucinogenic species.

Destroying angel mushroom

Among the wild edible mushrooms that grow in the city, the most sought after are yellow morels (*Morchella esculenta*). These delicious, honeycombed-patterned mushrooms, which sell for as much as $30 a pound at gourmet stores like Dean & Deluca, are rare but have been collected by the dozens among the tulip trees in Manhattan's Inwood Hill Park. One mushroom hunter even discovered a patch in a vacant lot on the Lower East Side. More easily found than the elusive morels are two varieties named after fowl: the chicken mushroom (*Laetiporus sulphureus*), a yellow-orange mushroom that grows on tree trunks and tastes like chicken breast; and "hen of the woods" (*Grifola frondosa*), so called because it resembles a brown-and-tan hen sitting at the base of a tree. This savory mushroom (which is also used for treating cancer in Asia) is often found growing on old oak trees in Central Park.

Alongside such delicacies, New York City's parks produce mushrooms that can kill. The aptly named destroying angel (*Amanita virosa*) is a ghostly white mushroom that grows under oak trees in places like Brooklyn's Prospect Park. Usually about 5 inches high with a slender stalk and flat top, this lethal mushroom contains a poisonous compound called amanitin that shuts down the kidneys and liver. Even a single bite of a destroying angel, if untreated, can cause a painful death. Another poisonous mushroom, the jack-o'-lantern (*Omphalotus illudens*), is not quite so potent. Usually it causes only intense gastric distress. However, this large orange mushroom is renowned for another characteristic: its luminescence. Growing on tree stumps and on mulch in street tree plots throughout the city, the jack-o'-lantern glows in the dark, giving off a faintly visible green light.

Causing visions of a different sort are hallucinogenic, or mind-altering, mushrooms, of which the city has at least three. The big laughing gym (*Gymnopilus spectabilis*) is an orange-and-yellow mushroom that grows on decaying wood, and causes what the *Audubon Society Field Guide to North American Mushrooms* calls "unmotivated laughter and foolish behavior." Specimens of this species, which is said to taste unbearably bitter, have been found growing in street tree plots right in the middle of Manhattan.

Another hallucinogenic mushroom is the girdled panaeolus (*Panaeolus subbalteatus*). This small brown mushroom, though inconspicuous, contains the vision-inducing compound psilocybin. The girdled panaeolus grows, often abundantly, in gardens and lawns, where it breaks down fertilizer used to enrich the soil.

The city's most notorious psychoactive mushroom is the *Amanita muscaria*, or fly muscaria. Yellow-capped with white polka dots, it is the classic fairy-tale toadstool. Growing in many parts of the world, this mushroom is used by Siberian tribes during rituals to induce intoxicating trancelike states. Although New York City's fly muscaria species differs from the well-known red-capped variety that grows in northern Europe, it has the same toxic effects, including sweating, delirium, and a comalike sleep. Fly muscaria usually grows under pine and hemlock trees in parks and cemeteries, where groves of these evergreens have been planted.

These three hallucinogenic species, as well as many edible mushrooms, can easily be mistaken for deadly ones. In fact, poisonous look-alikes present the main hazard to mushroom collectors. One New York City group, however, navigates the treacherous and sometimes delicious world of wild mushrooms. Members of the New York Mycological Society, many of whom have survived decades of "mushrooming," strongly advise those new to foraging never to consume any mushroom before checking it out with an expert. Newcomers can join the society on its mushroom walks through city parks and nearby areas in spring, summer, and fall. When mushrooms are not in season, the society throws a winter banquet consisting solely of dishes made with wild mushrooms. Revived in the 1960s by the composer John Cage after a period of inactivity, the mycological society also holds lectures at the American Museum of Natural History on various facets of fungus science and culture. Inquiries about membership should be addressed as follows: Paul Sadowski, 205 East 94th Street, Apt. #9, New York, NY 10128; or call 212-962-6908 for information about walking tours.

HAY FEVER HELL

Every spring it's the same story. Just when love is in the air, thousands of New Yorkers start blowing their noses, wheezing, and getting itchy, puffy eyes. About one out of every 14 New Yorkers suffers from hay fever—but hay has nothing to do with it. The real culprits are pollinating oak and ailanthus trees, various local grasses, and the notorious ragweed, which ends the allergy season every August with a bang and the sneezes of about half a million city residents.

Whereas the majority of the world's plant species are pollinated by insects that transfer pollen from flower to flower, allergy-causing plants use less sophisticated methods to reproduce—simply letting loose massive amounts of pollen into the air in the hopes that it will land on a tree or plant of the opposite sex. The inconspicuous, dull green that usually characterizes the flowers of such plants is what necessitates the release of so much pollen; because insects are not attracted to their dreary blossoms, these plants have to rely on wind dispersal. Some wind-pollinating trees release as many as 6.4 billion pollen grains per season. However successful this approach may be for the plants themselves, such effusive methods have consequences for humans: dusty coatings up to an eighth of an inch thick on sidewalks and cars beneath wind-pollinating trees in springtime, torture for allergy sufferers, and billions of dollars in allergy medicine sales.

Long Island Jewish Hospital, in New Hyde Park, Queens, has been conducting pollen counts since 1990, in which technicians take pollen measurements from greased slides placed on the hospital's roof every day during allergy season. Three general types of pollen—ragweed, tree, and grass—as well as mold spores, are measured. During spring and late summer, measurements usually range from 10 to 100 pollen grains per square meter of air. When these counts push above 200, however, allergy sufferers start sneezing. In general, the highest counts occur in spring when trees are dropping powdery pollen and in fall when ragweed strikes. On May 15, 1992, the city logged its highest count to date. On that day pollen grains saturated the skies, and the count skyrocketed to 6,862—so high that the hospital's technicians thought they had made an error. Unfortunately for allergy sufferers, the reading was correct, and what could have been a beautiful spring day turned into a pageant of clogged sinuses and empty tissue boxes.

THERE *IS* A SEASON: FALL COLORS

New Yorkers are inveterate leaf peepers. Come October, the bed-and-breakfasts from the Berkshire Mountains to Bar Harbor, Maine, are packed with urban escapees determined to see the fall colors at their most glorious. It is a little-known fact, however, that you never have to leave New York City to experience the changing of the seasons. The same process that creates fall foliage in New England also occurs in the city; you just have to know where to look.

In the summer, leaves are green because they are packed with chlorophyll, the green-colored pigment used by plants to absorb sunlight. However, in areas that have four seasons and a hard winter, chlorophyll is not needed year-round. When the days start to shorten in fall, plants get the message that they should stop making chlorophyll, and underlying pigments, specifically xanthophylls and carotenoids, that were masked by the chlorophyll are slowly revealed. Under optimum conditions, the combination of these pigments and the breakdown of chlorophyll is what gives particular plants their unique fall hue. Trees like birches and tulips sport bright yellow leaves, beech trees turn bronze, and the leaves of oaks turn red and reddish brown.

In the city, leaves begin changing color in late October and early November, later than the surrounding suburbs and countryside. Biologists believe that New York City trees turn color later because the day is artificially lengthened by all the lights. But it is not the delay that gives the fall foliage of the city's street trees a bad reputation. The natural color palettes of the city's most common street trees—Norway maples, London planes, and honey locusts—are limited to pale yellows. And street trees like the native pin oak, which have the potential to turn red in fall, often turn brown instead. For red to emerge in an autumn leaf, there must be a chemical reaction between sugar and sunlight inside the leaf, and often the city's stressed-out trees are deprived of sugar. Thus, even in places like Central Park, the red-spectrum colors sometimes don't emerge.

The city's best fall colors are found in the areas with the healthiest trees and the most native species. Brilliant reds light up forested sections of the Bronx, Queens, and Staten Island, where the woodlands are populated not with street trees but with native red maples, sweet gums, sassafras, tulips, beeches, and oaks. In these less trampled areas, trees are given the chance to absorb the materials they need to produce fall color.

New York City leaf peepers also should learn to look down instead of up. Often the ground cover, particularly along the city's coast, puts on a more spectacular show than the trees. For example, the Jamaica Bay Wildlife Refuge is filled with Virginia creeper, poison ivy, and the salt marsh plant, slender glasswort—all of which turn brilliant reds, scarlets, and purples in fall. Sumac, which also grows at the refuge, is another fall winner; its leaves turn scarlet while its berrylike fruit turns from yellow to red. Common vines like oriental bittersweet and porcelain berry produce white and yellow berries, and the flowers of fall-blooming seaside goldenrod are bright yellow. Combined with the electric blue sky and dark blue waters that surround the refuge, this bayside display is one of the most colorful and intricate that fall has to offer.

CHAPTER 6

RITES AND MYSTERIES
The City's Natural Phenomena

New York City has consistently managed to defy and reorder nature, but despite the artificial lights that extend the day, and the constant traffic and construction, many of nature's cycles continue unabated: The tides roll in and out every day, the moon goes through its monthly cycle above the skyline, and the trees still blossom every spring. Along with these routine cycles, however, the city possesses some more esoteric natural phenomena—each following a rhythm all its own.

THE ATLANTIC FLYWAY

NEW YORK CITY ALOFT

The hub of national and international travel in the Northeast, New York City is also a stop along one of nature's great transportation routes, the Atlantic Flyway. Stretching along the Atlantic coast from Nova Scotia to Florida, the fly-

way is a migration path for millions of songbirds, waterfowl, birds of prey, and seabirds during the spring and fall.

More than 150 species of birds use the flyway, each with its own schedule, point of origin, and final destination. Some, like the yellow warbler, breed in northern Canada and winter in the Caribbean. Others, like the white-throated sparrow, come from the Great Plains, cut across the middle of the county, and turn right when they hit the East Coast on their way to Mexico. The flyway has nonavian lanes as well. Three species of migratory bats travel along the Atlantic flyway, as do several migratory insects, such as the monarch butterfly and the green darner dragonfly.

For many New Yorkers, the Atlantic Flyway is an unseen phenomenon. Hawks make their way south soaring over the tallest buildings, often out of the range of human eyesight. Tiny songbirds slip into the city at night and spend a couple of days hidden in treetops before taking off again. Many birds that travel in large flocks—such as red-throated loons—pass by over the ocean, miles offshore. Often the only clue that flocks of birds are passing is the faint honking of Canada geese as they fly 500 feet over the city in V formation.

However, there are a surprising number of places where the flyway directly intersects with New York City. In fall, before they head for the Carolinas, huge flocks of tree swallows—containing as many as 10,000 birds—gather at the Jamaica Bay Wildlife Refuge, a popular resting site for migratory birds. Bald eagles—until recently an endangered species—have been documented passing over Central Park's Belvedere Castle in recent Novembers, with as many as 48 living representatives of the U.S. national emblem counted in a single day. Even an autumn sighting of a small flock of sanderlings scurrying along the surf in the Rockaways is impressive; these members of the sandpiper family stop here on an itinerary that takes them from the Arctic to as far as Tierra del Fuego on the southern tip of Argentina—a distance of 10,000 miles.

During these long-distance trips, birds employ a variety of methods to navigate. They follow topographic features like coastlines, mountain ranges, and river courses. They navigate by the stars and the sun and even use Earth's mag-

---

Wild Fact

WINTER PLAYGROUND

For most birds, flying south for the winter means escaping the snowbelt and enjoying the sunny weather of the Caribbean and South America. One Arctic bird, however, has selected New York City as the perfect cold-weather getaway. Every December, hundreds of snow geese (*Chen caerulescens*) take off from the wilderness surrounding the James and Hudson bays in northern Quebec. After flying south for 2,000 miles, they finally come in for a landing at the Jamaica Bay Wildlife Refuge in Queens. Here, these beautiful all-white birds spend the winter months cruising the refuge's West Pond in small flocks, eating aquatic plants, and pinwheeling in for seaplane-style landings.

According to bird biologists, the city's raw, wintry weather suits the snow geese just fine. With their downy feathers and heavy-duty insulation, these Arctic birds are most comfortable when the temperature is below 40°F.

> ### *Wild Fact*
>
> ### BLINDED BY THE LIGHT
>
> Most birds migrate long distances at night and orient themselves by the position of the stars. Sometimes, however, city lights befuddle them. On foggy nights, when the stars are obscured, high-flying migrators look down and see beacons from skyscrapers, radio towers, and airports. Believing they have headed off course, whole flocks of birds will descend and slam into tall buildings and other structures.
>
> William Beebe, a famous ornithologist with the Bronx Zoo during the first half of the twentieth century, once spent what turned out to be a foggy night at the top of the Statue of Liberty to observe the spring bird migration—at a time when the torch in the statue was lit like a beacon. What he saw instead was a massacre. Confused by the light, birds swarmed into the statue, smashing against the observation deck. Some survived and clung, panting, to Beebe's coat, but in the morning, he counted 271 dead birds on the ground. Since then, the torch on the Statue of Liberty has been dimmed.

netic field as a guide. Many birds, such as waterfowl and songbirds, fly at night, when the air is less subject to turbulent air currents; nighttime radar scans at John F. Kennedy Airport routinely pick up flocks of migrating birds as they pass over the city.

During the spring migration, songbirds fly as far as 400 miles a night and by the time they reach New York City may have logged more than 2,000 miles, including exhausting stretches over the open waters of the Gulf of Mexico. Each night a migrating songbird may expend as much as 25 percent of its body fat. If a migrant happens to be over the city when dawn breaks, it will descend out of its flight pattern (or "drop out," as ornithologists put it) to refuel. These birds will take refuge in any wooded spot available, which is why Central Park—seen from above as a spot of green amid a mass of concrete—is a stopover for so many exotic-looking birds

Whereas songbirds hug the coastline while they migrate, birds of prey follow several different routes, depending on the species. Merlins, kestrels, and sharp-shinned hawks also take the coast, simply migrating alongside their food supply. Bird-watchers looking for these predatory species often spy them hunting for migrating songbirds along the city's seashore.

Meanwhile, red-tailed and broad-winged hawks take a different flight path, traveling down the Hudson River, which is a feeder route to the Atlantic Flyway from upstate New York and Canada. These hawks expend little energy while migrating, using northwest wind currents to carry them high overhead. Over the Bronx at places like Wave Hill, as many as 1,000 broad-winged hawks have been seen crossing the Hudson River on their way to New Jersey in a single day.

Biologists theorize that birds began migrating to take better advantage of food supplies and avoid overpopulation in their breeding grounds. Generally, they move from areas of high population and low food supply to areas of low population and high food supply. Many local birds—house sparrows, pigeons, and starlings, for example—don't bother to migrate, however. These birds—all introduced species—have no reason to leave, because garbage cans and handouts from bird lovers offer an endless supply of food, even during the winter.

THE RUNNING OF THE SHAD

Return to the Hudson River

Every spring, nine species of fish run the gauntlet up the Hudson River—beneath the Verrazano-Narrows Bridge, past the Statue of Liberty, and up the entire liquid length of Manhattan. All of these fish are native New Yorkers—born and raised here—and after spending the rest of the year roaming the wide-open ocean, they have an urge to return to their hometown for a little spring fling. Among the most impressive of these long-distance travelers, and certainly the most trumpeted, is the American shad.

Reaching lengths of 2½ half feet and weights of 9 pounds, the shad is the king of the herrings, a sleek silvery fish that has never given up on New York City. In April and May, when the water warms to 58°F, the shad swim by the hundreds of thousands into New York Harbor on the way to their spawning grounds upriver, turning the lower Hudson into a veritable fish superhighway. Seventy miles past the city, at Kingston, in a ritual that has gone on for more than a century, the shad are met by a few seasoned fishermen who string 500-foot-long fishing nets across the river and haul their catches into small boats. A few shad are cooked and eaten right at the river's edge; the rest are sold at the Fulton Fish Market and at the city's finer fish stores. Considered a delicacy by gourmets, the shad and shad roe (the fish eggs of the females) usually end up in the hands of the city's most discriminating chefs.

Today, most New Yorkers are more familiar with the taste of Pacific salmon and Maryland crab than they are with the delicate, sweet flavor of shad. In the old days, it was different. In the 1930s, dining on shad and shad roe was considered such a rite of spring that Manhattan's chefs sometimes put as

CULINARY DELIGHT

How can anything fished from the Hudson River be considered a delicacy? Even though the waters around New York City are becoming less polluted, health advisories are still issued on the types and number of fish that may be eaten without risk. None of these restrictions, however, apply to the shad. Part of the shad's modus operandi is that it does not eat while on its spawning run; thus it avoids taking in any pollutants it encounters in the river.

However, one small problem remains: bones. The shad is affectionately referred to as a porcupine turned inside out. According to ichthyologist C. Lavett Smith at the American Museum of Natural History, each fish contains 769 bones. Needless to say, most amateurs will want to start with a filet. Fortunately—though the shad come but once a year—deboning specialists at the Fulton Fish Market provide bone-free shad to the city's better fish stores.

Cooking Shad

Shad has a rich, almost nutty flavor and its flesh has a melt-in-your-mouth quality that makes it perfect for baking or broiling. The traditional method of preparing shad, however, was by "planking" it outdoors: nailing it to an oak plank, putting strips of bacon around it, and placing the plank next to the coals of an open fire. The recipe given here, which comes from the Savoy Restaurant in Soho, calls for planking the shad indoors. According to owner-chef Peter Hoffman, the best shad to use is one that was caught in the Hudson River the night before.

Oven-Planked Shad

- 1   *1-inch-thick oak plank brushed with olive oil (if you can't find a plank, use an iron skillet)*
- 2   *large deboned shad filets*
- 1   *tablespoon melted butter*
-     *salt and pepper*

Preheat oven to 400°F. Place filets skin side down on oiled plank. Brush with melted butter and season with salt and freshly ground pepper. Cook shad about 25 minutes, or until flesh begins to brown. Serve on plank with roasted new potatoes and springtime asparagus.

American shad

CAVIAR ON THE HUDSON

The shad aren't the only anadromous fish in town. Every April and May, Atlantic sturgeon (*Acipenser oxyrhynchus*)—enormous fish up to 12 feet long and weighing up to 800 pounds—return from their ocean wanderings to spawn in the deep waters of the Hudson River. Swimming past the Statue of Liberty, they ultimately arrive at their spawning grounds near Hyde Park, about 100 miles north of the city line.

Although the world's most expensive and highly coveted caviar comes from the eggs of the beluga sturgeon that live in Russia's Caspian Sea, some first-rate caviar can be found right here in the Hudson River. A single female Atlantic sturgeon bursting with as many as a million black caviar eggs can sell for as much as $3,000, and in recent years an increasing number of Atlantic sturgeon have been ambushed by commercial fishing nets.

Unfortunately, because of heavy fishing during the last century, sturgeon have already disappeared from many rivers where they once spawned on the Atlantic coast—an ironic fact, considering that sturgeons are members of one of the world's longest-surviving families of fishes, tracing their lineage back 200 million years to the early Jurassic period.

Until recently, conservation biologists recognized the Hudson River as the Atlantic sturgeon's most successful remaining spawning ground. Now, this magnificent fish is declining in the Hudson River as well. In 1996, the New York State Department of Environmental Conservation banned sturgeon fishing until further notice, in the hopes that this prehistoric fish will have a chance to recover.

Atlantic sturgeon

many as seven different shad dishes on their menus: Shad a la Cordon Bleu, Baked Shad Roe with Fine Herbs, and Broiled Shad with Bacon and Grilled Tomato were just a few of these old-time favorites. To revive some of this spirit, shad bakes are now held every spring on the banks of the Hudson River, and Manhattan's more forward-thinking restaurateurs are putting locally caught shad back on the menu with some new twists, such as Sorrel-Wrapped Shad, Sliced Shad Roe Served atop Bitter Greens, and Shad Filets with Red Pepper and Saffron Sauce.

Shad, or *Alosa sapidissima* (Latin for "most delicious herring"), has been a culinary phenomenon for as long as New York City has existed—but it has been a natural phenomenon for even longer.

Most fish live either in fresh water or salt water. Shad, however, are one of a few species of "anadromous" fish that can live in both worlds. Born in freshwater rivers, shad spend their adult years in the ocean and return to their home river only to spawn. Though shad born in the Hudson River are intimately wedded to the waters around New York City, they travel an enormous distance during the rest of the year. After spawning, they swim out past the Battery and head up to Canada's Bay of Fundy. When the weather becomes colder, they migrate down the coast and spend the winter in the waters off Virginia and North Carolina. By the time they return to New York Harbor in the spring, they have completed a round-trip journey of 2,400 miles. Unlike salmon, which return to their home rivers only once—to spawn and die—shad live as long as 15 years, returning to the river spring after spring.

No one knows exactly how the shad find their way home every year. What is known is that they remain loyal to the Hudson despite many difficulties. Although shad are native to the entire eastern seaboard, they have been eliminated from many other rivers by pollution, hydroelectric dams, and overfishing. Even cleaner waters won't make them come back—because there are no wild fish born in those rivers left *to* come back.

Today, biologists believe that the Hudson River has more shad than any river on the East Coast, but even Hudson River shad are under pressure. Historically, when the shad were running in May, New York Harbor was choked with fish, and hundreds of commercial netters flocked to the riverbanks, often making small fortunes on their catches. Since the 1940s, however, the Hudson's shad population has been riding a roller coaster.

After rebounding in the 1980s, it appears the shad are now on the decline again. Large commercial fishing vessels are snagging the shad on their wintering grounds—before they even begin their return trip. Hudson River biologists are currently working to establish regulations for this offshore fishing industry so that more of the shad will have a chance to make it home.

A LITTLE ROMANCE

THE MATING OF THE HORSESHOE CRABS

It's the oldest love story in the book—literally. Every May and June when the moon exerts its most powerful attraction, horseshoe crabs head up onto New York City's beaches for an annual rendezvous that they have been keeping for the last 310 million years. On city shores from Marine Park in Brooklyn to Orchard Beach in the Bronx, the full and new moons herald the highest tides of the month, and the helmet-shaped horseshoe crabs—some as big as hubcaps—sense that it's time to ride into town for *amore.*

Out in the harbor, a moonstruck male links onto the back of a female's shell with specially adapted, hooked legs. Occasionally, a second, third, and even fourth male will hitch onto the towline, and when the amorous crabs hit the beach, they look like a sinewy, brown subway train pulling in for a station stop.

Once on the beach, the horseshoe crabs don't waste time. Each female digs a nest at the high-tide line and proceeds to lay about 300 tiny green eggs. Close on the female's heels, the males scramble to be the first to fertilize the eggs. Afterward, both males and females are carried back into nearby waters by the retreating tide.

Over the next few days, the moon's power wanes, and the level of each tide gets lower, never quite reaching the line in the sand where the incubating eggs are buried. Two weeks later, when the moon once again exerts its strongest gravitational pull, the crab eggs hatch and the next high tide flows in—right on schedule—to sweep the newborns out to sea.

Such impeccable timing may be what has kept horseshoe crabs around for so long. Essentially unchanged in their shape and habits since they first came onto the scene during the Paleozoic era, horseshoe crabs are considered "living fossils" by biologists. Resembling no other living animals known today, horseshoe crabs have outlived such formidable species as the trilobites with which they once shared the ancient seas, as well as every species of dinosaur.

Technically, horseshoe crabs (*Limulus polyphemus*) are misnamed. According to taxonomists, they are not crabs at all, but distant cousins of spiders and scorpions. With brown armor-plated shells, spiky tails, and 10 insectlike legs, horseshoe crabs can look fearsome, and many beachgoers shun them, thinking that they sting or pinch. In fact, horseshoe crabs are one of the seashore's most harmless creatures. Their long, spiked tails are used not as weapons, but as levers to help them right themselves if they accidentally flip upside down onto their backs.

Most of the time horseshoe crabs wander around on the bottom of the coastal shelf—anywhere from the low-tide line to water 75 feet deep—where they scavenge for food and eat burrowing mollusks. Highly adaptable, they can survive in a wide range of conditions, and biologists note that they are among the last creatures to be driven out by pollution.

New York City is not the only place where horseshoe crabs can be found *flagrante delicto.* Delaware Bay, 150 miles south of the city, is the best-known and most heavily frequented rendezvous point. There, hundreds of thousands of horseshoe crabs congregate on the beaches to lay their eggs, many of which are eaten by the hordes of shorebirds that arrive simultaneously. On long-distance migrations to the Arctic, these birds are desperately in need of fuel, and biologists believe that their migration is timed so that the birds can take advantage of the crabs' protein-rich eggs.

Thousands of serious bird-watchers travel to Delaware Bay every May to observe this spectacle, but it can also be seen on a smaller scale in New York City. Here, at places such as the Jamaica Bay Wildlife Refuge, hundreds of rare, interesting, and just plain hungry birds, including ruddy turnstones, semipalmated plovers, red knots, dunlins, laughing gulls, and Canada geese can be found feasting on the eggs of the city's horseshoe crabs.

Every spring, as many as a dozen "crab walks" are led by park rangers along New York City's shores, and occasionally these expeditions allow for a little scientific study. In previous years, biologists from the National Parks Service have asked New Yorkers to help them tag horseshoe crabs in order to learn more about the crabs' habits. So far, horseshoe crabs tagged in Jamaica Bay have been found to stray, on average, about 18 miles down the coast. Some crabs, however, have been known to wander farther afield, and one rogue was found 1,000 miles away, swimming in the warm waters of the Bahamas.

THE FLIGHT OF THE MONARCHS

BUTTERFLIES AT THE BEACH

Every November, 60 million monarch butterflies congregate at mountain elevations above 12,000 feet in central Mexico. Covered with fir trees, these cool mountaintop forests act as natural refrigerators, where the butterflies chill out—literally—to wait out the winter. In 12 distinct colonies—some as small as half an acre—on Mexico's Trans-Volcanic Ridge, the monarchs sit, wings folded, looking like orange leaves in the dark forest. Though individually each butterfly weighs a bare fraction of an ounce, the combined weight of monarchs here is estimated at more than 30 tons. In some places, the monarchs sit so thickly on the trees that the branches droop and sometimes even break.

What do a bunch of butterflies in such a far-flung locale have to do with the Big Apple? According to researchers, a few of these colorful creatures are New York natives. In the summer of 1995, one New York–based monarch on which a tiny identification tag was placed was rediscovered in the Mexican winter colonies—having flown at least 2,100 miles to get there.

For more than a century, naturalists have observed that monarch butterflies (*Danaus plexippus*) leave for the winter. In the fall, these blowsy, 4-inch-wide butterflies can be seen in groups, flitting purposefully along the coastline. In places like Kansas, large groups of south-flying monarchs appear each September, moving downstate like a slow-moving cold front. But until entomologists discovered the Mexican winter colonies in 1975, no one knew where the monarchs were going. Today, biologists believe that the entire eastern U.S. population funnels into this tiny area in central Mexico.

The butterflies make this incredible journey, because they are tropical at heart. They cannot survive the frigid winters of the northern United States and Canada, and because they live as long as 8 months—a geologic age in butterfly terms—they have to go south in the cold months, just as most birds do.

Starting in September, monarchs from as far north as Nova Scotia begin flying south. Though their style of flight looks lilting and delicate, they average about 50 miles a day during their migration flight. Locally, this phenomenon can be observed at several of New York City's beaches and bayside parks. In September, at Jacob Riis Park, Fort Tilden, the Breezy Point Tip, the Jamaica Bay Wildlife Refuge, and Great Kills Park, masses of vivid orange-and-black butterflies can be seen clinging to the yellow flowers of seaside goldenrod—as many as 40 to a plant. Although the best place to see the monarchs is along the coast, they can show up anywhere, even flying in small groups down Manhattan's Fifth Avenue.

Altogether, the monarchs' trip takes 30 to 45 days. Once they arrive at their Mexican wintering grounds, they spend about 4 months in hibernation, blanketing the fir trees in layers up to six butterflies deep. These isolated mountain forests were chosen for their near-perfect climate conditions: above freezing but below 60°F, and highly sheltered. For most of the winter, the monarchs remain extremely still, living off of their fat reserves.

In March, as the weather begins to warm, the monarchs begin making tentative, exploratory flights. Then, they mate, and flutter off like orange-and-black confetti—with the future of all the East Coast's monarchs resting on the success of their return trip. After a journey of about 10 days, the returning monarchs arrive in the southern United States, lay their eggs, and collapse. Their eggs turn into caterpillars, which in turn become chrysalises, which in turn become adult butterflies. This second generation then continues the flight north, laying the eggs of the third generation along the way. Throughout the spring and summer, each succeeding generation heads farther north by stages. By late June, the north-traveling monarchs have reached New York City, and by August, the great-grandchildren of the original migrants have made it all the way to Canada. It is this final generation that will return to Mexico. Instead of expending their energy on mating, the great-grandchildren start bulking up on nectar—energy they will need for the long flight south.

How these fourth-generation butterflies navigate their way across more than 2,000 unfamiliar miles to their small and secluded wintering colonies is still under study. Somehow the directions are embedded in their genetic code and, thus, guide the monarchs that are seen flitting through the city in fall all the way to Mexico.

THE BROOD

THE EMERGENCE OF THE 17-YEAR CICADAS

Every 17 years, Staten Island hosts one of the strangest natural occurrences on the planet. Millions of "periodical" cicadas—1½-inch-long winged insects with bulging red eyes—appear out of nowhere and take over the island. In parks and suburbs, in fields and high in the treetops, the cicadas overwhelm the landscape, smashing into car windows and buzzing about in short blundering flights. And though they *look* strange, it is the noise they make that drives people buggy.

The chorus of the 17-year cicadas has been likened to the sound effect used for flying saucers in movies or to the whine of a million tiny car alarms. When the cicadas come out, people can't sleep. They can't think. They can't take it.

Fortunately, or unfortunately if you're an insect lover, this won't happen again until the year 2013. Whereas most natural cycles occur on a daily, monthly, or yearly basis, periodical cicadas (*Magicicada septendecim*) are on a completely different time clock. One of the longest-living insects in the world, they spend more than 99 percent of their lives underground, emerging only when they are exactly 17 years old. The last time the periodical cicadas hit the streets was in June 1996. Before that it was 1979, 1962, 1945, 1928, and so forth, as far back as anyone can remember.

At present, the cicada nymphs—ghostly white wingless creatures with crablike claws—are ensconced in little burrows 2 feet underground. Beyond the reach of sunlight and insulated from seasonal temperature fluctuations, they receive no apparent clues about what time of day it is or what time of year. All the while, these youngsters are living off the juices of tree roots. Scientists theorize that the taste of tree sap, the "ingredients" of which change depending on the season, allows the cicadas to count the years until it is time to emerge. Another theory is that these insects have a yet-to-be-understood 17-year internal timer.

However they know it is their year, the teenage cicadas will start tunneling closer to the surface in the spring of 2013. There, they will be able to sense outside temperatures, and in late May or early June, when soil temperatures reach a balmy 64°F, they will begin to emerge. On that day, starting at sunset, the cicadas will come out en masse in Staten Island's parks and on people's front lawns—each leaving a dime-sized hole in the ground behind it.

With all the new housing going up on Staten Island, some of the cicadas may find that the ground above their heads has been paved over, and these cicadas will never see daylight. Millions and millions, however, will make it to the surface, and once there, they will climb the nearest vertical objects—usually trees, but sometimes telephone polls and lampposts—where they will shed their young skins and take on their final, adult forms, becoming red-eyed, black-bodied bugs with 3-inch-long translucent wings.

For periodical cicadas, the brief world of adulthood lasts 6 weeks at the most, and in that short time they have only two things on their minds: singing

> **Wild Fact**
>
> ## QUIZZZZZZZ
>
> In 1902, the *New York Times* compared the din of the 17-year cicada's song to:
>
> a. The filing of 10,000 saws.
> b. The beating of tom-toms on a giant scale.
> c. The simultaneous tuning of all the fiddles in the world.
> d. All of the above.
>
> (Answer: d)

and mating. To attract females, the male cicadas gather in what scientists call chorus centers, producing an eerie whirring noise that reaches levels up to 100 decibels. This droning song is made by the vibration of tymbals, built-in kettle drums in the cicada's abdomen. Somehow this racket attracts the girls to the boys, and after the cicadas mate, the female cicadas lay eggs in twigs on the tips of tree branches.

Once the future of the next generation—or brood, as it's officially called—is secured, all the adult cicadas die off, falling to the ground in a gruesome pile. Six weeks later, their eggs hatch, and the white nymphs crawl back down (or fall from) the trees to the ground, where they begin tunneling down with their crablike front claws—not to be seen again for another 17 years. So the cycle continues.

When first observed by naturalists, periodical cicadas were mistaken for locusts because they emerged in such biblical proportions. However, it was later discovered that they are more closely related to aphids, and unlike locusts, the cicadas don't eat a thing, not a single leaf, when they come to the surface in their adult form.

It also took a few years for naturalists to figure out the timing of these amazing insects. In the 1920s, one naturalist convinced postmasters all over the eastern United States to report when the cicadas emerged in their districts. From this data, the 17-year cicadas were divided into 13 different broods—with each brood coming out on a slightly different cycle. Staten Island's periodical cicadas are part of Brood 2, along with cicadas that emerge simultaneously in parts of Georgia, North Carolina, Virginia, Pennsylvania, Maryland, New Jersey, and Connecticut. The nation's largest group, Brood 10—which used to emerge in Manhattan, Brooklyn, and Queens before being crowded out by urbanization—comes out in different years (1970, 1987, 2004, and so on). Although Brood 10 no longer makes an appearance in New York City proper, its otherworldly whine is evident in the city's suburbs from Long Island to New Jersey.

New York City's own cicadas will not reappear until the year 2013. For those who can't wait, however, the Staten Island Institute of Arts and Sciences near the Staten Island ferry terminal in St. George has a collection of 60,000 cicadas preserved in small wooden specimen boxes.

CHAPTER 7

WILD PLACES
Exploring Nature in New York City

This chapter is a guide to 33 parks, nature areas, and wildlife refuges—all located within the five boroughs. Some are located in the center of the city, where elements of the natural world manage to survive. Others are in more pristine spots, where the crush of the city can be momentarily forgotten.

In many of New York's natural areas, the landscape and the life that inhabits it may seem unfamiliar. To help urban ecotourists gain their bearings, 10 walking tours (Wild Walks), with maps, have been designed for nine of the city's larger parks (Central Park merits two tours). Directions to the parks, most of which can be reached by mass transit, are provided for all 33. Additionally, smaller maps of 6 other wild areas have been included.

Many people are ill at ease about going to parts of the city where they don't know their way around. In general, the city's natural areas are not magnets for crime; many of the parks described here could even be characterized as "safe." However, park visitors should exercise the same caution they would anywhere else in New York City. Stick to daylight hours and consider bringing along a companion. Or, if you're uncomfortable going alone, go with a group. The Urban Park Rangers at the Department of Parks and Recreation (1-800-

201-PARK) and National Parks Rangers at the Gateway National Recreation Area (718-318-4340) organize free nature tours every weekend, year-round.

One final caveat: Some of the parks listed here are wilder than others. Along with the pretty scenery, there may be mosquitoes, ticks, and other biting insects—not to mention unpredictable weather conditions. Depending on the place and the season, dress appropriately and don't forget to bring insect repellent, sunscreen, bottled water, and snacks.

MANHATTAN: THE WILD HEART

Scholars have suggested several meanings for the Native American word *manhattan*. According to Robert Steven Grumet's *Native American Place Names in New York City, manhattan* may mean:

> island,
> hilly island,
> small island,
> cluster of islands with channels everywhere,
> reeds,
> place for reeds, or
> place where timber is procured for bows and arrows

Before Europeans settled here, Manhattan's shores were marshy and convoluted—indented by tidal creeks—and above these rivers, the high grounds were rugged with boulder-strewn forests. Today, the island's shores have been filled in and smoothed; in place of marshes Manhattan has the United Nations and the World Financial Center. The wooded hills have been leveled; instead of timber, Manhattan is synonymous with Madison Avenue and the Upper West Side. Land-filling and the street grid have transformed what was once an island wilderness. Yet in and around the architecture, behind the crowds and the endless roar of the streets, Manhattan's wild heart still quietly beats.

Central Park

When architects Frederick Law Olmsted and Calvert Vaux finished laying out their blueprint for Central Park in 1858, just 3 years before the Civil War, the plan for the first large-scale park in the nation was considered nothing short of revolutionary. Central Park was going to be free and accessible to all. It was going to be paid for with public funds. And—perhaps oddest of all—it was going to be built in the middle of nowhere.

In 1857, the city proper reached only as far north as present-day 23rd Street, and the 1¼-square-mile plot of land that is now Central Park was rough, inhospitable country. Six streams meandered across the site toward the East River, but some never made it to the shoreline—ending instead in mosquito-infested swamps. Poison ivy grew everywhere, and the only people who lived on the land were unlicensed pig farmers and squatters.

To complete Olmsted and Vaux's design, every inch of the land had to be sculpted. First the farmers were unceremoniously booted off their property. Then workers in "rock gangs"—using 20,800 pounds of gunpowder—had to blast through innumerable outcrops that interfered with plans for carriageways and lawns. Finally, 500,000 cubic yards of topsoil were brought in to reshape the grounds, and 270,000 trees were planted.

Built in Manhattan's backcountry more than 130 years ago, Central Park today is bounded by Fifth Avenue and Central Park West—home to some of the most expensive real estate in the world. The park itself is a National Historic Landmark, and more than 16 million people visit annually. Although what had been a forbidding landscape is now a cultivated green playground for the city's tired masses, many natural features remain. The following tours cover two of Central Park's most natural areas, the Ramble and the recently revitalized Great North.

Wild Walk: The Ramble

On the edge of Central Park's Lake, Olmsted and Vaux preserved the well-wooded, hilly Ramble in the center of the park as a haven for birds and other wildlife. The first area of the park opened to the public, it was greeted by the *New York Times* in 1859 as "the most delightful spot . . . beautifully varied with

Red-bellied woodpecker

picturesque rock-work and cool secluded nooks." Today, its mazelike trails, beneath a thick canopy of shady trees, remain the most popular natural area in the park.

Entering at West 81st Street next to the Diana Ross Playground, cross beneath the stone bridge and turn right, heading straight past the Delacorte Theater. Here you will see a stairway—cut from Manhattan's native bedrock—that leads to the **Shakespeare Garden** **1**, which is planted with trees and flowers mentioned in Shakespeare's works. Among these plantings are marigolds from *A Winter's Tale*, holly from *As You Like It*, and camomile from *Henry IV*.

From the garden, head up to **Belvedere Castle** **2**, a fanciful nineteenth-century tower built atop an enormous stone crag called Vista Rock. Venture onto this rugged precipice and take a closer look at the rock—schist—which is dotted with shiny flecks of a mineral called mica. Although it is hard to imagine, this stone outcrop and others in the park are the eroded nubs of an ancient mountain range that once (about 400 million years ago) rose as high as the Alps.

Inside Belvedere Castle is the Henry Luce Nature Observatory, featuring hands-on exhibits about wildlife in the park. If you climb the narrow stairs to the top of the castle's tower, you will be treated to a spectacular view of Turtle Pond, the canopy of trees blanketing the park, and the distinctive outlines of the park's Gold Coast along Central Park West, including the towers of the San Remo, the Beresford, and the Ardsley.

Back on Vista Rock, a small fenced-off area houses Central Park's National Weather Service monitoring station. When NBC's Al Roker announces, "The temperature in Central Park is 60 degrees," this is where the temperature is recorded. When official weather monitoring first began here in 1869, measurements were taken by hand and sent by telegraph to the Smithsonian in Washington, D.C. Today, readings of temperature, precipitation, wind speed, wind direction, visibility, air pressure, and humidity are updated every minute by automatic sensors, and the information is sent straight to forecasters' computers. Because weather measurements have been taken here for so long, all of New York City's official records are made and broken in Central Park. Over the years, the park has seen everything from 106°F heat to −15°F cold.

Next to the monitoring station, two paths lead to **The Ramble** **3**, a 37-acre woodland and mecca for local bird-watchers. Ever since the Ramble was listed in a 1994 issue of *Travel & Leisure* as one of the best bird-watching spots in the nation, binocular-toting birders from around the world have flocked here to see some of Central Park's 275 species. Though birding goes on in this woodland year-round, the Ramble is overrun in spring by "warbler mania" (described in Chapter 4). Birding tours are held almost every day—all on the lookout for brightly colored songbirds that stop here on their migration north.

Wander down the paved pathway from Belvedere Castle into the forest of oaks and black cherries. Massive outcroppings of dark rock loom over the paths, giving the Ramble a primordial feeling. At the bottom of the hill, **Bank Rock Bridge** 4 stretches over the upper lobe of the lake, offering a pastoral view and a good place to look for turtles and waterbirds. Instead of crossing the bridge, head up the stone steps and down a narrow path leading through a keyhole-shaped arch built from slabs of native bedrock. Take the path down to the view of the **Central Park Lake** 5, where you can see a rustic wooden shelter known as the Ladies Pavilion across the water and families of mallards navigating their way among the rowboats. From the lake, cross the wooden bridge over **The Gill** 6, a 1,000-foot-long artificial stream running through the woods. Climb up the steps and cross two rustic wooden bridges to reach **Azalea Pond** 7. This small water hole has become a giant snack bar for the park's birds. Hanging on several trees above the water are bird feeders that are stocked with seeds by Central Park's many avian fans. Look for any number of birds making a play for a free handout—from red-bellied woodpeckers that nest in the park to pigeons just visiting from the streets.

From here, head for the lake and the **Loeb Boathouse and Cafe** 8, where you can record any sightings in their nature log (ask the maître d' for it).

Wild Fact

UNNATURAL SELECTION

Nay, I'll have a starling shall be taught to speak nothing but "Mortimer."
—William Shakespeare

Central Park hosts a free Shakespeare festival every summer and has a Shakespeare Garden devoted to plants mentioned in Shakespeare's plays. The park was once also the repository of an obsession with the bard that changed the face of North America. In 1890, Eugene Scheifflin, a Shakespeare fanatic and the leading member of the American Acclimatization Society, decided that all the songbirds mentioned in Shakespeare's works should be introduced into the United States. On March 6, 1890, he let loose 40 pairs of the European starling—the bird mentioned in *Henry IV*—in Central Park. Within a few years, the starlings (*Sturnus vulgaris*) had spread from coast to coast, and they are now one of the most common birds in the nation.

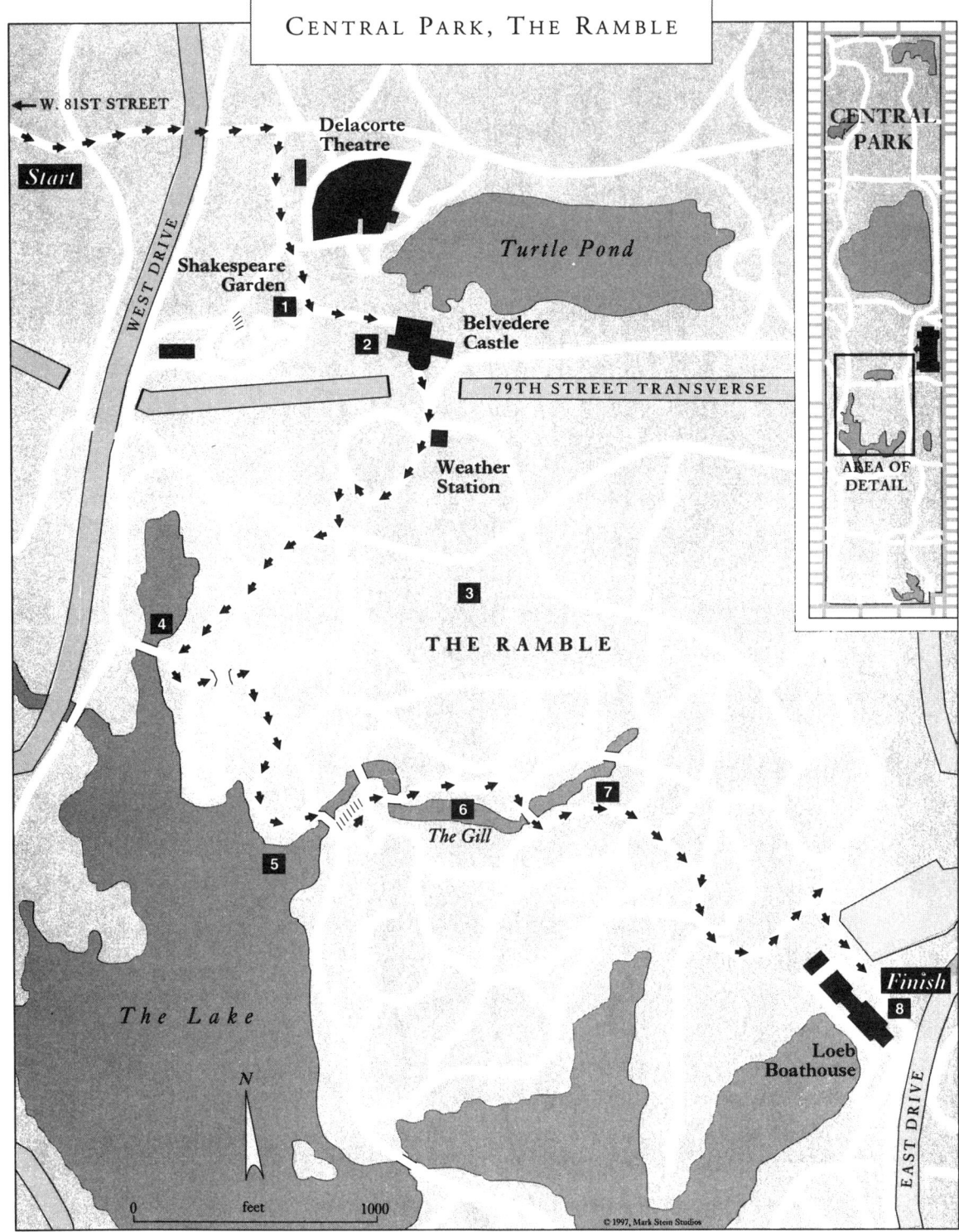

Occasionally the log has unusual entries, including groundhogs and turkey vultures, as well as elaborate updates on a family of red-tailed hawks that have taken to nesting nearby on a Fifth Avenue apartment tower.

Take note: It's easy to lose yourself in the Ramble. To reorient yourself, simply follow any running water downstream to the Lake.

HOW TO GET THERE: **By mass transit:** *Take the B or C train to the 81st Street/Museum of Natural History station at Central Park West. Or, take the 1 or 9 train to the 79th Street station. Walk east on 79th Street for 3 blocks and turn left on Central Park West to reach the park's 81st Street entrance.*

WILD WALK: THE GREAT NORTH

Frederick Law Olmsted, the park's codesigner, had great affection for the northernmost section of Central Park because it epitomized his ideas about creating a "natural and rustic" setting within the confines of New York City. During the park's construction in 1859, Olmsted actually lived here with his family in an old convent—behind what is now the Conservatory Garden—in order to better superintend the fulfillment of his designs. At that time, a meandering brook called Montanye's Rivulet flowed down the park's western ridge, crossed what is now Fifth Avenue, and emptied into the East River. As part of the park's construction, Montanye's Rivulet was redirected to form a watercourse that now follows the rivulet's original streambed from the 100th Street Pool to the Harlem Meer. Although the park's engineers refined the scenery—they added "greatly to its natural wildness" by hauling in huge boulders and building waterfalls—the Great North, in large part, preserves Manhattan's original, rugged topography.

For many years, the northern part of the park was virtually abandoned. However, a massive landscape renovation completed in 1993 by the Central Park Conservancy, a nonprofit organization dedicated to maintaining the park, restored the Great North to its former glory. Shadier, quieter, and more forested than the better-known southern end, the Great North remains partially undiscovered—one of New York's more pleasant surprises.

From the park's entrance on West 96th Street, follow the main drive past the 100th Street entrance and stop to contemplate the picturesque **100th Street Pool** [1], considered by many park lovers to be the most beautiful spot in all of Central Park. Weeping willows, red maples, and a cinnamon-colored bald cypress are reflected in the water's surface, an impressionistic effect that Olmsted and Vaux were particularly fond of.

From the pool, stone steps lead down the side of a 14-foot-high **waterfall** **2** that gurgles into the **Loch** **3**, a naturalistic but artificially fed stream that flows alongside the path. To reach the Upper Loch, head under the Glenspan Arch—built out of 1- to 20-ton blocks of fieldstone found in the immediate vicinity—and cross the wooden footbridge to the right bank.

Until the renovation of this area was completed in 1993, the Upper Loch was choked with silt and the surrounding woods had been taken over by non-native plants such as Norway maple and Japanese knotweed—both exotic species that crowd out woodland plants and create a monotonous monoculture where little else can grow. To combat this arboreal invasion, the park's horticulturists have planted "wet-footed" native trees such as red maples, sweet gums, tupelos, and tulips along the high banks of the Loch—many of which are now taking off on their own and reseeding. In low-lying areas, streambed plants such as ostrich ferns and skunk cabbage—which probably grew naturally along Montanye's Rivulet 150 years ago—have also been reintroduced.

A little farther along the path, a 3-acre hillside **meadow** **4**—formerly overgrown with exotic weeds—has been replanted with native wildflowers such as purple asters and black-eyed Susans that once blanketed the lowlands of Harlem. Bird-watchers now report that the meadow is beginning to attract rare grassland species—from bluebirds to the elusive Le Conte's sparrow.

As you walk, Manhattan's bedrock and the 95-acre North Woods rise steeply to your left. The park's original designers left this portion of the park undisturbed in deference to its "natural ruggedness," as well as to the high cost of leveling it. Here along the rocky hills, the forest habitat is naturally drier, with oaks and black cherry trees growing in sparser stands—in some cases even taking root in cracks in the bedrock.

Ostrich fern

After passing a second waterfall, the path travels under **Huddlestone Arch** **5**, a stone bridge constructed from blocks of native schist that are dramatically flecked with mirrorlike grains of mica. From here, bear left around the Lasker Swimming Pool and Ice Skating Rink and you will encounter the **Harlem Meer** **6**, a delightful 13-acre reflective pond. Clogged and desolate before the renova-

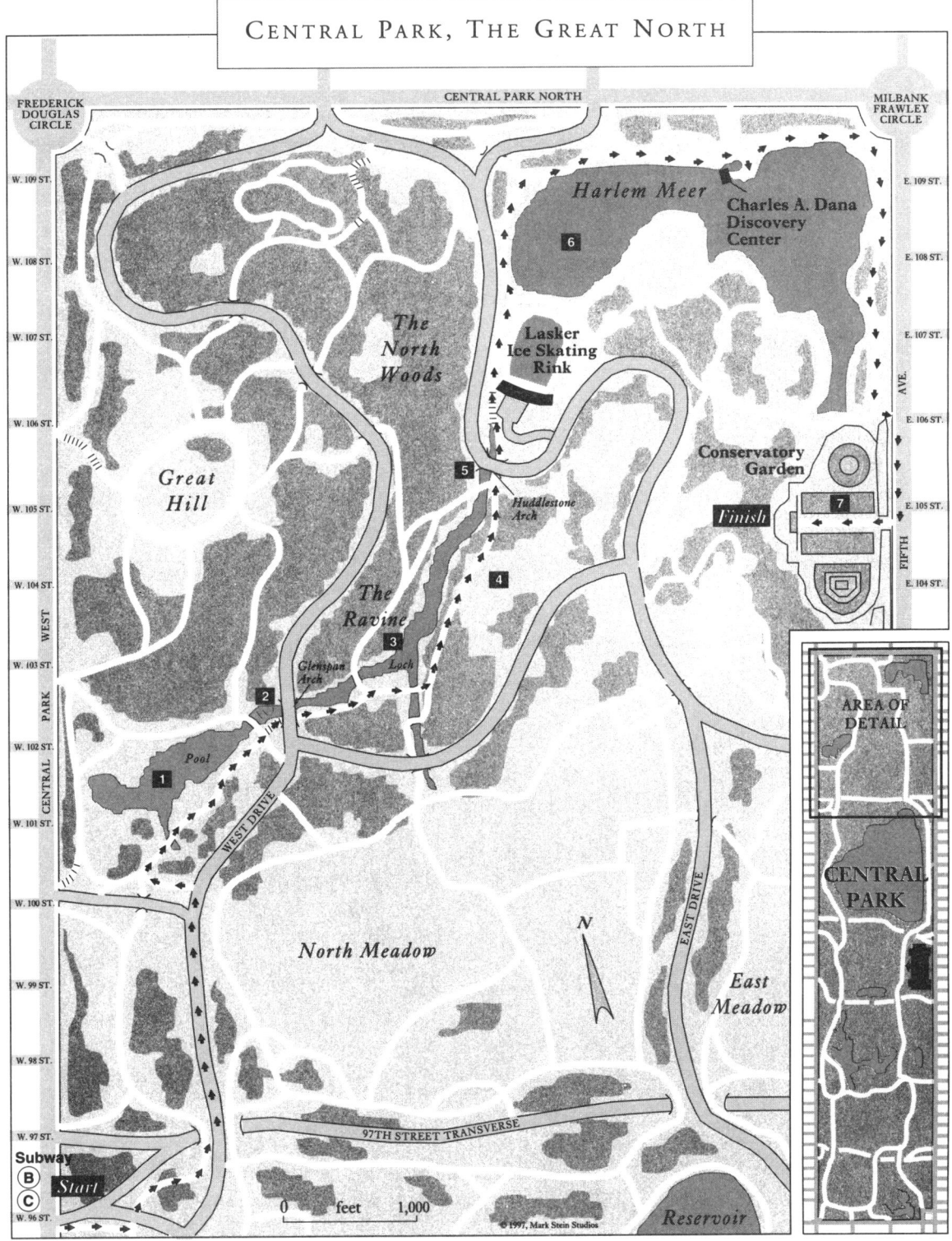

tion, the Meer has been beautifully revamped and replanted with wetland plants like cattails and rushes. Follow the path to the neo-Victorian Charles A. Dana Discovery Center, where from the outdoor terrace, you have the best view of the Meer. In spring, tree swallows flash their electric blue wings as they skim over the water, cormorants sun their wings on the roof of the center, and kids fish for sunfish and largemouth bass with bamboo poles on loan from the Parks Department.

Continue following the path around the Meer, and exit briefly onto Fifth Avenue. Reenter the park at 105th Street through the Vanderbilt Gate into the **Conservatory Garden** **7**, the Great North's grand finale. In addition to the formally arranged English-, French-, and Italian-style flower beds, the 6-acre Conservatory Garden is best known for its arcades of crabapples that bloom luxuriously with pink-and-white flowers each spring.

HOW TO GET THERE: *By mass transit: Take the B or C train to the 96th Street station at Central Park West. Or, take the 1, 2, 3, or 9 train to the 96th Street station, and walk east on 96th Street to reach the park's 96th Street entrance.*

INWOOD HILL PARK

At the borough's northern tip, Inwood Hill Park is the little-known home of Manhattan's last stand of native forest. Growing from the high bluffs overlooking the Hudson River down the slopes to the park's wetland, some of the trees here reach 100 feet high and have lived for more than 200 years. The park's most beautiful section is a wooded valley where, half a millennium ago, Native Americans had a village called Shorakopock, which (depending on whom you consult) meant either "a sheltered safe place" or "in between the hills." It was at the foot of this valley that the Dutch reputedly bought Manhattan Island from its original inhabitants for the equivalent of $24.

WILD WALK: INWOOD HILL PARK

From the park's entrance at 218th Street and Indian Road, follow the paved pathway (on the right) to the **Promenade on the Harlem River Ship Canal** **1**. To the right is the Columbia University boathouse, where the school's crew team launches early-morning practices. Across the channel is a huge white letter *C*—for "Columbia"—painted on a 200-foot-high outcrop of 1.1-billion-year-old gneissic rock. To the left, the Henry Hudson Bridge frames a view of the New Jersey Palisades in the steel arch of its span. Here at the northernmost tip of Manhattan Island, you can gaze across the ship canal to the Bronx—the very edge of the North American continent.

Continue along the path to the park's **Urban Ecology Center** 2, which houses exhibits on Inwood Hill's geology and natural history. From the center, take the pathway across the footbridge for a close-up view of **Manhattan's last salt marsh** 3. This 12-acre estuary is the only surviving example of the marshes that once ringed Manhattan Island all the way from Inwood Hill to Wall Street. At high tide the little bay is flooded with water, but at low tide the water is sucked from the marsh into the Hudson River, unveiling a moonscape of mud. At these times, ducks cruise through narrow rivulets of water, while herring gulls, hunting for insects, leave their footprints on the mudflats. Beyond the marsh, you can see the tall trees of the forest climbing the steep ridge of Inwood Hill. Follow the path around the marsh, and turn left at the hill's base.

As you head into the forest, you will come to **Shorakopock Rock** 4, a boulder that marks the site of the Big Apple's first and biggest real estate rip-off. According to legend, it was here that New York's original inhabitants in 1626 relinquished Manhattan to the Dutch Governor, Peter Minuit, for some beads and trinkets valued at a mere 60 guilders ($24). At that time the island was almost completely wooded, and a cement circle around the rock represents the 20-foot girth of a giant tulip tree that grew at the site of the deal and that, in 1933, finally died at the ripe old age of 280.

From Shorakopock Rock, follow the center trail into the forest. Immediately, towering above the path, you will see oak, beech, and tulip trees. This wooded section of Inwood has moist, limestone-rich soils and is considered one of the healthiest tracts of forest land in the city. Although saplings, ferns, and woodland flowers grow here, the forest is best known for its 100-foot-tall tulip trees. Named for their tulip-shaped, yellow-orange flowers, which bloom in late spring, tulip trees can also be recognized by their long, straight trunks—once hollowed out by the Native Americans to make canoes.

As you walk farther into the forest, you will find yourself delving deeper into New York City's past. Long before the Europeans arrived, Manhattan was

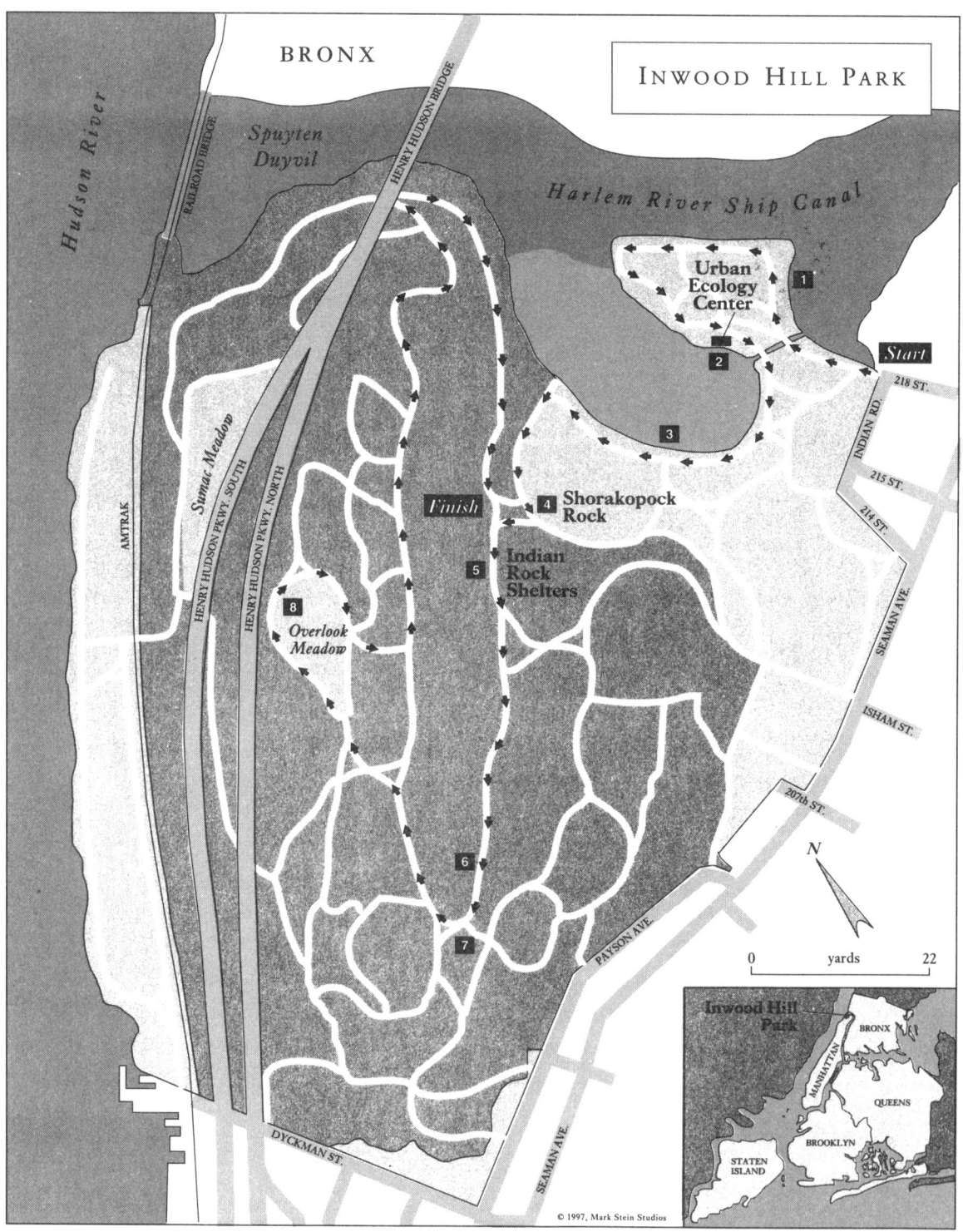

overrun by the Wisconsin Ice Sheet—the work of which can still be seen today. On the steep hillside to your right, look for the **Indian rock shelters** **5**, slabs of bedrock ripped up and piled atop each other by the grinding force of the glacier. In these cavelike crevices, Native Americans cooked clams and oysters, leaving behind artifacts like stone tools and pottery shards.

Bear right at the next intersection. As the path leads steeply up the hillside, you will see what looks like a giant's thumbprint in a rocky outcrop next to the trail. This is a **glacial pothole** **6**, drilled out by pebbles swirling in eddies of water beneath the glacier as it began to melt 20,000 years ago. At the top of the path, you will be greeted by further evidence of the glacier's passage: a smooth, rounded rock, a *roche moutonnée* **7**, that looks like the back of a whale breaking the surface of the water. This car-sized outcrop of Manhattan's bedrock was ground down and polished by huge boulders dragged southward by the traveling mountain of ice.

From here, turn right, climbing uphill through a less dense section of the woods. Follow the ridge until you reach a fork in the trail marked by a lamppost. There, take a left. Bear right at the next intersection, passing an enormous beech tree with initials carved in its trunk. Turn left again at the next opportunity and head for the **Overlook** **8**, where you have a sweeping view of the Hudson River 200 feet below and the steep, forested wall of the New Jersey Palisades beyond.

Continue on the path (heading straight through the first intersection) back to the trail along the ridge, and turn left. As you walk along the path, you can see into the tops of tall trees growing in the valley below. Soon, the wooded trail will start to slope downward, winding beneath the Henry Hudson Bridge and giving you a beautiful view of the waters below. Follow the trail back to Shorakopock Rock.

HOW TO GET THERE: *By car: Take the Henry Hudson Parkway to the Dyckman Street exit; then head east on Dyckman for 5 blocks to Broadway. Take Broadway north for 4 blocks to 207th Street and then go west for 2 blocks to Seaman Avenue. Look for parking here and then walk to Inwood's entrance at 218th Street. By mass transit: Take the 1 train to the 215th Street station. Walk up Broadway to 218th Street and take a left. Go up the hill, passing Columbia University's football field, to the park's entrance.*

> **Wild Fact**
>
> **CROSSING THE BORDER**
>
> Today, Inwood Hill Park defines the very northern tip of Manhattan, but the Manhattan of yesteryear was just a wee bit bigger. Once the northernmost section of Manhattan, Marble Hill was cut off from the rest of the island in 1895 by the construction of the Harlem River Ship Canal. The original path of the waterway (then called Spuyten Duyvil—"in spite of the devil"—Creek) meandered north of Marble Hill, but this natural curve was filled in following the digging of the ship canal. That's why even though Marble Hill is physically wedded to the Bronx and the continent beyond, the neighborhood is still legally part of Manhattan—and its denizens still vote in Manhattan's elections.

RIVERSIDE PARK

A 324-acre narrow ribbon of green that extends 4 miles, from 72nd Street to 153rd Street, along the Hudson River, Riverside Park is the emerald of the Upper West Side. Designed at the turn of the twentieth century by Frederick Law Olmsted (Central Park's cocreator), Riverside Park features the rustic feeling and clever layout that are Olmstedian hallmarks. Although the park abuts a busy Manhattan neighborhood, you would never know it. Tall trees and embankments block the sight and sound of the city. The only view is of the Hudson River and the New Jersey Palisades on the opposite shore.

Enter the park at West 72nd Street and Riverside Drive, and head down the path and through the pedestrian tunnel that leads to the park's riverfront promenade. This placid terrace offers an intimate view of the Hudson River's lapping waters and is lined with crabapple trees that bloom with frothy white blossoms each spring. The promenade also parallels the docks of one of the city's most unusual communities: the 79th Street Boat Basin. At this city-owned marina, dozens of houseboats are anchored, and residents have to walk across gangplanks to reach their front doors. Continue along the promenade, through a second pedestrian tunnel, and head up the stairs on the right to the foot of "Mount Tom," an enormous old outcrop of dark, mica-encrusted schist—the bedrock of Manhattan. According to local lore, Edgar Allan Poe lived nearby in 1844—when he was working on *The Raven*—and would sit atop Mount Tom gazing at the Hudson River for hours at a time.

From Mount Tom, you have several choices. You can stroll along the wide lower promenade or along winding Riverside Drive, with its limestone mansions, block-long apartment houses, and century-old American elm trees. As you walk north, the elevation begins to climb, and if you follow the park's shady paths up to Riverside Drive and West 120th Street, you will find Riverside

Church, a mountainous neo-Gothic structure perched atop a ridge overlooking the Hudson. For $1, you can take the elevator up to the observation deck in the church's 392-foot-high bell tower. Here, you'll be treated to a panoramic view of the city, the Hudson itself, and the New Jersey highlands beyond. Along with a 74-bell carillon, Riverside Church is host to a pair of the city's endangered peregrine falcons, which make their home in the church's tower.

HOW TO GET THERE: *By mass transit: Take the 2 or 3 train to the 72nd Street station. Walk west on 72nd Street for 2 blocks to the park's entrance at Riverside Drive.*

Hudson River Park and the Battery Park City Esplanade

Starting at the foot of Battery Park City's glass-and-granite towers, this liberating park and promenade on Manhattan's Lower West Side stretches for 1.2 miles along the Hudson River. Extending from First Place to Chambers Street (with a connecting 3-mile bike- and walkway that now runs all the way to 41st Street), the park puts you right on the Hudson—providing the perfect opportunity to watch the tides roll in, the freighters chug by, and the sun go down on the New Jersey shore across the water.

Along the esplanade are several open-air restaurants, the North Cove Yacht Harbor, and the dock for the trans-Hudson ferry, which makes the 2¼-mile trip across the water to Hoboken. There are also plenty of opportunities to contemplate the river's ecosystem. Leaning over the railing, you can see submerged eelgrasses swaying in the dark water below—a testament to the river's improving health. Sometimes you can find anglers reeling in striped bass, flounder, and even the occasional seahorse—much to the surprise of office workers who take their lunch breaks here.

If you walk along the bikeway to Pier 26 (6 blocks north of Chambers Street), you can view river life up close inside the Estuarium, a down-to-earth aquarium featuring American eels, blue crabs, and dozens of other specimens captured in tidal waters just off the pier. Run by The River Project (a nonprofit group devoted to the protection and restoration of the Hudson River's environment) and open on weekends during the summer, the Estuarium gives visitors a diver's-eye view of the creatures that inhabit the waterway and is further proof that the Hudson River is alive and kicking.

HOW TO GET THERE: ***By mass transit:*** *Take the 1 or 9 train to the Cortlandt Street station. Head upstairs into the World Trade Center plaza and walk across the North Bridge, a pedestrian tube that crosses over West Street and connects the World Trade Center plaza to the World Financial Center's Winter Garden. Head down the polished, pink granite stairs and through the front doors to reach the esplanade.*

FORT TRYON PARK

In 1917 John D. Rockefeller, Jr. purchased 67 wooded acres above the Hudson River in northern Manhattan. To safeguard the beautiful river vistas, his family also bought a slightly larger chunk of real estate across the Hudson—the cliff tops of the New Jersey Palisades. Today, from its promenades and terraces, Fort Tryon Park features the same scenery—the high walls of rock and slow-moving waters—that Rockefeller first admired more than a century ago.

Designed by Frederick Law Olmsted, Jr. (the son of Central Park's codesigner), Fort Tryon is filled with 8 miles of intricately winding paths. The most scenic of these is the promenade along the delicately terraced Heather Garden. Starting at the park's southern gateway, at Margaret Corbin Circle, this 600-foot-long overlook, bordered by a fieldstone wall and lined with flowers, is one of Manhattan's most peaceful spots for strolling.

Fort Tryon is also home to the Cloisters, the northernmost outpost of the Metropolitan Museum of Art. Built from bits and pieces of old European monasteries, the Cloisters displays the museum's prestigious collection of medieval art, including 500-year-old tapestries depicting unicorns—a wild creature otherwise not found in New York City.

HOW TO GET THERE: ***By car:*** *Take the Henry Hudson Parkway north to the Fort Tryon Park exit, which leads directly into the park. Parking is available next to the café (on the park's main drive) and at the Cloisters Museum.* ***By mass transit:*** *Take the A train to the 190th Street station. This subway stop is so far* underground (165 feet) that you have to take an elevator to the exit at Overlook Terrace and Margaret Corbin Circle. To reach the park's main promenade, head straight through the circle and into the park. To reach the Cloisters, follow the park's main drive.

JAMAICA BAY

Jamaica Bay, a pocket of the Atlantic Ocean between Brooklyn and Queens, is one of the most beautiful places in New York City. Home to an intricate network of islands, channels, and marshes, the calm waters of the bay and its shores are the harbor of choice for hundreds of species of waterbirds, huge schools of saltwater fish, and the occasional visiting dolphin.

Today, Jamaica Bay can be enjoyed from dozens of wild spots, but life on the bay hasn't always been so serene. As the city expanded in the early part of the twentieth century, Jamaica Bay's waters became contaminated with raw sewage and garbage. Its once-busy fishing industry was closed in 1921 because of pollution, and the joke was that if you fell into the water, you would dissolve before you drowned. Just when the bay was at its worst, however, environmentalists rallied to save it. Today, about half of the shoreline has been preserved as parkland—much of it part of the Gateway National Recreation Area, established in 1972 as the first urban national park in the nation. In the same year, the Clean Water Act made dumping in the bay illegal. Since then water quality in the bay has steadily improved, culminating in what has been dubbed the "miracle on the bay."

JAMAICA BAY WILDLIFE REFUGE

Part of the Gateway National Recreation Area, the Jamaica Bay Wildlife Refuge is better known as Birdland. On an island in the middle of the bay, the refuge was established in 1953 when about 60 types of birds were found here. Now, after 40 years of restoration of the native habitat, the refuge is visited or called home by more than 320 different bird species. Although the cast of characters changes depending on the season, some of the notables include beautiful white snow geese that fly in by the hundreds for the winter, flocks of fork-tailed tree swallows that ascend from the refuge like plumes of smoke during the fall migration, and summer shorebirds like the squat, red-billed American oyster catcher.

Year-round, even when freezing winds whip off the bay in January, the birds are here in force. Along with them, bundled-up bird-watchers can be spotted carrying high-powered binoculars and short-range telescopes along the refuge's scenic trails.

WILD WALK: JAMAICA BAY WILDLIFE REFUGE

Extremely well maintained by the National Parks Service, the flat, clearly marked trails of the Refuge lead to vista after vista overlooking the bay. To begin, exit through the back of the **Visitor Center** **1** and turn left onto the sunny trail loop to the West Pond. Growing alongside the trail are tough, seaside shrubs like bayberry and sumac; their natural oils protect them from the salty air and give the refuge a tangy smell. Because the soil here is extremely sandy, plants at the refuge must contend with desertlike conditions. Another common plant—one that New Yorkers are usually surprised to see growing along the trails here—is the prickly-pear cactus.

From the Visitor Center, the trail loop leads to the **South Marsh** **2**, an unbroken vista of tidal inlets, where you can spy wading birds such as great egrets—pure-white, long-legged birds that sometimes fly like graceful pterodactyls across the marsh.

A short distance farther along the trail is the 45-acre **West Pond** **3**, a mix of fresh and salt water where flocks of birds rest during their migrations, sometimes staying for the entire season. At times there are so many birds—representing so many different species—that the West Pond looks and sounds like a PBS nature documentary. Some of the more unusual birds that regularly visit here are black skimmers, red-legged seashore birds that fly close to the surface of the water—their beaks skimming the surface in search of fish. There are also semipalmated sandpipers, small stilt-legged birds that frequent the water's edge and probe the muddy shoreline for food with their long beaks.

If it's open, take a detour onto the sandy **Terrapin Trail** **4**, which is closed in June and July to protect the eggs laid on the beach by diamondback terrapin turtles. Although it's hard to see these shy turtles in the water, they are sometimes on display in aquariums at the Visitor Center. The Terrapin Trail skirts a low-growing meadow of beach grass, little bluestem, and salt-spray rosebushes and leads to a point overlooking the bay where salt-marsh grasses grow on island tussocks. From the Terrapin Trail, finish the main loop, walking along the edge of the West Pond and through the refuge's cooler zone, the **North and South gardens** 5, where evergreens and willows shade the path. The gardens' evergreens are occasionally visited by saw-whet owls, miniature owls that are known to stop by the city in winter.

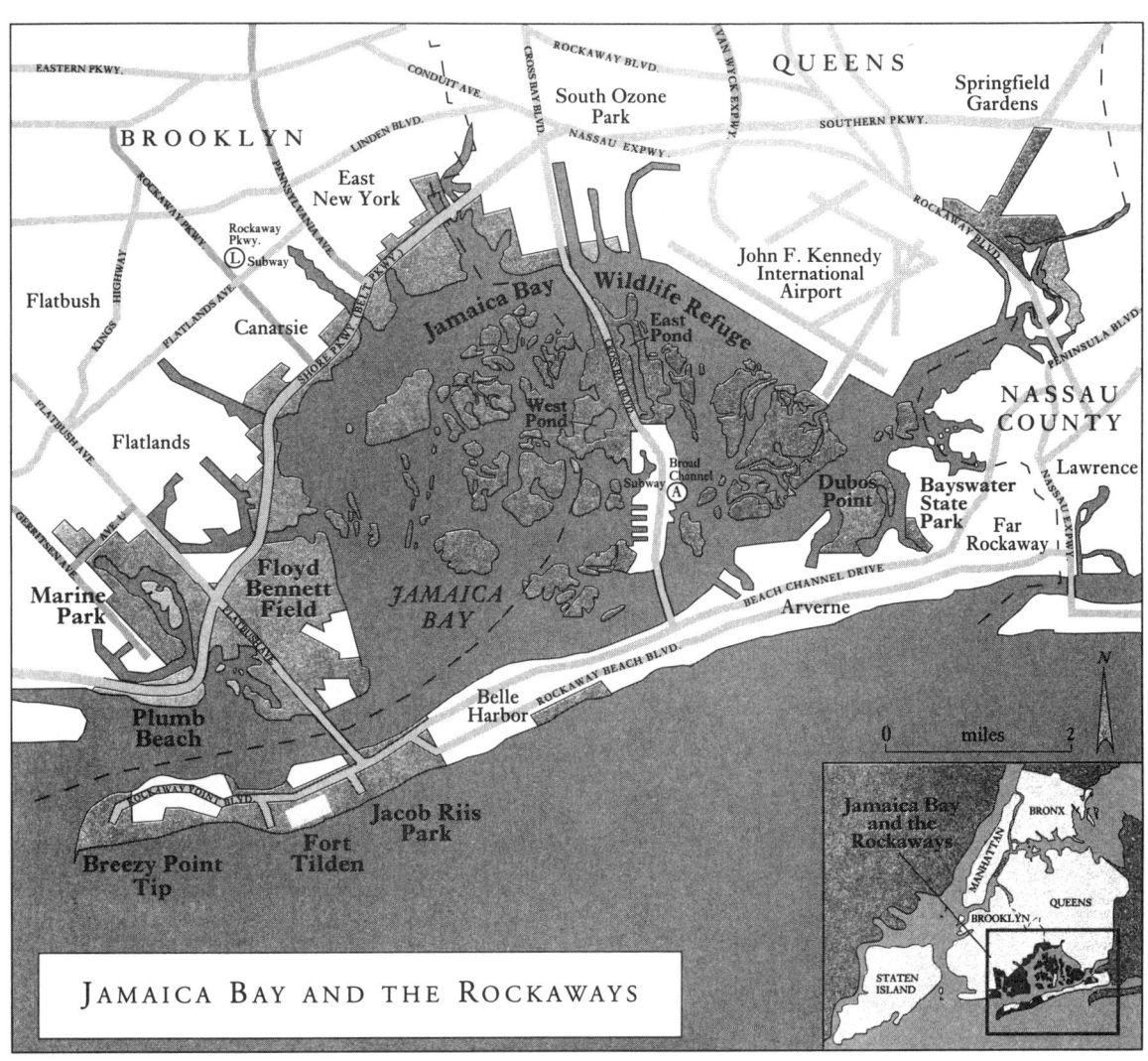

> ### Wild Fact
>
> #### MOSES PARTS THE WATERS
>
> The vast ponds at the Jamaica Bay Wildlife Refuge are not "natural," but were created as part of a political deal. When the Transit Authority (TA) wanted to dredge part of the bay in order to build an embankment for the subway system in the early 1950s, Parks Commissioner Robert Moses insisted that the TA dig the ponds in exchange for a dredging permit. The TA complied, and the ponds now attract 113 species of waterbirds, including snow geese, black ducks, and great blue herons. Now one of the most pleasant ways to get to the refuge, the A train glides across the bay for a full 3 miles, barely above the water, giving you a panoramic view and the feeling that you have left the city far behind.

After returning to the Visitor Center, begin the tour of the East Pond. The East Pond section is less traveled, giving one the feeling of being on a far-flung expedition. Start by entering at the **trailhead 6**, directly across the highway from the Visitor Center. Walk through a grove of black willows and turn right at the sign marked **East Pond Trail 7**. In this woodland of white European birch and willows, look for brief glimpses of great blue herons, gulls, and other birds as they fly over the treetops. As you continue, the terrain becomes more marshy and you soon encounter a boardwalk bordered by 12-foot-high, bushy-topped reeds.

From the boardwalk, follow the wood-chip trail until it reaches a wooden bench overlooking the 100-acre **East Pond 8**, a slightly salty freshwater lake that thousands of migrating birds use as a resting spot during late summer. Year-round, look for double-crested cormorants—dark seabirds that resemble vultures—perched, with wings spread, on top of pilings in the middle of the water. Also look for the silvery "A" train on the opposite shore, zooming behind the trees.

From this vista, double back, continuing straight on the trail. This path takes you to the boardwalk leading to **Big John's Pond 9**, a small freshwater pool named after the bulldozer operator who dug it out. At the end of the boardwalk, a wooden blind offers peephole views of the animals attracted to the pond, including turtles basking on logs and even muskrats swimming through the water. As part of a program to reintroduce New York City's native amphibians and reptiles, Big John's Pond is now home to thousands of tiny tree frogs called spring peepers. On spring nights, their shrill chorus—which sounds eerily like sleigh bells—can be heard ringing through the marsh.

To return to the Visitor Center, continue on the trail and take the first left back to the highway.

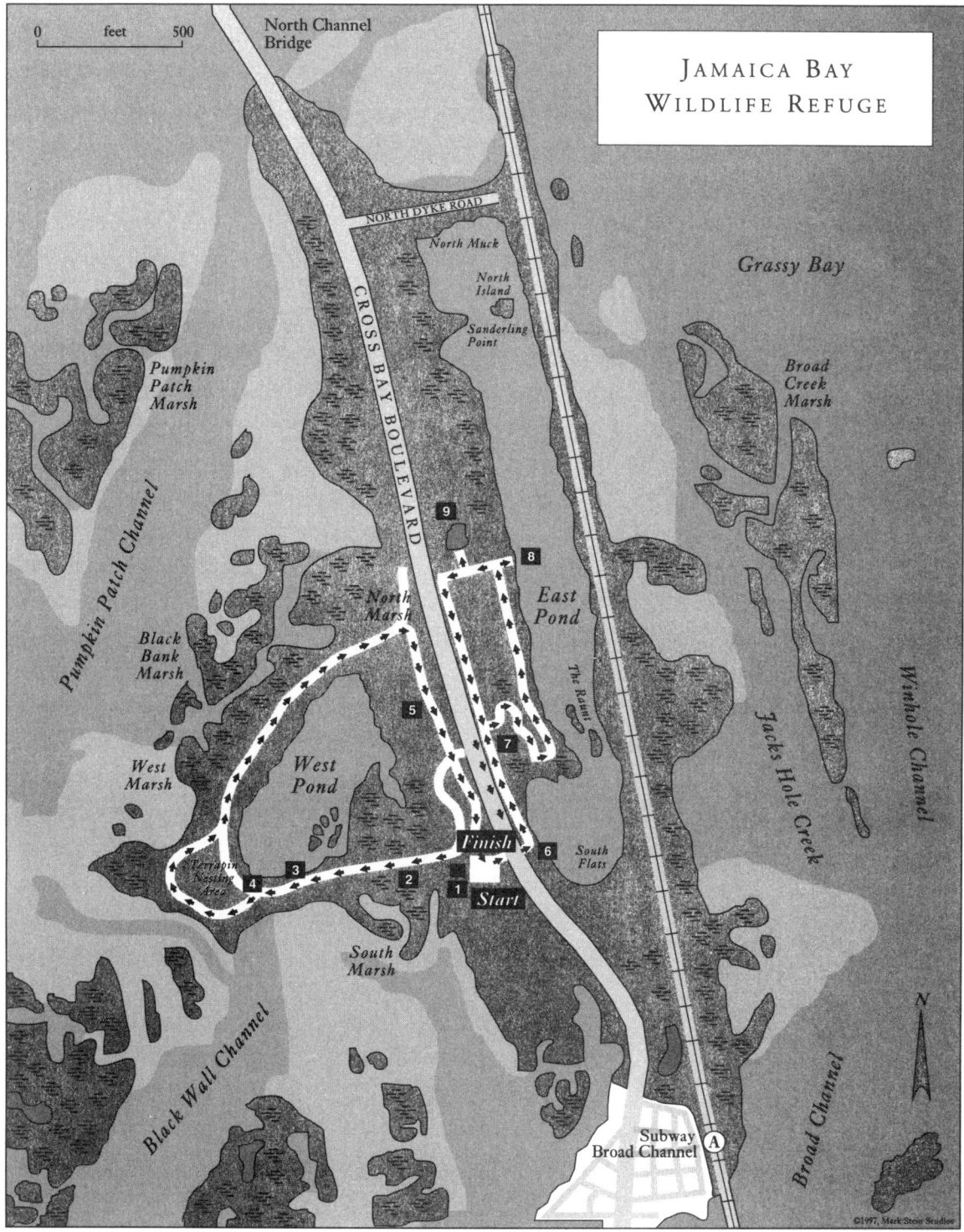

HOW TO GET THERE: ***By car:*** *Take the Belt Parkway to Exit 17 (Cross Bay Boulevard). Cross the North Channel Bridge and look for signs to the Wildlife Refuge on the right.* ***By mass transit:*** *Take the A train to the Rockaways and exit at the Broad Channel station. Head west on Noel Road for 1 block and turn right on Cross Bay Boulevard, walking three-quarters of a mile to the Visitor Center.*

FLOYD BENNETT FIELD

At the end of Brooklyn's Flatbush Avenue, Floyd Bennett Field is a truly odd spot. Built atop what used to be a group of islands at the edge of Jamaica Bay, Floyd Bennett Field was the city's first public airport. Celebrity aviators like Amelia Earhart and Howard Hughes flew in and out of this airport when commercial air travel was in its infancy. Today, runways still crisscross the airfield, which is now divided among a hodgepodge of activities: a U.S. Coast Guard station, an NYPD heliport where police pilots practice combat-style landings, and a flying field where model-plane aficionados pilot their "gas hawks" by remote control.

As for nature, there's plenty. Located on Jamaica Bay, Floyd Bennett Field is now part of the Gateway National Recreation Area. It has a nature trail on 40 acres of young forest, beautiful shoreline vistas, two public campgrounds, and even a grassland bioreserve. Be prepared, however. The distances separating the sites in this old airfield are great, so you really need a car, bike, or skates to get around.

WILD WALK: FLOYD BENNETT FIELD

Entering at the main gate on Flatbush Avenue, head one-half mile down **Floyd Bennett Drive** **1** and bear left, passing the U.S. Coast Guard station. Turn left again down one of the old runways, and you will find yourself in the 140-acre Brooklyn **Grassland** **2**. Botanically speaking, this is one of Brooklyn's richest natural areas. Dozens of wildflowers, such as toadflax and sheep sorrel, color the grasslands in blues, reds, whites, and yellows from spring to fall. Also growing here are more than a dozen unusual grasses with names like panic grass, little bluestem, purple love grass, and fall witchgrass. These grasses provide a haven for wildlife, particularly open-country birds that fly in from as far away as North Carolina, Florida, and the Gulf of Mexico. In spring you can see marsh hawks diving and barrel-rolling over the grasses and a pair of endangered peregrine falcons using the airport's abandoned control tower as a lookout. To keep the area from turning into a thicket, the grassland is mowed and occasionally burned as part of the New York City Audubon Society's ongoing Grassland Restoration and Management Project.

To continue, backtrack to the main road and head for **Raptor Point** 3, where you can park and walk down a ¼-mile length of sandy beach littered with white clam shells. Here, with a distant view of the Manhattan skyline, anglers cast into Jamaica Bay for winter flounder, an odd-looking flat fish with both eyes on the right side of its face. Farther up the beach, look in the tidal pools formed by depressions in the sand for brown-shelled marine snails, called mud dog whelks, and hermit crabs massing together to scavenge on discarded fish heads.

Continue down the main road, past the model-airplane field to the trailhead for the **North Forty Nature Trail** 4. This sandy trail winds through an emerging forest that is so dense with small shrubby trees, thorny berry bushes, and vines that you feel as if you are walking in an overgrown maze. Among these impenetrable thickets roams a population of transplanted eastern box turtles—imported in an attempt to reintroduce this "lost" reptile species to Brooklyn. So far, more than 300 of these miniature land turtles have been trucked in from Queens and Long Island, many of them wearing radio tracking devices so that biologists can keep tabs on them. Also on the North Forty Trail is a pond with a wooden blind for wildlife viewing. In warmer months, glossy ibises—wading birds with long curved bills and brilliant green wings—preen themselves in the pond's fresh waters.

Completing the loop on Floyd Bennett Drive, head past historic Hangar Row and park in the lot by the main entrance. Walk out the main gate and across Flatbush Avenue to the trails of **Dead Horse Bay** 5. Proceed through the corridor of giant reeds and take the first right, passing blackberry brambles and stands of spice-scented bayberry bushes, to the beach. Look for ribbed mussels fixed to holdfasts and bits of brilliant green sea lettuce—a favorite food of the huge flocks of Brant geese that winter on Jamaica Bay. As you walk you may find what look like soup bones in the sand. In fact, they are the bones of horses.

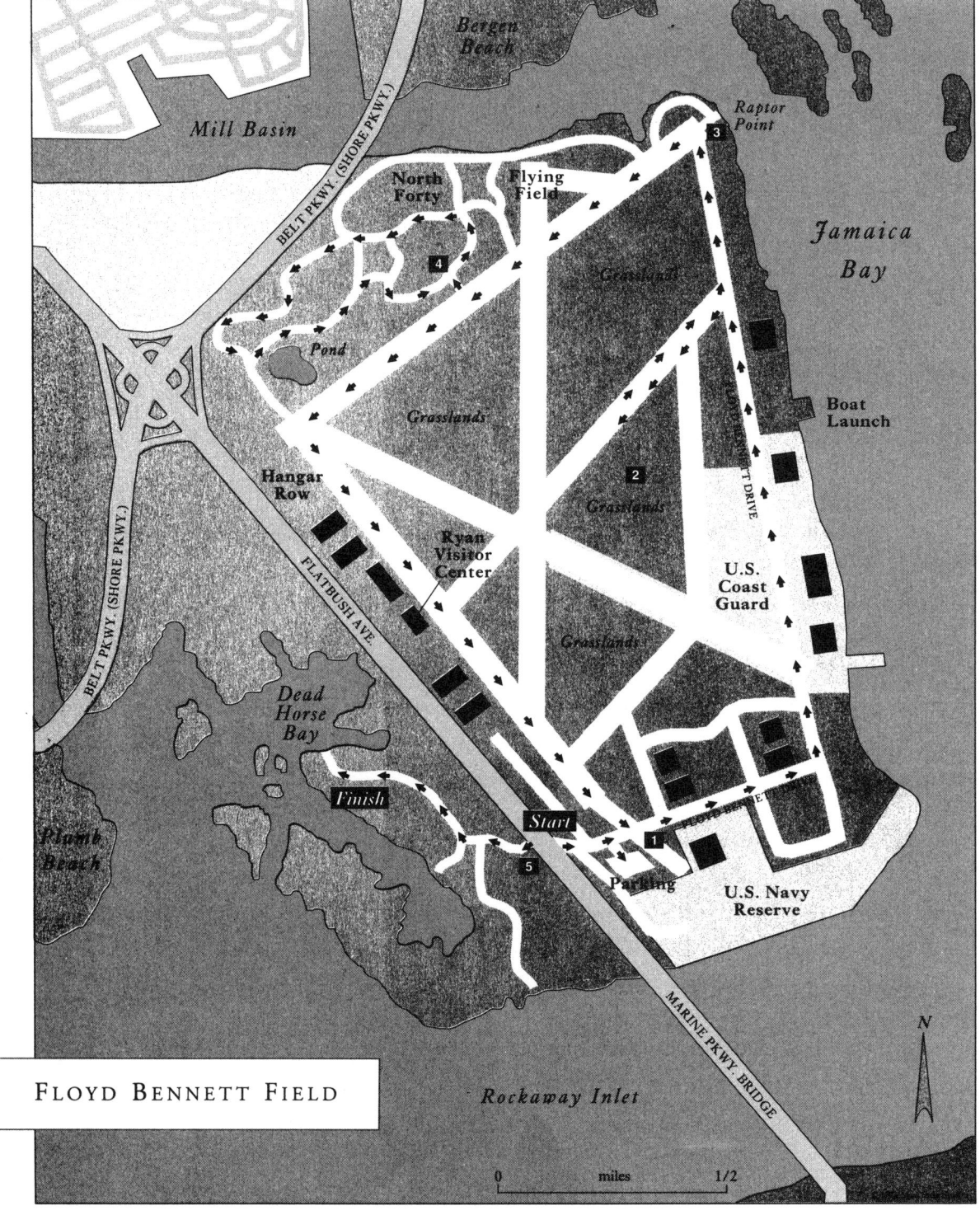

During the nineteenth century, whenever one of New York City's carriage horses died, it was sent down Flatbush Avenue to be "processed." Here, the horse's skin was tanned, its meat was turned into dog food, and its bones were tossed into the aptly named bay.

HOW TO GET THERE: *By car: Drive to the southern end of Flatbush Avenue and take the last left before the Marine Parkway Bridge. By mass transit: Take the 2 train to the Flatbush Avenue station. Then catch the Q35 bus to the last stop before the Marine Parkway Bridge. The field's entrance is just across Flatbush Avenue.*

THE BREEZY POINT TIP

To reach this wildlife refuge—on the very end of the Rockaway Peninsula—you have to drive through the Breezy Point Cooperative, a private community that bears more than a slight resemblance to a locked-down compound. Driving west on Rockaway Point Boulevard, you first pass the cooperative's guardhouse, and once you're "inside" all the side streets are gated; residents use card keys to enter. However, if you're going to the Breezy Point Tip, a division of the Gateway National Recreation Area, you won't need a pass to get through.

Just past the cooperative, the National Parks Service maintains one of the prettiest and most refreshing spots in New York City. A 2-mile-long, horseshoe-shaped beach curves from the peninsula's sheltered bay side all the way around to the Atlantic shore. Here, facing the incoming waves, sand dunes provide a haven for the city's most persistent endangered species: a tiny beach bird called the piping plover. Every spring more than a dozen pairs of plovers fly into Breezy Point to lay eggs on the edge of the dunes. Also nesting here are colonies of common terns and black skimmers—two distinctive-looking seabirds, both with webbed orange feet and long, reddish bills. During their spring courtship season, they can be seen performing mating rituals: feeding each other on the beach and chasing each other in zigzagging flights above the waves.

To explore the shore, head down the refuge's unpaved road, passing by the cabanas at the members-only Breezy Point Surf Club. At the end of the road, you will come face to face with the endless prospect of the Atlantic Ocean. Here, the narrow beach is pounded by the surf and speckled with unbroken

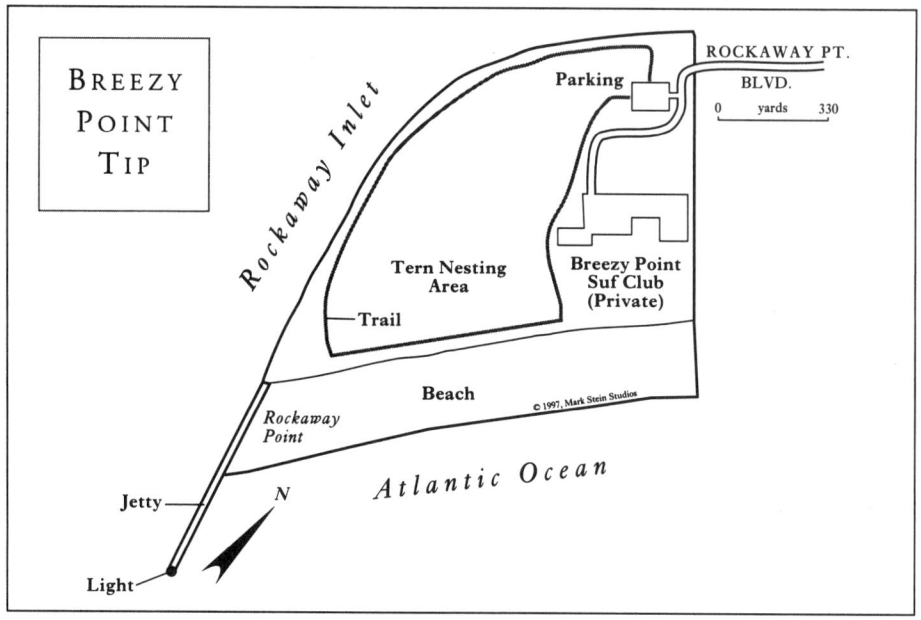

seashells—from purple-splotched quahogs to delicate bay scallops. Turning right, you can walk along the sand to the tip's bay side, where you'll be treated to an unexpected view of the Coney Island Parachute Jump and the Wonder Wheel across the water.

Although the dunes behind the beach are closed to visitors—both because they are a bird sanctuary and because they are extremely fragile—the sandy path back to the parking lot cuts through a small section and affords a glimpse of how beautiful the dunes really are. American beach grass, which anchors the dune ecosystem, is the dominant plant here, and it is complemented by bayberry bushes, seaside goldenrod, and wild sumac. Clear days in autumn—when these plants burst into sun-washed fall colors—are among the nicest times to visit. And if you come after September 15, you won't need to buy a permit to park in the lot.

HOW TO GET THERE: **By car:** *Take the Belt Parkway to Exit 11S. Head south on Flatbush Avenue to its terminus, over the Marine Parkway Bridge, and get off at the Breezy Point/Fort Tilden exit onto Rockaway Point Boulevard. Continue west on Rockaway Point Boulevard for about 3 miles to the very end, where there is a National Parks Service parking lot. A parking permit is required* *from May 15 to September 15 and can be obtained at the park's headquarters at Fort Tilden (see below for directions). The entrance to the trails is just to the left of the parking lot entrance.* **By mass transit:** *Take the* **A** *train to the Rockaway Park/Beach 116th Street station. Then catch the* **Q35** *bus to the park.*

FORT TILDEN

Built in the Rockaways to protect New York Harbor from enemies invading by sea during the War of 1812, Fort Tilden served as an active military base until 1974. Now part of the Gateway National Recreation Area, it is one of the city's most ecologically rich parks, featuring crashing surf and sand dunes amid decaying barracks and bunkers.

Whereas most New Yorkers experience the beach as a broad band of sand covered with umbrellas, sunbathers, and volleyball nets, Fort Tilden is more reminiscent of Cape Cod. It is the only park in New York City where you can see a naturally functioning beach ecosystem, complete with blue mussels and barnacles clinging to rock jetties, surf clams buried in the sand, 20-foot-high dunes covered with beach grass, and—behind the dunes—a sand- and salt-influenced forest of gnarled pines, holly bushes, cottonwoods, and quaking aspens.

Interspersed with the wild elements in this setting are remnants of the fort's military past. Most notably, two enormous concrete bunkers—overgrown with seaside vegetation—are still camouflaged in the dunes. During World War II, these bunkers, called Battery Harris East and Battery Harris West, housed 70-foot-long cannons capable of firing 1-ton shells 30 miles out into the ocean. Now that the fort has been decommissioned, the bunkers are used as platforms by bird-watchers, who station themselves here to observe the Northeast's annual hawk migration. Following the same route every autumn, thousands of hawks, falcons, and even bald eagles fly by this lookout, and during a single day, as many as 1,100 of these birds of prey have been seen winging their way along the coast.

Sprawling over 317 acres, Fort Tilden's diversions include a mile-long beach, a small pond, playing fields, old army barracks, makeshift bicycle paths, and nature trails. It takes a while to get the lay of the land, and when you first arrive, the park's natural charms are not immediately apparent. From the main parking lot you must cross the "Drill Grounds" to reach the beach. Or, if you

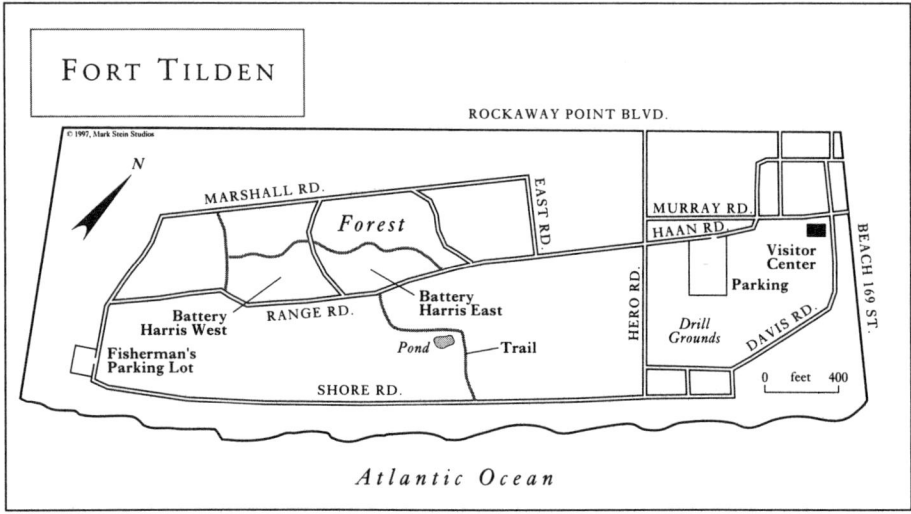

have a car or bicycle, head out to the far parking lot (called the Fisherman's Lot) and walk across the park's Shore Road to explore the surf. From the Fisherman's Lot you can also walk down the Range Road to reach the many intersecting trails through the forest and sand dunes. For more information, stop by the fort's Visitor Center.

HOW TO GET THERE: *By car: Take the Belt Parkway to Exit 11S. Head south on Flatbush Avenue, cross the Marine Parkway Bridge, and take the Breezy Point/Fort Tilden exit. At the first traffic light, turn left into Fort Tilden. Follow the signs to Fort Tilden's two parking areas. From May 15 to September 15, there is a $4 parking fee and a permit is required for the Fisherman's Parking Lot. By mass transit: Take the A train to the Rockaway Park/Beach 116th Street station. Then catch the Q22 bus, which stops in front of the park. Or, take the 2 train to the Flatbush Avenue station and catch the Q35 bus to the park.*

BAYSWATER STATE PARK

On the grounds of a former waterfront mansion in Far Rockaway, Bayswater State Park was once the home of A. M. Heinsheiner, a Wall Street magnate who commuted to Manhattan in his own private boat. Today, all that remains of his opulent house and garden, built in 1907, are a freestanding stone conservatory and an *allée* of turn-of-the-century pine trees. These ghostly remains stand on what is now a 12-acre wildlife preserve managed by the New York City Audubon Society.

When you first walk through Bayswater's main gate on Mott Avenue, the city suddenly seems vastly spacious. A wood-chip path meanders through a meadow of goldenrods and 4-foot-high yellow switchgrasses, leading to unobstructed views of Jamaica Bay and electric blue skies overhead. Surrounded by a lush green salt marsh and mudflats that are regularly flooded by the tides, this bayside area is particularly popular with anglers, who cast for bluefish from the park's crumbling seawall.

This strangely solitary and scenic spot became a state park in 1991, thanks to the efforts of Buffer the Bay, an environmental project cosponsored by the New York City Audubon Society and the Trust for Public Land. Buffer the Bay's goal is to conserve Jamaica Bay's overall ecosystem by advocating the preservation of bordering uplands. Bayswater is one of six Buffer the Bay hot spots to be turned into ecopreserves since the project began in 1987.

Though owned by the state, Bayswater is currently managed by the New York City Audubon Society. The park's Mott Avenue gate is unlocked each morning by a neighborhood couple, Mickey and Barbara Cohen, who act as Bayswater's stewards—monitoring the park's wildlife (which includes pheasants and muskrats), leading birding tours, and organizing shoreline cleanups.

HOW TO GET THERE: *By car: Take Flatbush Avenue south to its terminus at the Marine Parkway Bridge. Cross the bridge and turn left onto Beach Channel Drive (heading toward Far Rockaway). Follow Beach Channel Drive for 7 miles, and then turn left onto Mott Avenue. Follow Mott Avenue for 1 mile, until you reach the park's front gate. Parking is available on the street.* **By mass transit:** *Take the A train to the Far Rockaway/Mott Avenue station. Walk north on Mott Avenue for about 13 blocks to the very end, where the park's entrance is located.*

Dubos Point Preserve

Located in the Rockaways on a small peninsula jutting into Jamaica Bay, Dubos Point Preserve is a 26-acre natural oasis in an industrial neighborhood otherwise distinguished by trash-clogged vacant lots, junkyard dogs, abandoned cars, and an auto-wrecking yard.

One of six bayside parks created over the last decade to protect Jamaica Bay's waters and wetlands, Dubos Point is best known for its extensive flats of green salt-marsh grasses. Here the desolation doesn't seem to bother the wildlife. In the lush, low growth behind the preserve's sandy shoreline, wading birds—such as snowy egrets and yellow-crowned night-herons—can be seen stalking. Terrapin turtles lay their eggs on the beach. And a bird considered rather uncommon, the "salt marsh sharp-tailed sparrow," (it also has the longest name of any bird in North America) makes its nests in the grassy tussocks.

No marked trails have been laid out at Dubos Point, and there is no official entrance. In fact, visiting is advisable only for the hard-core urban explorer. To enter the park, you have to crawl through a hole in the fence on Decosta Avenue or climb over a guardrail constructed to prevent illegal car dumping. The best way to navigate the preserve is to walk along the shoreline. Avoid visiting the preserve in summer, because swarms of salt-marsh mosquitoes that emerge in July and August can make things very unpleasant.

HOW TO GET THERE: *By car: Take Flatbush Avenue south to its terminus at the Marine Parkway Bridge. Cross the bridge and turn left onto Beach Channel Drive (heading toward Far Rockaway). Follow Beach Channel Drive for about 4 miles, turning left on Beach 63rd Street. After 3 blocks, turn right on Decosta Avenue, which dead-ends at the park. By mass transit: Take the A train toward Far Rockaway and get off at the Beach 67th Street station. From the station, walk north on Beach 67th Street for 3 blocks (toward the bay) and turn right on Decosta Avenue. Follow Decosta for 4 blocks to the preserve.*

MARINE PARK

In Brooklyn's flatlands, Marine Park is best known for its softball diamonds, where teams representing local bars and businesses face off. However, just south of the playing fields, more than half of this 798-acre park is a wetland wildlife preserve. Here, a nature trail runs along Gerritsen Creek, one of several freshwater inlets that flow from Brooklyn and Queens into Jamaica Bay.

Along the water's edge, the ebb and flow of the tides into the creek create the ideal conditions for a salt marsh. In summer, red-winged blackbirds dart in and out of the giant reeds beside the inlet, and as it turns colder, small sea-going ducks, such as buffleheads, seek shelter in the creek's calm waters. However, Gerritsen Creek is far from pristine. Massive concrete pylons left over from an aborted 1960s town house project are the first things you'll see at the trailhead. In places, the trail itself is in disrepair—fire bugs periodically set ablaze the wooden boardwalks that span the trail's marshier spots. Despite the problems, residents of the Marine Park neighborhood swear by these wetlands, and they have organized a community watch, which keeps vandalism to a minimum.

The officially designated nature trail begins across the street from the main parking lot on Avenue U. A mile-long loop, it skirts the mudflats along the edge of the creek and then cuts through a field of giant reeds and seaside goldenrod. However, a second trail across the creek—starting at Avenue U and Burnett Street—offers an even better view of life on the marsh. On nice days and in the evenings, local parents come here with their kids to fish for winter flounder and snappers, observe the shifting tides, and look for estuary animals such as the horseshoe crabs that occasionally come to visit.

HOW TO GET THERE: *By car: Drive south on Flatbush Avenue and turn right on Avenue U. Continue ½ mile. Just past 33rd Street you can park near the playing fields and walk across the avenue to the trail. By mass transit: Take the D train to the Avenue U station, and catch the B3 bus to Burnett Street and Avenue U. Walk back on Avenue U to the parking lot and across the avenue to reach the trailhead.*

PLUMB BEACH

Named for the tart wild beach plums that ripen here in late September, Plumb Beach—along the Brooklyn shore of the Rockaway Inlet—is one of New York City's newest "natural" features. Five years ago, the shoreline here had become so eroded that Atlantic Ocean tides were literally lapping at the Belt Parkway. To prevent the road's inundation, millions of tons of sand were pumped in from Rockaway Channel, and a beach, complete with sand dunes, was created.

On hot summer days, the mile-long shoreline (part of the Gateway National Recreation Area) is packed with sunbathers, who often defy the park's no-swimming policy. However, the park also attracts nonhumans.

In spring, horseshoe crabs converge at the high-tide line to mate and lay eggs in the sand. In summer, flocks of sandpipers race along the shoreline, dodging the waves. In fall, raccoons hit the sand dunes to harvest the olive-sized beach plums. But you never really know who or what is going to turn up. Dead bodies have been discovered among the poison ivy plants, behind the dunes; and when a ship illegally carrying hundreds of refugees from China was scuttled off the Rockaways in 1992, an escapee, covered in ticks, was found hiding in the dunes by park police.

Usually, park visitors stick to the swath of beach just yards in front of the park's headquarters, which are housed in an old army bunker—shaped like a foreign legionnaire's cap. But serious nature lovers may want to head left into the dunes to explore the park's sand shrubland—and look for beach plums.

HOW TO GET THERE: *By car: Take the Belt Parkway east and just after the Knapp Street/Sheepshead Bay exit, turn into the Plumb Beach parking lot on the right, where you will find the park's headquarters. **By bicycle**: Beginning at Knapp Street in Sheepshead Bay, a bike path parallels the Belt Parkway. Ride east for 1½ miles to reach the Plumb Beach parking lot.*

BROOKLYN

Brooklyn's three major green spaces—a Victorian-era graveyard, an Olmstedian park, and a world-renowned garden—are all beautiful examples of landscape design. Dating from a bygone era sometimes loosely referred to as Old New York, they are strung together like green emeralds on a line of hills that were too steep to be farmed when there was agriculture in the borough and too far from the center of things to be already developed when New Yorkers claimed them as public spaces. Tamed to suit the aesthetic tastes of the times in which they were built, Greenwood Cemetery, Prospect Park, and the Brooklyn Botanic Garden each represent idealized concepts of nature and bear only a shadowy resemblance to Brooklyn's original, rough-hewn landscape.

Within all three, however, are hints of the truly wild. When you leave the lawns behind and walk into the woods in Prospect Park, you'll find chipmunks and downy woodpeckers living as if they were in a state forest instead of Brooklyn's most popular park. Cottontail rabbits peep out from beneath trimmed azalea bushes at the Brooklyn Botanic Garden. And at Greenwood Cemetery, bluebirds—New York's official state bird—sometimes can be seen singing from atop the headstones.

PROSPECT PARK

The leading park in Brooklyn, 526-acre Prospect Park is best known for family barbecues, bicycling, live music, and softball games. Despite these myriad activities, the park is never terribly crowded, and its meadows, lake, and rolling terrain exude a serenity that is hard to come by elsewhere in New York City.

Designed by Frederick Law Olmsted and Calvert Vaux, the creators of Central Park, Prospect Park fulfilled their dream of a park that, though smack in the middle of the city, would appear rural to those inside it. In that spirit, when the park first opened in 1867, its woodlands housed a dairy to which parkgoers could hike and drink milk—fresh from the cow. Although the dairy was torn down in the 1930s and the cows are now part of history, Prospect Park remains distinctively rustic to this day.

WILD WALK: PROSPECT PARK

The gateway to Prospect Park at **Grand Army Plaza** [1] is a busy traffic circle and one of the most architecturally imposing sights in New York City. The plaza's central feature is the 80-foot-high, 80-foot-wide Soldiers' and Sailors' Memorial Arch—a granite behemoth modeled after the Arc de Triomphe on Paris's Champs-Élysées. Built in 1892 and adorned with lofty bronze sculptures, the arch commemorates the Civil War's dead and the Union's victory. On weekends when the Urban Park Rangers give tours, visitors can ascend the stairs to the top of the arch for a glorious view of the park and the brownstone-studded streets of neighboring Park Slope and Prospect Heights.

Across the street from the arch is Prospect Park's main entrance, flanked by four 50-foot-high Doric columns and 16 snake-handled bronze urns. On Saturdays, there is a farmer's market here, where New York State apples, goat cheese, and fresh milk are sold. To enter the park, follow the paved path closest to Prospect Park West and pass through the wooden tube of Prospect Park's 129-year-old Meadowport Arch.

Emerging from the arch, you'll see the longest, uninterrupted vista of parkland in the five boroughs, the three-quarter-mile-long **Long Meadow** 2. One of the few places in the heart of the city with a view of wide-open sky, this grassy expanse is shared by kite flyers, frisbee tossers, soccer players, and dog walkers. Surrounded by tall trees, the grounds of the Long Meadow have been designed as a rolling, undulating expanse of green. Here you can stroll across the turf and experience what the park's designers, Olmsted and Vaux, called "a sense of enlarged freedom."

About half a mile across the Long Meadow are **The Pools** 3, two freshwater ponds fed by a small, artificial waterfall. Overgrown with reeds and cattails in the summer, the ponds attract red-winged blackbirds, ducks, and all kinds of frogs. In fact, if you walk around the pond's edges, particularly in reed-choked spots, multiple splashes may precede your footsteps, as the frogs—sensing an intruder—leap into deeper water. (Note: The Prospect Park Alliance, a nonprofit group devoted to improving the park, has slated The Pools for a facelift, so they may be temporarily fenced off.)

Camperdown Elm, Prospect Park

Circling behind The Pools, a flagstone path leads through **The Ravine** 4, a stream-cut woodland modeled after the scenery of the Adirondack Mountains. Here, among the century-old oaks and evergreens, you can spot a surprising number of animals, including cottontail rabbits, squirrels, chipmunks, hawks, and woodpeckers. Part of a continuous 250-acre woodland that runs through the hilly center of the park, the Ravine—

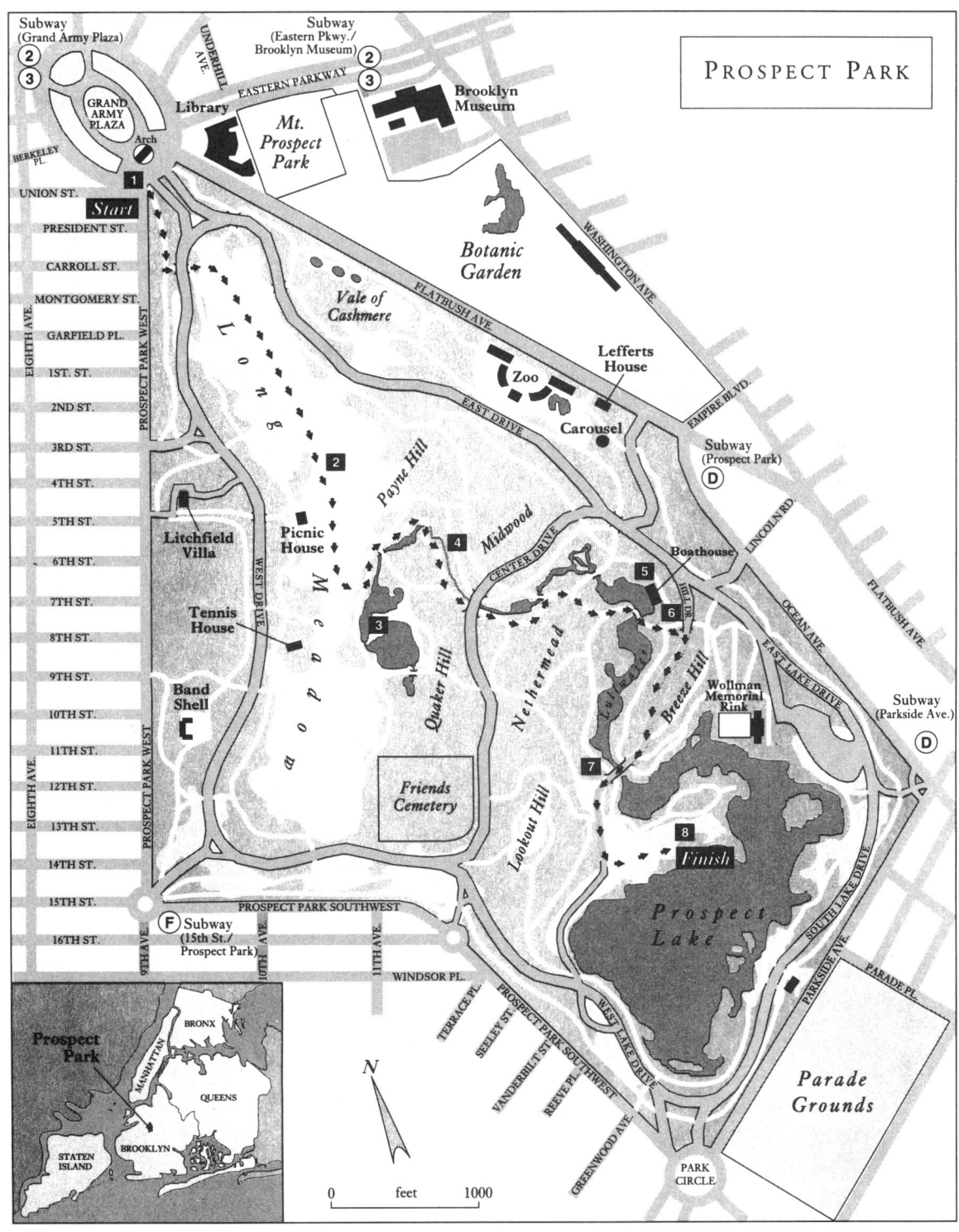

> ### Wild Fact
> #### END OF THE LINE
> During the last great Ice Age, the Wisconsin Ice Sheet crept southward from Canada, grinding down hills, slicing through river valleys, and finally coming to a halt right in the middle of Brooklyn and Queens. Here, the ice sheet deposited a vast load of rock and silt, creating a long hill known to geologists as the terminal moraine. Formed about 20,000 years ago, this mini–mountain range now runs straight through Prospect Park from the Midwood to Lookout Hill.
>
> When the park was designed in 1866, every footpath and carriageway culminated at Lookout Hill's 185-foot-high pinnacle. Today, the stairways leading up from the shore of Prospect Lake are ramshackle and overgrown; nonetheless, if you're bold enough to climb to the top, the view remains. Look north toward Manhattan and you can imagine a landscape buried under a mountain of ice. Look south and you can see what the meltwaters of the retreating glacier left behind: a vast, flattened landscape stretching 5 miles from Flatbush to Coney Island.

despite its forestlike appearance—is an ailing ecosystem. Decades of soil erosion and compaction prevent its venerable trees from reseeding and starting new saplings. To save what is referred to as Brooklyn's last forest, horticulturists from the Prospect Park Alliance have collected hundreds of thousands of seeds from the park's trees and shrubs. Work crews are rebuilding the Ravine's eroded hillsides and hand-planting seedlings propagated in the park's greenhouse. Most notable among the plantings are native trees, including sweet gum, tulip, white ash, hickory, and white, red, and black oaks.

Following the Ravine's tree-lined brook, the flagstone path leads under the Nethermead Arches and past the old Music Grove to the park's **Boathouse** 5. A landmark Venetian-style building, the Boathouse overlooks the Lullwater, a meandering watercourse choked with mats of white water lilies and other aquatic plants. In summer, dozens of large iridescent dragonflies buzz over the surface, while schools of bass and minnows cruise below. On hot, sunny days, the view from the Boathouse is sleepy and serene, and it's a great place to have a quiet picnic.

Behind the Boathouse, you can visit the fenced-in **Camperdown Elm** 6, the park's botanical mascot. Probably the most "unnatural" natural attraction in the park, this 120-year-old tree is a rare variety of weeping elm grafted onto a Scotch elm. To the left of the Camperdown Elm, a steep dirt path leads up to Hill Drive. Turn right on the drive and make your way toward **Terrace Bridge** 7, where you can look down on the Lullwater and see mute swans paddling below.

Continue on Hill Drive another ¼ mile and then walk down the hill to the **Peninsula** 8 for a view of 50-acre Prospect Lake. Look for small gray ducks called coots diving to the bottom in search of aquatic plants, as well as for swans, mallards, and the ever-present flocks of herring gulls circling above. During coastal storms, all manner of odd waterfowl show up on Prospect Lake. Even the occasional loon can be seen resting here on the way back to isolated lakes in Maine or Vermont.

From here, retrace your steps to Grand Army Plaza or, if you want to take a different route, follow the path around the lake and walk back to Grand Army Plaza on the park's East Drive.

HOW TO GET THERE: *By car: Take Flatbush Avenue south to Grand Army Plaza. Turn right on Prospect Park West, where street parking is available. By mass transit: Take the 2 or 3 train to the Grand Army Plaza station and exit on the south side of Flatbush Avenue. Walk 3 blocks up Plaza Street West to the park's entrance at Grand Army Plaza.*

Greenwood Cemetery

This Victorian-era necropolis once doubled as New York City's first large-scale public park. Opened in 1840—33 years before the completion of Central Park—Greenwood's grounds were quickly thronged with people, who came in horsedrawn carriages to escape the smoke and congestion of Manhattan. While famous New Yorkers such as Samuel F. B. Morse, the inventor of Morse code, and Boss Tweed, the inventor of machine politics, were being buried here, still-breathing residents were clamoring over the wooded paths in search of recreation. Today, Greenwood is still open for business, but living visitors are much scarcer than they once were, so raccoons, bats, crows, pheasants, and other beasts now have the run of this 478-acre graveyard.

Though Greenwood is privately owned, amateur naturalists are welcome, as long as they check in at the main

---

Wild Fact

STRANGE VISITATIONS

Along with the inherent spookiness of its stone crypts, Greenwood Cemetery is home to some strange goings-on. At the entrance at 25th Street and 5th Avenue, a flock of exotic green parrots known as monk parakeets *(Myiopsitta monachus)* has built a giant nest out of sticks and mud in the spire of the cemetery's Gothic-revival tower. No one knows how these raucous, 12-inch-tall birds arrived in New York City—they may originally have been pets or escapees from a shipment at John F. Kennedy Airport. But the only way these natives of Argentina have managed to survive the city's cold winters is by huddling together in their oversized communal nest.

> ### *Wild Fact*
> ### STRANGE VISITATIONS II
>
> In 1853, a group of misguided bird lovers from the Brooklyn Institute (the future founders of the Brooklyn Botanic Garden) set free several pairs of European house sparrows *(Passer domesticus)* inside Greenwood Cemetery. The bird lovers longed for the sound of the sparrows' cheery song in springtime, and they hoped that the birds would thrive in their new land. Then completely unknown to the American landscape, the sparrows did indeed thrive (they grew fat and prosperous by picking the hay seeds out of horse droppings), and they became one of New York City's—and the entire nation's—most ubiquitous creatures. Today, these chirping sparrows can be seen on almost every street in New York City, building their nests under air conditioners, in air vents, and in the eaves of City Hall from twigs, coffee stirrers, and cellophane.

gate. From there, turn right on the entry road to reach Valley Water—a pretty pond with white lily pads—and follow Valley Avenue to the Sunset Path, which leads over Sunset Hill to the Sylvan Water. Home to mallard ducks and the type of geese that give us French pâté, the Sylvan Water faces the cemetery's rolling hillsides, which—reflecting the Victorian love of the exotic—are planted with hundreds of different specimen trees from Japanese maples to Siberian firs. In fall, many of these century-old trees turn vivid colors, and the sight of their brightly festooned branches drooping over the crypts is strangely affecting.

HOW TO GET THERE: *By car: From the Manhattan Bridge, head south on Flatbush Avenue for about 2 miles, and turn right on 5th Avenue. Continue on 5th Avenue for 2 miles until you reach the main gate of the cemetery at 25th Street. Turn left. Parking is available on the road in front of the cemetery office.* **By mass transit:** *Take the Brooklyn-bound R train to the 25th Street station (at 4th Avenue). Walk 1 block east on 25th Street to the cemetery's main gate at 5th Avenue.*

Brooklyn Botanic Garden

The Brooklyn Botanic Garden (BBG) often catches first-time visitors by surprise. Here, in the same borough where "flowers" and "birds" are pronounced "flowuhs" and "boids," you'll find French and Italian gardens, prim hedgerows, and arbors dripping with purple wisteria.

Not content simply with offering stunning vistas and an explosion of seasonal flowers, the BBG boasts 17 theme gardens. These include a medieval herb garden, water lily pools, a native-plant garden, and an indoor rain forest—all elegantly crammed into 52 exquisitely landscaped acres. Although it would take an entire day—or multiple visits—to explore everything, first-timers can easily tour the garden's highlights in a couple hours.

From the entrance on Eastern Parkway, head through the Azalea Walk (also known as the Osborne Section) and down the steps at the walk's end. On your left, an arbor path leads to the Cranford Rose Garden (home to a hybrid tea rose named after Elizabeth Taylor), past the Cherry Esplanade (featuring 30 species of cherry trees), and to the formal Japanese Hill-and-Pond Garden.

Although the Japanese garden is intended as a haven for human contemplation, wild animals have discovered it as well. Here, wading birds are notorious for poaching fat orange carp from the pond, mallard ducks waddle across the pedestrian paths, and an army of dark green turtles sun themselves on the pond's decorative stepping stones.

The BBG is the best place in New York City to stay in tune with the cycle of the seasons. From the first hint of spring through summer's last gasp, there is a nonstop sequence of blossomings. It starts with well-ordered beds of brightly colored tulips in March and ends with showy, late-blooming roses in October. The most celebrated seasonal event, however, is the garden's Cherry Blossom Festival. When the Cherry Esplanade is in full bloom in late April, soft winds toss puffy, pink cherry blossoms

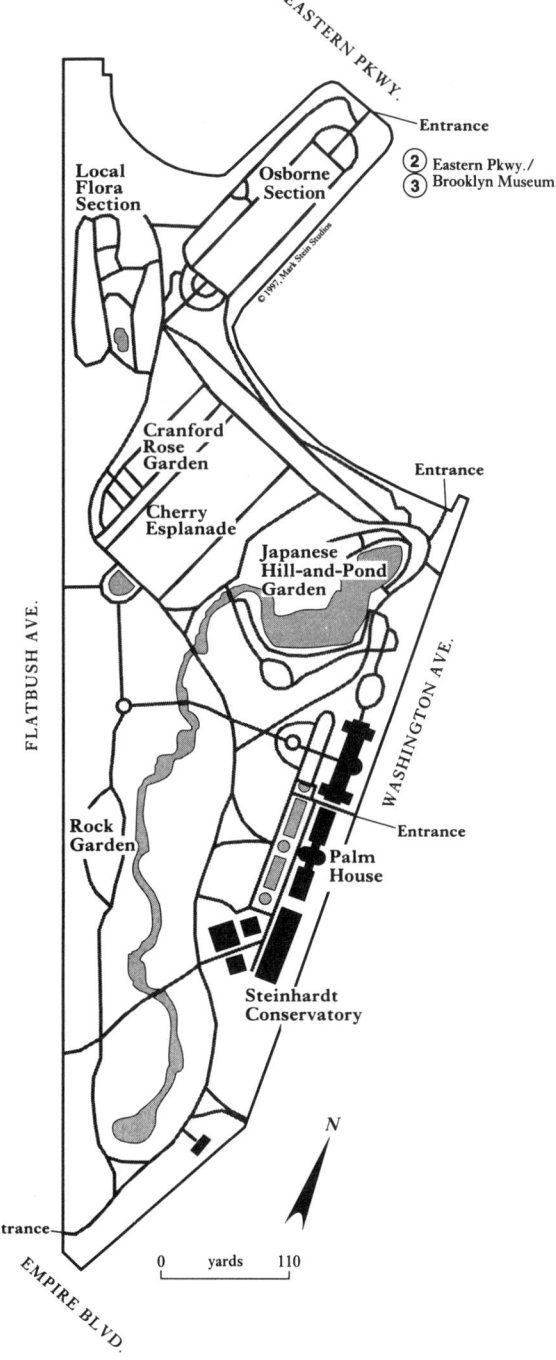

BROOKLYN BOTANIC GARDEN

> ### *Wild Fact*
>
> ### ROCKY ROOTS
>
> Originally, the land on which the Brooklyn Botanic Garden stands was a gardener's nightmare—hilly and chock-full of hoe-busting boulders. Before even the first seed was planted in 1910, 8,000 rocks—from 50-pound stones to 12-ton boulders—had to be extracted from the soil. This giant effort is now immortalized in the BBG's Rock Garden, where visitors can examine hunks of schist from Manhattan, white marble from Spuyten Duyvil, and hard plutonic diabase from the New Jersey Palisades.
>
> How did all these non-Brooklyn rocks end up here? According to geologists, they were passengers on the Wisconsin Ice Sheet. Ripped from bedrock farther north during the last Ice Age, they were slowly dragged along and finally dumped at the ice sheet's southernmost limit—right in the middle of Brooklyn.
>
> Although most of the stones in the Rock Garden came from nearby, some originated farther afield. The long-distance champion is "Rock #23," a hunk of granite from the southeastern Adirondacks that, embedded in the glacier, traveled 250 miles before being dropped off here about 20,000 years ago.

down on the heads of visitors—many of whom come from as far away as Japan to celebrate spring in Brooklyn.

HOW TO GET THERE: *By car: Take Flatbush Avenue south to the Grand Army Plaza traffic circle. Follow the circle halfway around and exit onto Eastern Parkway. Take the parkway for one-quarter mile to Washington Avenue, turn right, and look for the garden's parking lot on the right. By mass transit: Take the 2 or 3 train to the Eastern Parkway/Brooklyn Museum station, which is right in front of the garden's entrance.*

THE BRONX

Often portrayed as the embodiment of urban decay on the nightly news, the Bronx is New York City's most maligned borough. However, when it comes to green space, the Bronx deserves a cheer—it boasts the highest concentration of parks anywhere in the city. In fact, the Bronx's two mega-parks—Pelham Bay (2,764 acres) and Van Cortlandt (1,146 acres)—rank as the city's first and third largest, both dwarfing their Manhattan cousin, 843-acre Central Park. With so much open space, the Bronx also attracts lots of wildlife. Although no one believes it until they see it, great horned owls nest in the woods in Pelham Bay Park, painted turtles live in the Bronx River, and even the American bald eagle has been spotted in the wilds of this underrated borough.

Pelham Bay Park

Named for the now nonexistent Pelham Bay, this park is home to Orchard Beach, one of the most heavily used strips of sand in the city. To build the beach and a parking lot of almost equal size, Parks Commissioner Robert Moses had Pelham Bay filled in in 1936, connecting three offshore islands to the mainland in the process. Despite Moses' reconfiguration of the natural landscape, Pelham Bay Park sustains several viable ecosystems, and the park's Hunter "Island" is one of the most stunning natural areas in the city. Its green salt marshes are visited by thousands of wading birds, and its rocky New England–style coastline presents a picture-perfect scene complete with sailboats and fishermen.

WILD WALK: PELHAM BAY PARK

Constructed with sand brought in by barge from Sandy Hook in New Jersey and the Rockaways, **Orchard Beach** [1] was billed as the "Riviera of New York" when it opened on July 25, 1936. Today, its white sand and gently lapping surf still attract as many as 30,000 sunbathers on hot summer days. If you walk down to the end of the beach's mile-long **Promenade** [2], you can see sailboats docked at neighboring City Island—a maritime village within New York City—and from the woods beyond (in stark contrast to the otherwise bucolic scene) you can hear the sound of pistol fire from the police academy firing range on Rodman's Neck.

Head up the beach to see the vast, protected waters of Long Island Sound and its many rocky islands with names like Hog, Rat, and Chimney Sweep. Despite their barren aspect—or perhaps because of it—these windswept islands have had many uses over the years. In the 1800s, tiny Rat Island was employed at one time as an artists' colony and at another as a "pest house" where victims of yellow fever were sent to die. Hart Island has served as the city's potter's field since 1869 and is now the final resting place for more than a million of the city's unidentified and unclaimed dead. Nearby Huckleberry Island, owned by the New York City Athletic Club, is a sanctuary for marine birds.

Back on the Promenade, a sign indicates the start of the **Kazimiroff Nature Trail** [3]. Follow the trail and walk out onto the **rocky bridge** [4] span-

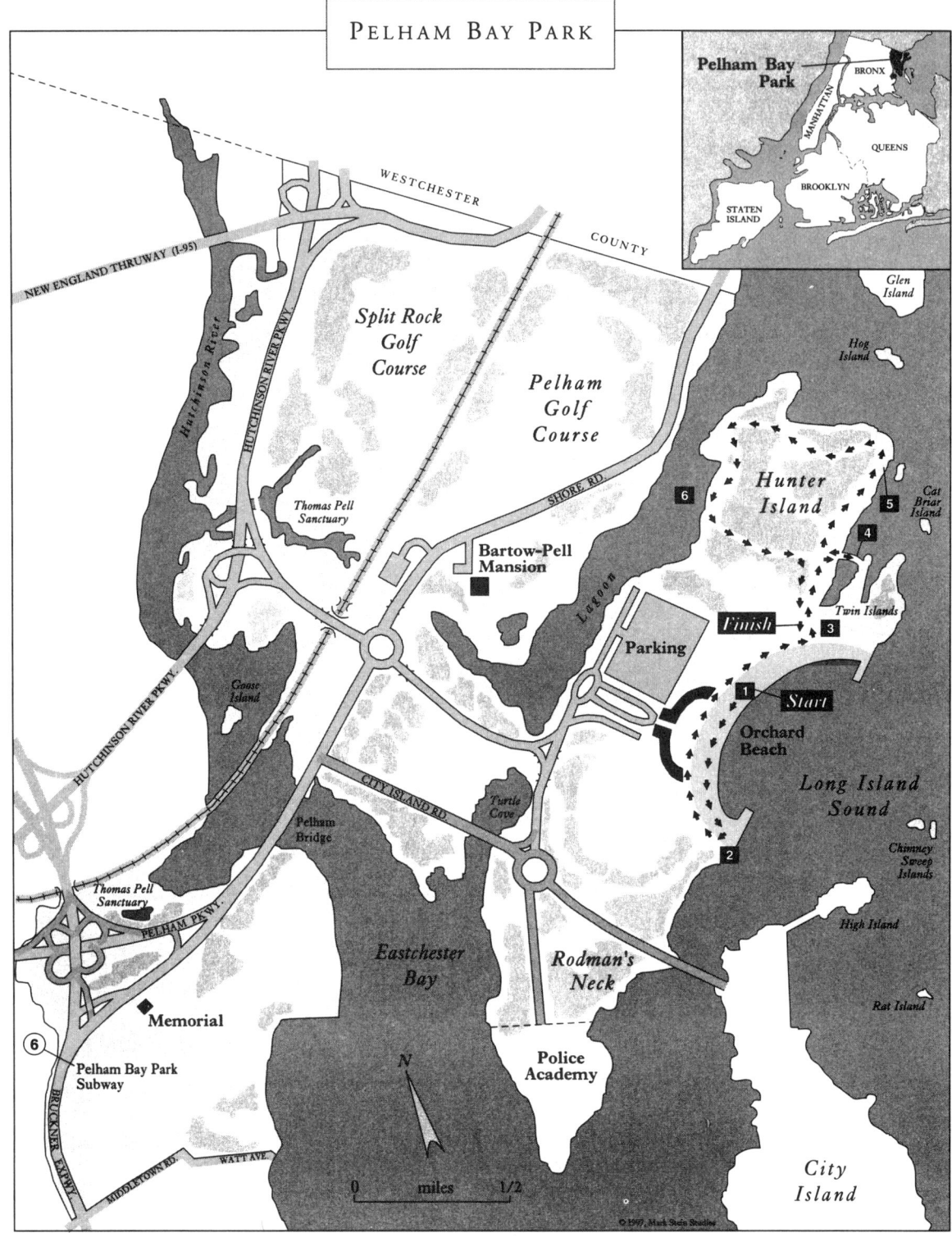

ning the inlet that separates Hunter Island from the Twin Islands. From here you can see the hip-high green grasses of the salt marsh ringing the islands' shoreline and the tall oak trees of their inland woods. Continue along the wooded shore, where in late summer you'll see flowers called white wood asters along with yellow droops of seaside goldenrod.

At the island's northeast corner, turn right and continue down the path to the rocky ledge of the **Hunter Island Marine Zoology and Geology Sanctuary** 5. Here you'll find one of the most surprising sights in the city: Beautiful, dark, sculptured rocks offset the blue waters of the sound, suggesting that you are on the rocky shoreline of Maine rather than in the Bronx. This ledge of bare rock was formed 400 million years ago and is made of gneiss. Melted, cooled, and remelted many times, the gneiss shows bands of white, gray, and black minerals swirled into psychedelic designs. Down at the water's edge, the rock is covered with brown rockweed and barnacles, and if you're here at low tide, you may also see tidal pools in the ledge with little minnows swimming in them, as well as clams and oysters clinging to the rocks.

Back on the trail, continue along the island's wooded shoreline all the way to the **Lagoon** 6, a swath of green salt marsh and mudflats where you can see wading birds fishing on stiltlike legs. In early autumn, the Lagoon is a favorite spot for migrating ospreys, a once-endangered species of hawk. These white birds hover 40 feet above the Lagoon and plummet like bombs into the water as they dive for fish. The trail alongside the Lagoon leads back to the walk's starting point.

HOW TO GET THERE: *By car: Take the Hutchinson River Parkway to the City Island/Orchard Beach exit. Follow the signs to the Orchard Beach parking lot. By mass transit: Take the 6 train to the Pelham Bay Park station and—during the summer—catch the special BX12 bus to Orchard Beach; during the rest of the year, take the BX29 bus to the City Island Road stop (at the traffic circle), and from there, walk north on the park road for about a mile to reach the Orchard Beach parking lot.*

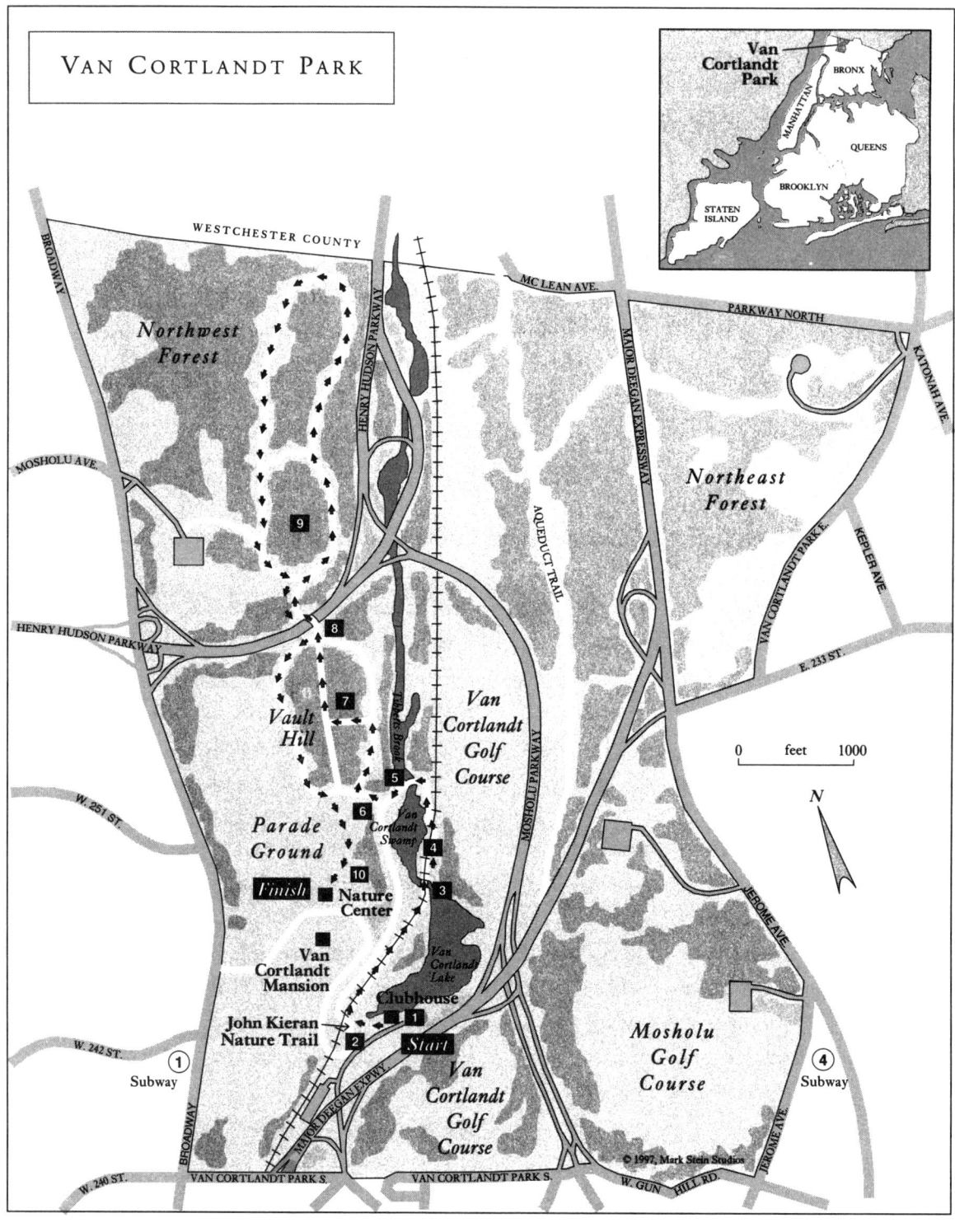

Van Cortlandt Park

In the northernmost end of the Bronx, Van Cortlandt Park is easily accessible and a one-stop-shopping sampler of the city's natural landscapes, featuring beautiful vistas, intricate topography, and an astonishing variety of New York's native ecosystems—from lakes and swamps to woods and grasslands.

With suburban Westchester County as its immediate neighbor, Van Cortlandt is often visited by wild animals not usually associated with the big city. Park rangers have seen red foxes with their pups in Van Cortlandt's woods. Birders report wild turkeys wandering near the park's golf courses, and most recently, coyotes have been spotted trotting into Van Cortlandt Park along the Major Deegan Expressway.

WILD WALK: VAN CORTLANDT PARK

Begin at the **clubhouse** **1** at the Van Cortlandt Golf Course, the nation's oldest public links. Next to the pro shop, a wooden deck overlooks Van Cortlandt Lake, a calm expanse where painted turtles bask on logs and families of Canada geese plow through the water. Behind the clubhouse, the **John Kieran Nature Trail** **2** follows the route of the Old Putnam Railroad—opened in 1880 as the first railroad to link New York City with Boston. Tall trees form a shady arch along the trail, where you can still see some of the old wooden ties. On the left, hidden in the shrubbery, look for big slabs of marble. These were part of an experiment to test which of 13 stone types proposed for the construction of Grand Central Station would weather the best. (In the end, the experiment was abandoned, and the architects selected the cheapest marble: Indiana limestone.)

Farther down the trail, a **railway trestle** **3** bridges the spot where Tibbetts Brook enters the lake. Running for 1½ miles through the park, Tibbetts Brook slows down here, forming Van Cortlandt Swamp, a freshwater wetland. Continue along the path. On the left, an **opening in the trees** **4** overlooks a small thicketed island. Here, you may spot wood ducks—Van Cortlandt's unofficial mascots. In their warm-weather finery, the red-billed male ducks are covered with glowing green and blue plumage, making them one of the most

Silvery checkerspot butterfly

Wild Fact

NOT SO WILY COYOTE

In 1995, coyotes finally made it to New York City. Trotting nonchalantly into the Bronx, one was spotted in both Van Cortlandt Park and Woodlawn Cemetery. However, this particular coyote may be sorry it made the trip. Now handsomely stuffed, it was found dead in Van Cortlandt Park—after being both run over and shot.

---

stunning sights in nature—let alone the Bronx. Though these waterbirds are known for being extremely shy, pairs of wood ducks have returned to nest in tree hollows and raise ducklings on Van Cortlandt Swamp every spring for the past 50 years.

Take the next left on the trail, and you'll come to a narrow **wooden bridge** **5** crossing the swamp. Using the bridge as a viewing platform, look for wood ducks and other waterfowl. In summer, the great blue heron—a 4-foot-tall wading bird with a 6-foot wingspan—is a frequent visitor.

Continue over the bridge and turn right, passing a huge **London plane tree** **6**—it has a 15-foot girth. Skirt the Parade Grounds where people play soccer and cricket, and hike up **Vault Hill** **7**, named for the tomb that the wealthy Van Cortlandt family built here before the American Revolution. As you ascend, you will enter one of the city's rare grassland ecosystems. Here, grasses like little bluestem and panic grass grow 3 feet high, along with wildflowers like goldenrod and meadowsweet—creating an ideal habitat for some of the city's 130 species of butterflies. In warm months, look for common species such as monarchs and mourning cloaks, as well as rarer ones like the silvery checkerspot.

Just before reaching the tomb itself, turn right and follow the broad dirt trail up and down through low-growing woods for about half a mile. This trail leads to a **bridge** **8** crossing the Henry Hudson Parkway and into the park's **Northwest Forest** **9**, home to owls, bats, chipmunks, giant silk moths, and other forest creatures. Walk toward the little brick building and turn right, continuing up the paved trail that circles the woods. Follow this winding path beneath shady oak and tulip trees, and you'll see dramatic rock outcrops looming overhead. Called Fordham gneiss, the rock is 1.1 billion years old, predating all but the earliest of Earth's life forms.

On your way out of the park, stop by the **Forest Ecology Center** **10** on the Parade Grounds, where you can check out the stuffed birds and other exhibits on the park's wildlife.

HOW TO GET THERE: **By car:** *Take the Major Deegan Expressway to the Van Cortlandt Park South exit and follow signs to the Van Cortlandt Golf Course. Parking is free in the lot farthest from the clubhouse.* **By mass transit:** *Take the 1 train to the last stop, at 242nd Street. Walk across Broadway to the park's Parade Grounds, head past the swimming pool and underneath the railway trestle to reach the Van Cortlandt Golf Course clubhouse.*

The New York Botanical Garden

One of the oldest and most significant scientific institutions in the city, the New York Botanical Garden (NYBG)—founded in 1891 by botanist Nathaniel Lord Britton—features 27 outdoor gardens on 250 sprawling acres. Here, you'll find an 83-bed formal rose garden, a 2½-acre alpine rock garden (with artificial waterfall), a 150-year-old snuff mill (now doing double-duty as a snack bar), and the palatial Enid A. Haupt Conservatory—an all-glass, Victorian-style greenhouse sheltering desert and tropical species. The garden's natural highlights are just as impressive, including the Bronx River and a 40-acre swath of native, uncut forest—both of which were wisely left uncultivated by the garden's original designers, Calvert Vaux (cocreator of Central Park) and Samuel Parsons, Jr.

Although individual trees within the NYBG forest have been chopped down, unlike most forests in the Northeast, the entire acreage has never been cleared for agriculture or timber. Five well-maintained trails wind beneath the shady boughs of old hickories, red and white oaks, maples, hemlocks, and tulip trees—some as old as 300 years. If you follow the Orange Trail, the sound of rushing water grows until you reach Hester Bridge—beneath which flow the racing, white waters of the Bronx River. The only freshwater river in the city, the Bronx River flows through a narrow stone gorge and over a small, constructed waterfall. Turning left on the opposite side of the bridge, the trail runs alongside the river, under stone overhangs, and past streamside wildflowers ranging from blue forget-me-nots in spring to the orange blossoms of jewelweed in late summer.

A cool respite from the surrounding urban crush, the NYBG forest is the only place in New York City where the native landscape has—seemingly—withstood the test of time. It is also one of the city's most studied natural

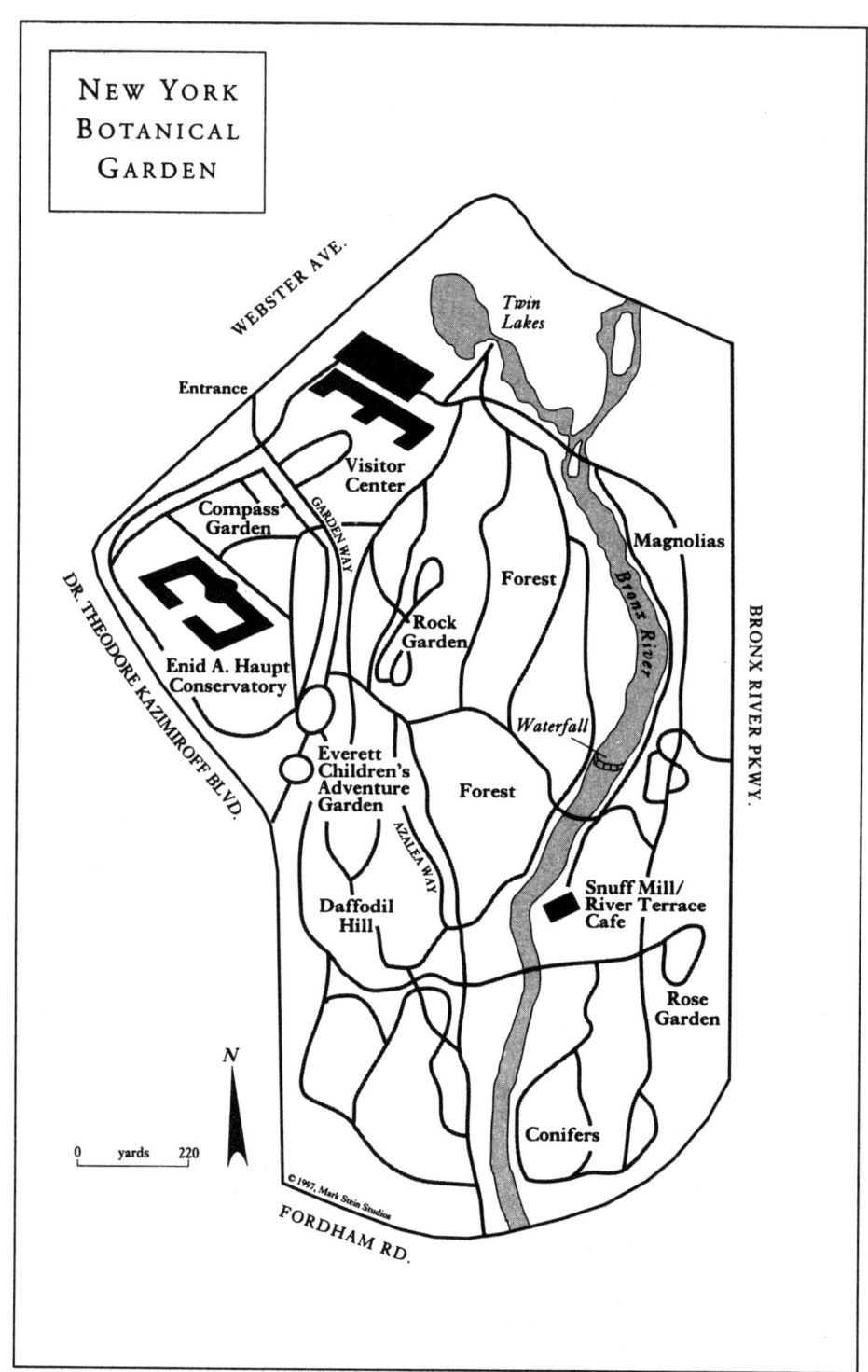

areas, and garden scientists are now facing the sad demise of the forest's old hemlock trees—short-needled evergreens with tiny pinecones and drooping limbs—at the hands of an invasive insect pest called the woolly adelgid. Though many dead and dying hemlocks can be seen alongside the trails, the NYBG forest is diverse enough to maintain its integrity—and never fails to impress.

To reach the forest from the main gate, walk down Garden Way and turn left onto Azalea Way, passing by the Everett Children's Adventure Garden on your right. Continue on Azalea Way until you reach the forest entrance.

HOW TO GET THERE: *By car: Take the Bronx River Parkway north to Exit 7W (Fordham Road) and bear right on Southern/Kazimiroff Boulevard to the garden entrance and parking lot. By mass transit: From Grand Central Station, take the Metro-North's Harlem Line to the Botanical Garden station. Or, take the D train to the Bedford Park Boulevard station and walk 8 blocks east to the garden's main entrance.*

Woodlawn Cemetery

Woodlawn Cemetery, where Mayor Fiorello La Guardia is buried and where hotel queen Leona Helmsley *will* be buried in a prebuilt mausoleum, is situated along the Fordham Ridge, a hillside underlaid by Fordham gneiss, the borough's 1.1-billion-year-old bedrock. Like Greenwood Cemetery in Brooklyn, this 400-acre necropolis is probably as "wild" as many of the city's parks. Four thousand trees cover Woodlawn's hilly grounds; the stars are 400 sugar maples, whose leaves turn luminous colors—bright reds, yellows, and oranges—in the fall.

HOW TO GET THERE: *By car: Take the West Side Highway to the Major Deegan Expressway. Take Exit 13 and follow East 233rd Street for three-quarters of a mile to the cemetery's main entrance (on the right). By mass transit: Take the 4 train and get off at the Woodlawn station to enter by the cemetery's Jerome Avenue gate. Or, take the 2 or 5 train to the 233rd Street station and walk 2 blocks west to the main entrance.*

Wave Hill

A former estate where Mark Twain and Teddy Roosevelt both briefly lived, Wave Hill is now a New York City cultural institution with immaculately landscaped formal gardens, greenhouses, and terraces. Perched on the steep Riverdale Ridge, a 200-foot-high crest of Fordham gneiss, Wave Hill's 28 acres offer some of the city's most scenic views—overlooking the wide blue waters of the Hudson River and the green-wooded Palisades beyond.

Wave Hill is most popular with horticulture fanatics, who flock to the Bronx to see its award-winning flower beds—featuring 3,250 species of plants. But those wanting something a little more wild should stop by Wave Hill's Forest Project, located in the estate's northwest section. Every summer since 1980, a group of New York City teenagers has weeded, planted, and tended a 10-acre plot—turning what once was a vine-choked morass into the beginnings of a healthy woodland ecosystem. Here, native oak and maple saplings are starting to sprout up on their own, and bird species that use the Hudson as a migratory route have recently begun dropping by during their spring and fall journeys.

HOW TO GET THERE: *By car: Take the Henry Hudson Parkway north to the 246th-250th Street exit, which leads onto a service road going north. From the service road, take the first left, at 252nd Street. Turn left onto Independence Avenue, then right onto 249th Street, which leads to Wave Hill's main gate and parking lot. By mass transit: Take Metro-North's Hudson Line to the Riverdale station. Follow the road uphill from the station's exit to Wave Hill's main gate on 249th Street and Independence Avenue.*

Riverdale Park

A narrow strip of land three-quarters of a mile long, Riverdale Park runs parallel to the Hudson River and the tracks of the Metro-North Railroad. Situated on the former grounds of turn-of-the-century estates, the steep hills of the park are scattered with marble property markers, stone fences, and other remains of the days when wealthy families like the Spauldings resided in this hilly Bronx neighborhood.

The most natural area in the park—a healthy 13-acre native woodland—is located at the southern end, near Palisade Avenue, where oak trees as old as

200 years tower above and sumac and ferns grow in their shade. These old trees, mostly red oaks, are themselves relics from another time, growing here when this spot was a wooded pasture during the early 1800s.

HOW TO GET THERE: **By car:** *Take the Henry Hudson Parkway north to the 232nd Street exit. Go west on 232nd Street for 2 blocks and turn right on Palisade Avenue, which leads to the park's Spaulding Lane parking lot.* **By mass transit:** *Take the 1 train to the 231st Street station and walk west on 232nd Street about 10 blocks, until you reach Palisade Avenue. Turn right on Palisade and look for the park's entrance on your left. Or, from Grand Central Station, take the Metro-North's Hudson Line to the Riverdale station. Walk 1 block south to the park's entrance on West 254th Street.*

QUEENS

The picture of Queens that comes to most people's minds is a concrete landscape clogged with miles of interlocking highways—some leading to its two airports, La Guardia and Kennedy, and others to Long Island. Although Queens has more than its fair share of expressways, highways, and parkways, what most New Yorkers don't know is that amid the automobiles are 4,900 square acres of city parkland—in total, more than that of any other borough.

Alley Pond Park

Not well known outside of Queens, Alley Pond Park is probably the best place to find out what New York City was like before people started crowding in and altering the landscape. Located on an inlet of Long Island Sound between the Douglaston and Bayside communities, this 654-acre park preserves many natural features that were typical of early New York, including spring-fed ponds, a tidal creek, hills formed by the last Ice Age, and old woods with tall oaks and tulip trees.

To really get a feel for the native scene, however, you have to stretch your imagination. Over the years the park has been sliced up into 13 puzzle pieces by such commuter thoroughfares as the Long Island Expressway, the

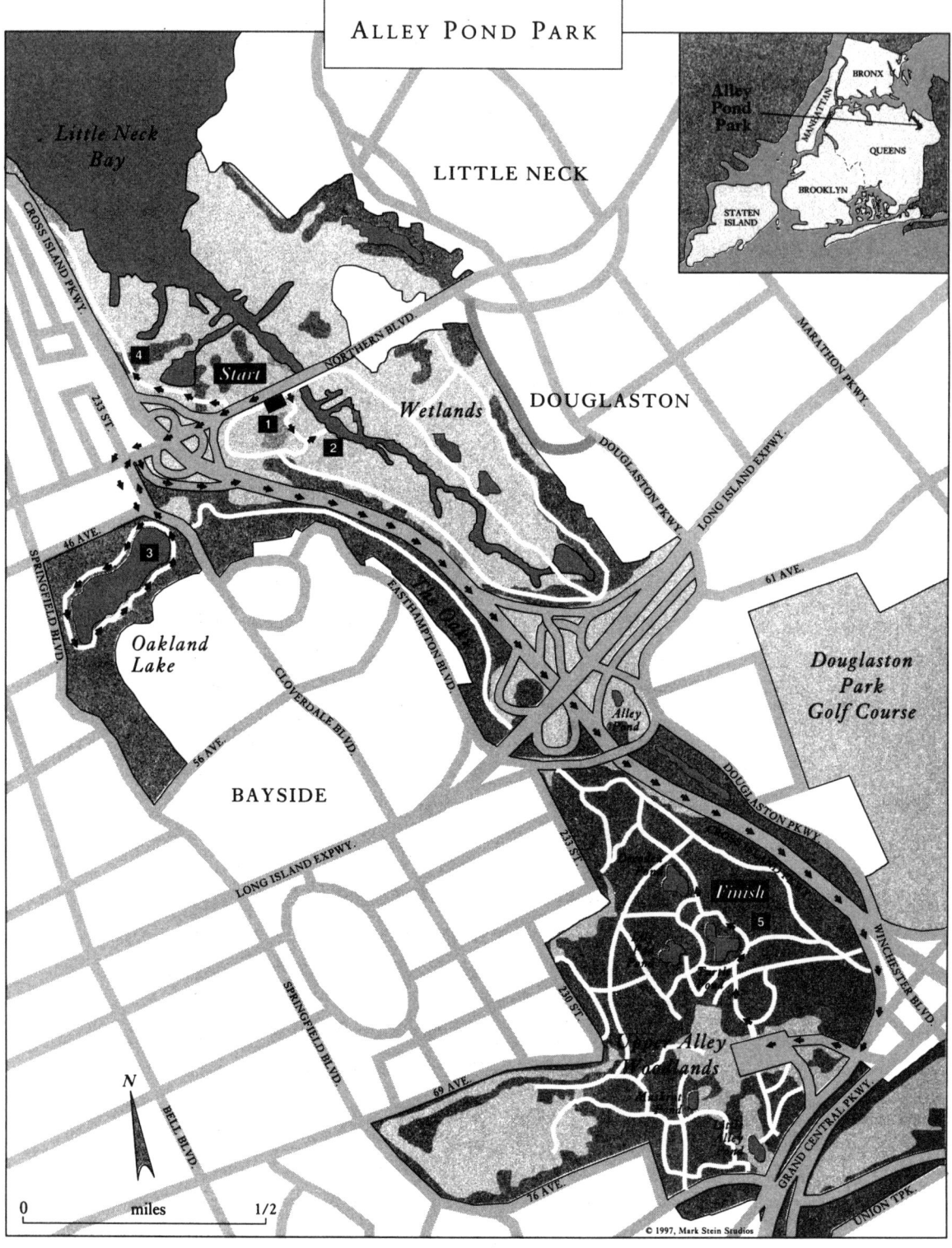

Long Island Railroad, and the Cross Island Parkway. In between these roads and cloverleafs, Alley Pond Park continues to support thriving ecosystems and some of the richest wildlife in the city—from muskrats and fiddler crabs to great blue herons and American toads.

Because the park covers such a large area, the walking tour is broken into four geographic sections: Alley Creek, Oakland Lake, Joe Michael's Mile, and the Upper Alley. If you want to see everything in one day, you should come by car. The park's lush woodlands in the Upper Alley are too far from the wetlands around Alley Creek to walk.

WILD WALK: ALLEY POND PARK

From the **Alley Pond Environmental Center** **1**, located in the Alley Wetlands, take the Cattail Trail over the wooden boardwalks and past 10-foot-tall giant reeds, called phragmites, to the observation deck over **Alley Creek** **2**. A true tidal creek, this ebbing and flowing stream is fed by natural springs and rainwater runoff inside the park and is also influenced by the tides from Long Island Sound. Twice a day, high and low tides can be observed from the platform, with low tides revealing mudflats and scurrying fiddler crabs. Mosquitoes are attracted to this swampy environment, so it is best to avoid this part of the park during the summer. However, spring, fall, and even winter are great times for close-up views of the magnificent wading birds that live in the salt marsh. Because the viewing platform places you right inside the marsh, you have an unobstructed view of sky, the green salt-marsh grasses, the meandering creek, and the hills in the distance. Here, it's not uncommon to see normally shy birds, such as snow-white terns and great blue herons, flying by without noticing they are being watched.

From the Alley Pond Environmental Center, it's a short walk to **Oakland Lake** **3**, a 40-foot-deep kettle of water created by a block of ice that "calved" off of the retreating Wisconsin Ice Sheet 18,000 years ago. Turn left on Northern Boulevard and left on 223rd Street to connect with the Gertrude Waldeyer Promenade, a wooded, ½-mile path circling the lake. As you walk along the shore, you may feel as though you are inside a Japanese painting. Although Oakland Lake is fed by rainwater and an underground spring, it seems more picturesque than wild. Mallard ducks look as if they have been posed under the

> ### Wild Fact
> ## ENDANGERED
>
> ### NEW YORKUS GIGANTICUS
>
> Alley Pond Park is home to one of the city's oldest and biggest trees. Growing in a remote section of The Oaks—a narrow swath of woods next to the Cross Island Parkway—is the "New York Giant," a 250-year-old tulip tree that, at 155 feet, is taller than the Statue of Liberty. Bypassed during the worst years of deforestation and witness to both the American Revolution and the Civil War, the Giant is surrounded by somewhat younger behemoths—oaks, beeches, and a few other tulips—that have all already seen their 200th birthdays.
>
> Though the Giant—which measures 16 feet around—and its oversized green pals are still standing, they are currently threatened by possible highway expansion. The state Department of Transportation has proposed having this area of Alley Pond Park "demapped" in order to cut down this rare tract of old forest and build an extra lane for cars on the Long Island Expressway.

shade of willow trees dipping their boughs in the water. White water lilies float obligingly on the surface in summertime. And a pair of mute swans top off the picture-perfect scenario by nesting every spring in the lake's shallow northwest corner.

Another spot you might want to visit is **Joe Michael's Mile** [4], which extends from the Cross Island Parkway to Little Neck Bay. The entrance to the "mile" is just to the left of the environmental center on the opposite side of Northern Boulevard. Popular with cyclists and skaters, the promenade opens onto the pebble beaches of Little Neck Bay, where you can look for wintering ducks—including unusual species such as goldeneyes, pintails, and buffleheads.

On the opposite end of Alley Pond Park, the landscape changes radically. While the area around Alley Creek and Oakland Lake is dominated by water and sky, the **Upper Alley** [5] is a moist, shady woodland of tall black oaks and beech trees. Here, a system of trails laid out by the Parks Department meanders through one of the prettiest pockets of woodland in the city. Alongside the trails, seasonal kettle ponds—usually dry by fall—provide microhabitats for all kinds of plants and animals. In spring, walking along this trail sometimes causes hundreds of frogs to leap for shelter into Decodon Pond, the park's largest kettle. The Upper Alley is also a favorite with wild mushroom hunters, who comb the forest floor for delicacies that bring a small fortune in gourmet stores. On a good day in summer, you may see dozens of different kinds of mushrooms, from spongy boletes (known in Italy as porcinis) to glowing-white—and hyperdeadly—mushrooms known as destroying angels.

HOW TO GET THERE: *To the wetlands—By car:* Take the Long Island Expressway to the Douglaston Parkway exit. Turn left on Northern Boulevard and drive 3 blocks to reach the park. *By mass transit:* Take the 7 train to the Main Street/Flushing station and catch the Q12 bus to the Northern Boulevard stop right in front of the park. *To the upland forest—By car:* Take the Grand Central Parkway to the Alley Park/Winchester Boulevard exit. Turn left on Winchester and immediately left onto the park road to the Nature Center parking lot. *By mass transit:* Take the E or F train to the Union Turnpike/Kew Gardens station and catch the Q44 bus to Winchester Boulevard. Walk northwest for about three-quarters of a mile along the Long Island Motor Parkway beneath the Grand Central Parkway overpass to reach the trails leading into the uplands.

UDALL'S COVE PARK PRESERVE

A 10-minute drive from Alley Pond Park, Udall's Cove is located in Little Neck, a picturesque neighborhood of New England–style houses on Little Neck Bay. Literally half a block from the city's border—20 steps will take you into Nassau County—Udall's Cove is one of the only parks in New York City that is dedicated solely to wildlife and habitat preservation. There are no ball fields here, no basketball courts, not even any paved walkways. There is, however, a parking lot from which two short paths lead to scenic overlooks of the 30-acre tidal inlet.

Leading straight from the parking lot, the first vantage point gives you a view of emerald green marsh grasses swaying in the shore breeze and the open waters of the cove beyond. The second overlook, found by veering onto the left-hand path through tangled underbrush, offers a close-up view of the salt marsh and its denizens. Here, from wooden pilings, you can see killifish swimming in the salty water, herons stalking the mudflats, and an old wooden boat filled with mud sitting half-submerged in a tidal creek.

The pilings and scuttled boat are remnants of the cove's once-thriving clamming industry. Until the late 1800s, boats headed into the shallows of Little Neck Bay and raked up bushels of hard-shell clams to sell to restaurants up and down the Atlantic coast. The local shellfish were so popular that today, 100 years later, clams served on the half shell are still called littlenecks in many seafood restaurants.

HOW TO GET THERE: ***By car:*** *Head south on the Long Island Expressway and exit at Little Neck Parkway. Take the parkway to the end (about 2 miles), which leads directly to Virginia Point, where the preserve's parking lot is located.* ***By mass transit:*** *Take the Long Island Railroad's Port Washington line to the Little Neck station and walk 2 short blocks down to the water and the preserve's parking lot.*

FOREST PARK

If it weren't for the desire of turn-of-the-century Brooklynites to have a rural retreat, Forest Park in eastern Queens probably would be thick with houses, not trees—more like Forest Hills, the adjoining residential neighborhood. In 1895, the people of Brooklyn (then still a separate city) purchased 538 acres of wooded land in Queens where they could scare up quail and ride horses along the park's steep, rocky ridges. One hundred years later,

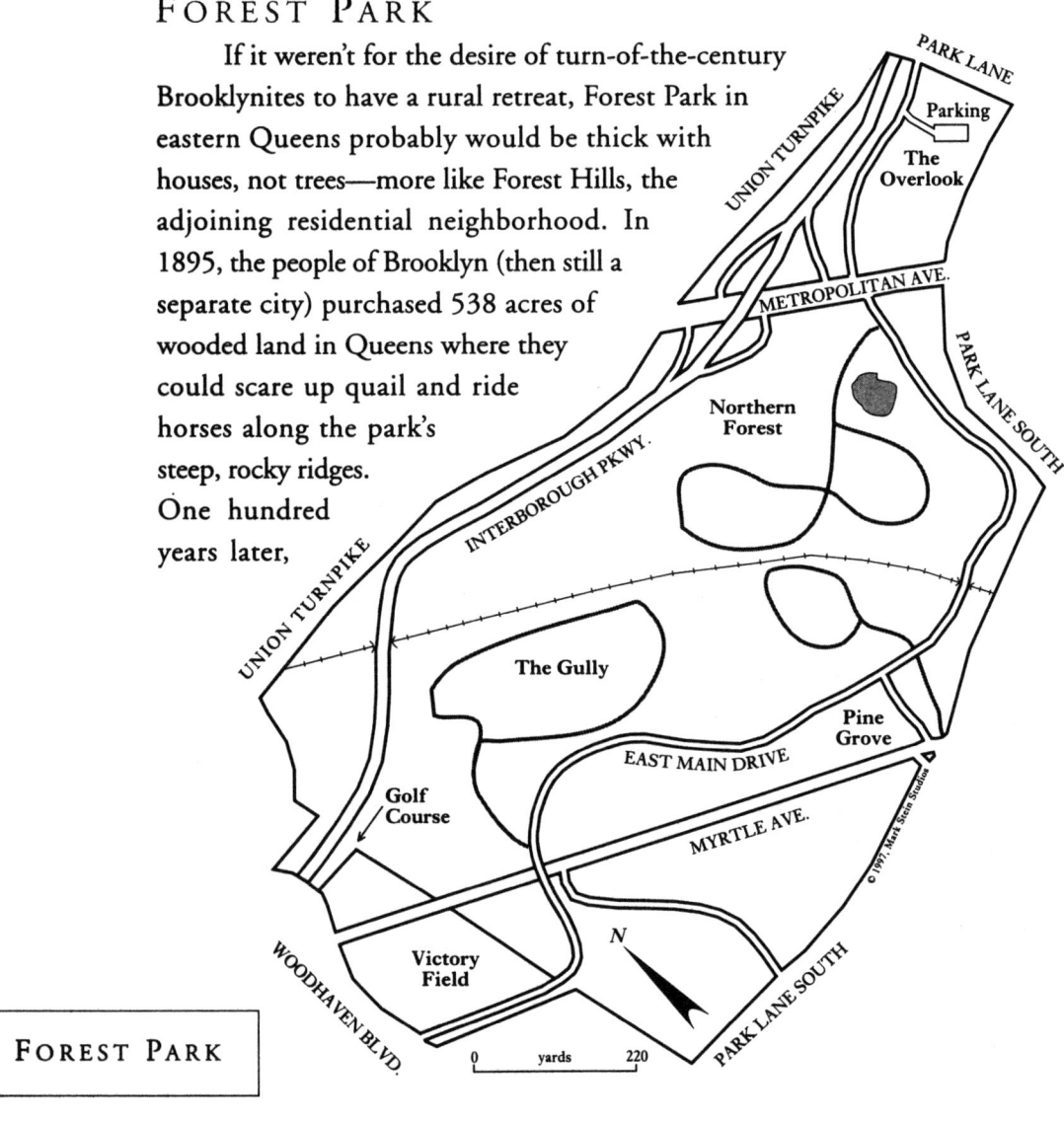

FOREST PARK

despite the addition of a band shell, golf course, and railroad tracks (which carry the Long Island Railroad's Montauk line), Forest Park still allows for "rusticating," as Victorian-era nature fans would have called it.

Though the "forest" in Forest Park has been reduced to 165 acres, naturalists say that it remains one of the city's healthiest and best-functioning woodland ecosystems. In the park's eastern half, massive oak trees, some believed to be more than 150 years old, drop their acorns on the paths below. Members of the Queens County Bird Club scan the tops of the trees for tiny migrating songbirds called warblers. And resident birds like the flicker, an intricately patterned woodpecker, raise their young in holes bored into the trunks.

To reach the forest, start at the Overlook, the park's headquarters, where a trail marked with yellow blazes begins behind the parking lot. Follow the Yellow Trail down the East Main Drive, across Metropolitan Avenue, and then turn right, into the woods. Within 200 feet, on the left, you will encounter a seasonal pond where local bird-watchers congregate. From here the trail winds up and down over small bumpy hills, known as "knob and kettle" terrain, a landscape that marks the fact that the park stands on the terminal moraine, the last stop of the Wisconsin Ice Sheet. Following the undulating topography, the Yellow Trail loops back to the park's main drive. However, if you want to continue exploring, you can (cautiously) cross the railroad tracks to reach The Gully, another section of the woods where there are more oaks, hills, and kettles.

HOW TO GET THERE: *By car: Take the Van Wyck Expressway south to the Union Turnpike exit. From the turnpike, turn left at the Markwood Place/Park Lane exit, which leads to the Overlook, the park's headquarters where there is a weekends-only parking lot. By mass transit: Take the F train to the Union Turnpike/Kew Gardens station. Then catch the Q37 bus to the Union Turnpike/Park Lane stop at the Overlook.*

Cunningham Park

In Cunningham Park's Southern Forest, the sunlight is obscured by the dense leaves of the trees, and the ground is covered with plush stands of wildflowers and ferns. On overcast days, when the mist rises off the park's small ponds, you can pretend you're in a Brazilian rain forest—even though you're just in Queens, cut off from the rest of the world by four heavily trafficked highways.

Spread over 358 acres, Cunningham Park contains a tennis center, the overgrown remains of the country's first highway (the Vanderbilt Motor Parkway), and a crowded court for bocce (an Italian form of lawn bowling). However, it is the park's surprisingly fertile, 60-acre woodland that draws botanists, who make regular expeditions here to hunt for ferns. So far, 18 different species have been identified—from pale green New York ferns to rattlesnake ferns, a rare species closely related to plants that existed more than 350 million years ago, during the Devonian period. These ferns grow in vast swaths, and the lushness of the greenery is due to the forest's unusually clay-rich and moisture-retaining soil, which acts like Super Gro on the park's native plants. Tulip trees, sweet gums, and red oaks shoot upward as high as 70 feet to form one of the leafiest forest canopies in the city.

Rattlesnake fern

The forest's shady interior also conceals a chain of small kettle ponds. These miniature wet worlds are surrounded by wetland-loving trees like red maples and attract pond-loving birds such as kingfishers and green herons. Somehow these wetland species manage to find Cunningham's tiny ponds despite their isolation in the midst of suburban sprawl.

Several looping trails lead through the Southern Forest—all of which can be reached from the forest's entrance, an inconspicuous paved pathway leading into the woods from busy Francis Lewis Boulevard.

HOW TO GET THERE: *By car: Head south on the Grand Central Parkway and exit onto Francis Lewis Boulevard, going north. At the next intersection, make a left onto Union Turnpike, which leads to the public parking lot at 196th Place. From the lot, walk back on Union Turnpike and turn right on Francis Lewis Boulevard. After about 20 yards, look for the trailhead on your left.* **By mass transit:** *Take the E or F train to the Union Turnpike/Kew Gardens station. Catch the* **Q46** *bus to Francis Lewis Boulevard. Walk back on Francis Lewis Boulevard about 20 yards to reach the trailhead on your left.*

STATEN ISLAND: COUNTRY IN THE CITY

With just 5 percent of the city's total population, Staten Island is the city's "country" borough. Although new houses are going up faster than you can say, "Save that tree," parts of the island remain rural in character, and the island's parks preserve what are by far the least disturbed woodlands in New York City.

THE STATEN ISLAND GREENBELT

Encompassing an area three times the size of Central Park, the Greenbelt is a network of wooded parks in the heart of Staten Island connected by 28 miles of hiking trails. Here, it is possible to walk for 4 hours in the forest without seeing another human being. What you *will* see are a canopy of huge oak trees, incredible panoramic views, spring-fed kettle ponds, and streams flowing through the woodlands.

In the 1960s, this swath of green was threatened by the proposed construction of a highway cutting through its middle. But Staten Island's citizens banded together to block the proposal, applying so much political pressure that the Greenbelt was officially turned into a nature preserve. However, all is not trees. In and around the Greenbelt's 2,500 acres are a golf course, scout camp, hospital, and several graveyards—most notably the Moravian Cemetery, where the Vanderbilt clan houses its 72-crypt tomb.

The following tour is a 3-hour-long introductory course that begins in High Rock Park, the Greenbelt's unofficial capital.

WILD WALK: STATEN ISLAND GREENBELT

From the parking lot on Nevada Avenue, head up the path through the iron gates into High Rock Park. Just on your left, a sign marks the start of the Swamp Trail, which circles **Loosestrife Swamp** **1**. A flat, ¼-mile loop, the Swamp Trail runs beneath wetland-loving trees like sassafras, sweet gum, and red maple. While most of the trail is pleasantly shady, at the halfway point a wooden boardwalk takes you right across the water. Surrounded by forest, this

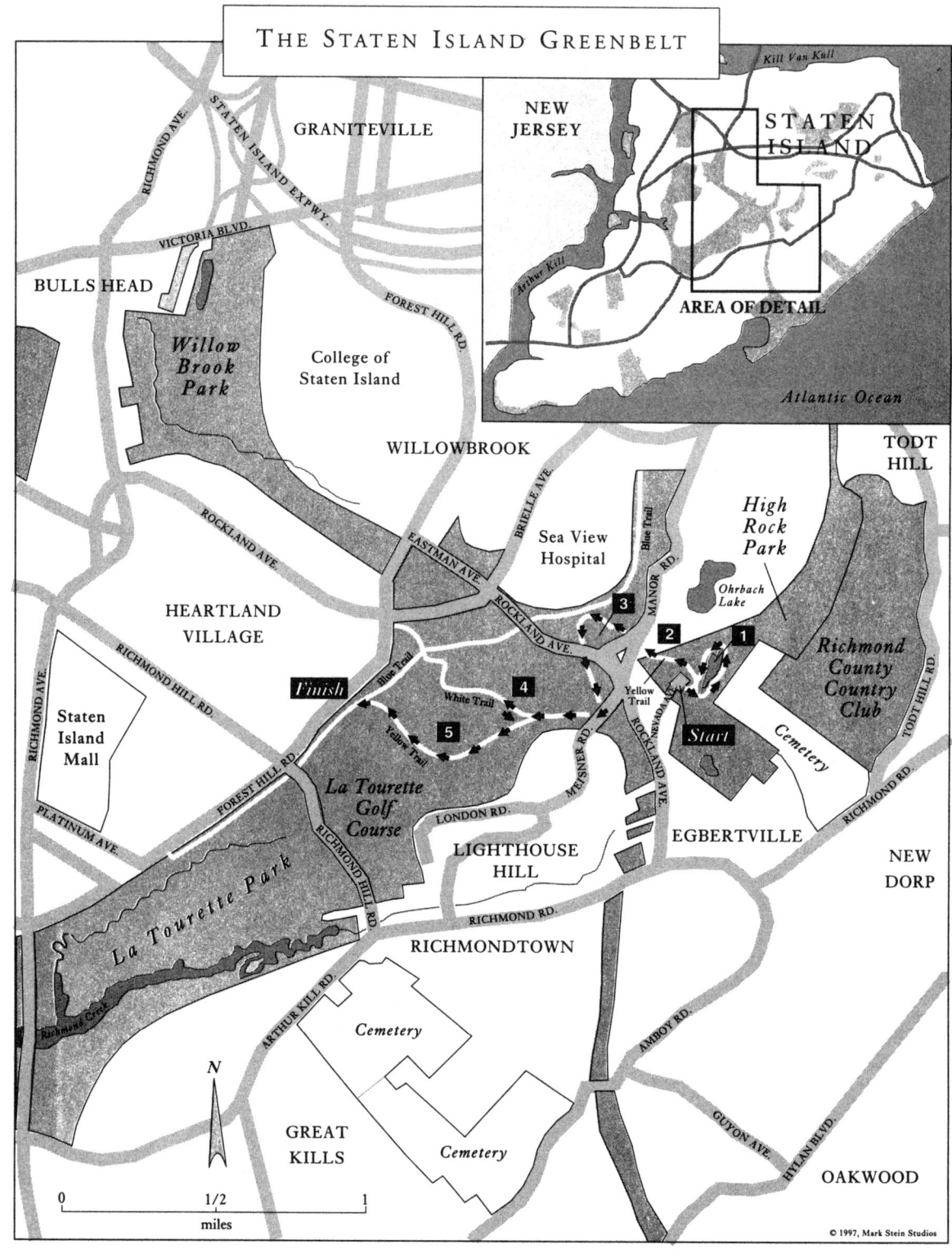

quiet, sun-filled spot is a good place to pause and look for wetland wildlife: red-winged blackbirds, dragonflies, painted turtles, and green frogs. It's also a good spot to observe the swamp's namesake plant—loosestrife—the flowers of which turn the whole marsh purple in midsummer.

After completing the Swamp Trail loop, look for a tree with yellow blazes—just to the left of the sign for the Swamp Trail—which marks the beginning of serious hiking on the Greenbelt's twisting Yellow Trail. Taking a left at the first fork, follow the Yellow Trail through an **oak-beech-hickory forest** **2**, climbing up and down beneath a lush, leafy canopy. Unless the weather is very dry, a steep-banked stream—lined with ferns and skunk cabbage—runs through here, completing the sensation that you have entered some far-flung country retreat. Just before the trail reaches Manor Road, look for a grove of rare wild persimmon trees, distinguished by their thin trunks and bark that is broken into small, rectangular blocks. In late fall, these trees drop red, podlike fruits, which, strangely, taste sweetest when they look a little rotten.

From here, cross Manor Road and pick up the Yellow Trail again. Walk about 30 feet down the trail, and take the first left, detouring up **Moses Mountain** **3**. Named for the famous Parks and Highway Commissioner Robert Moses, this 200-foot-tall "mountain" was made from the rock blasted out during the 1960s construction of the Staten Island Expressway. Over the years, the mound of fill has been colonized by grasses, wildflowers, and woody shrubs. As you walk up the hill, you will see chunks and boulders of a greenish rock called serpentinite. This is Staten Island's unusually soft, native bedrock, which geologists believe was formed 450 million years ago from deep ocean crust that was thrust up during a collision of continents.

After a steep climb to the top of the hill, you will be rewarded with a panoramic view of the surrounding Greenbelt—a soothing green blanket in summer and a stunning combination of reds, yellows, and oranges in fall. In October, bird-watchers come here for hawk watches, when they may see as many as 60 migrating raptors a day—from turkey vultures to red-shouldered hawks.

From the top of the hill, backtrack to the bottom of Moses Mountain and turn left to continue on the Yellow Trail. As you walk past the base of the mountain, you will see huge boulders of greenish serpentinite rock. Continue through the woods, which is dominated by beech and sweet gum trees, until you reach the intersection of Rockland Avenue and Meissner Road. Cross Rockland, and turn right onto Meissner, where you can pick up the Yellow Trail again. After about 5 minutes on this wooded path, you'll come to a fork, where the Yellow Trail continues on the left. However, take a short detour down the right fork, onto the White Trail, to see **Bucks Hollow Swamp** **4**. Here, great old oaks and a tangle of woody vines rise from the swamp's dark, shallow waters. In spring and summer, this extensive wetland is populated with frogs and turtles—and the occasional snake.

Head back to the Yellow Trail, which skirts the edge of the swamp. As you walk along the edge of La Tourette Park Golf Course, you may notice that the makeup of the forest has changed subtly. In these **moist woods** **5**, the oaks and beeches have given way to water-loving trees, like red maple and sweet gum. Ferns grow alongside the trail, and moss climbs up the sides of trees. Along the way, look for signs of the family farms, orchards, and vineyards that once covered parts of the Greenbelt. Remnants of fieldstone walls, old culverts, and nonnative garden plants are clues to the area's original settlement by large landowners.

Hiking for another ½ mile, you will reach the intersection of the Yellow and Blue trails. A one-way ticket, the Yellow Trail continues from here and ends anticlimactically at the Staten Island Mall. So you can make a choice: Either hike to the mall for a day of shopping, backtrack to High Rock Park along the Yellow Trail, or turn right on the Blue Trail, which leads to the Red-Bar Trail and back to the parking lot.

Take Note: The Greenbelt is a real forest, and it's easy to lose your bearings. All five of its major trails—the Yellow, Blue, Green, White, and Red-Bar—are marked with colored blazes painted on trees and rocks. However, the major trails often crisscross, and there are lots of unmarked paths. To stick with the walking tour, watch carefully for the yellow blazes. If you get lost, follow the trail to the nearest roadway to regain your bearings.

HOW TO GET THERE: ***By car:*** *Take the Verrazano-Narrows Bridge to the Staten Island Expressway (Route 278) and get off at the Todt Hill Road/Slosson Avenue exit. At the second light, turn left onto Manor Road. Follow Manor Road for 2 miles and turn left on Rockland Avenue. After 2 blocks, turn left onto*

Nevada Avenue, which leads into the High Rock Park parking lot. **By mass transit:** *Take the Staten Island Ferry to St. George and catch the S74 bus to the corner of Richmond Road and Rockland Avenue. Walk up Rockland for 2 blocks, and turn right on Nevada Avenue to reach the park's entrance.*

BLUE HERON PARK

Located on the site of what was once a French Huguenot farm in Annadale, a sparsely settled suburb on the southern end of Staten Island, Blue Heron Park contains 147 acres of woodlands, swamps, ponds, and streams—one of the city's richest forest ecosystems. Many wetland-loving trees, such as red maple, tupelo, and swamp white oak, grow in Blue Heron's moist forests, but most common are the sweet gums—tall trees with star-shaped leaves that litter the ground with their telltale spiky fruits—known as itchy balls to local kids. Beneath this shady canopy is a lush understory of flowers, shrubs, and saplings—further evidence of this ecosystem's health. Amateur botanists can have a field day trying to identify all the different species. White, wild Canada mayflowers blanket the forest floor each spring, and in July, hundreds of highbush blueberry bushes burst forth with delicious edible fruit.

Starting at the entrance off Poillon Avenue, several unmarked trails wind pleasantly through the park, fording streambeds and occasionally a roadway. Although the park is bordered by suburban homes, it's possible to walk here for hours without seeing another person. Despite Blue Heron's unusual beauty, it is rarely visited, making it one of the few attractions in New York where you can have the whole place to yourself.

HOW TO GET THERE: **By car:** *Take the Verrazano-Narrows Bridge to Hylan Boulevard, and turn left, going south on Hylan for about 5½ miles until you reach Poillon Avenue. (If you pass Huguenot Avenue, you've gone too far). Turn right on Poillon and look for the park's entrance on your left. (You can park in front of the guardrail.)* **By mass transit:** *From the Staten Island ferry terminal in St. George, take the Staten Island Rapid Transit train to the Annadale station. From the station's exit, walk southeast for about 6 blocks to Poillon Avenue. Turn left on Poillon to reach the park's entrance.*

Clay Pit Ponds State Park Preserve

Even to someone familiar with the many and varied wild areas in New York City, Clay Pit Ponds State Park Preserve comes as a complete surprise. The drive down Sharrotts Road toward the park has the feel of a remote country highway. In fact, there are so many stables for boarding horses here that some people call this area Staten Island's Wild West.

At the end of Carlin Street, the park's headquarters is located in an 80-year-old clapboard house. Just behind it are the trailheads for two well-marked and well-maintained hiking trails—the three-quarter-mile Abraham's Pond Trail and the 1-mile Ellis Swamp Trail. Both trails wind up and down over low,

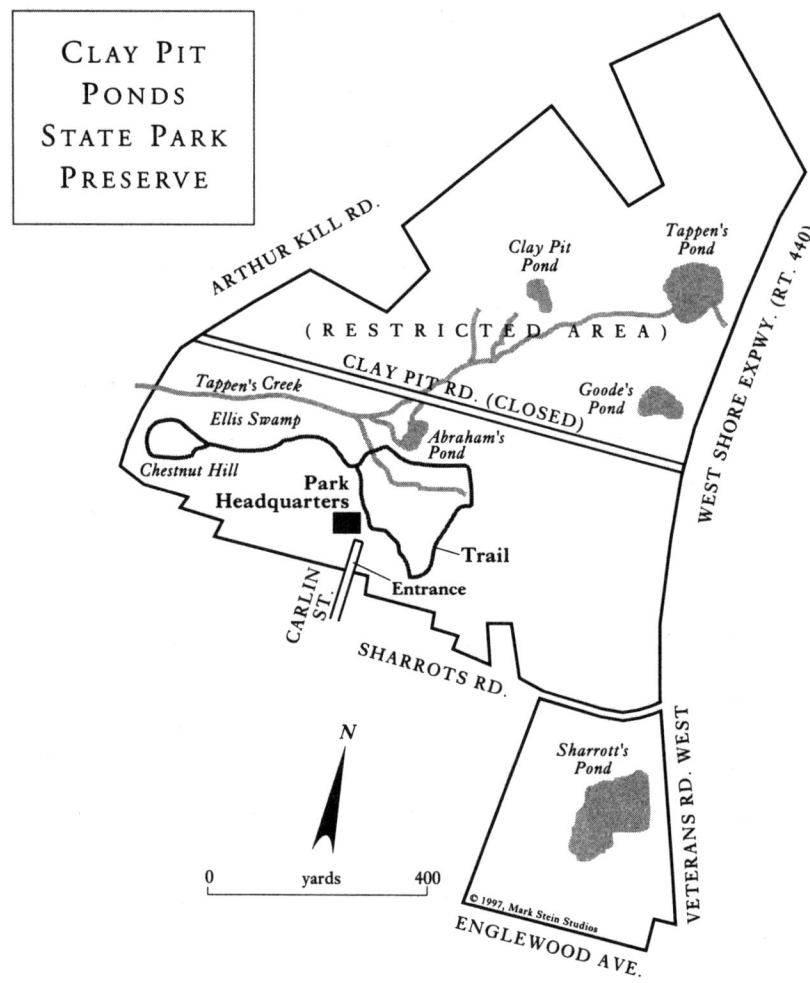

rolling terrain with numerous wooden bridges spanning marshy patches. Along the way are swamp forests, pine-and-oak barrens, gullies filled with ferns, and sandy spots where you can see prickly-pear cactus.

You will also come upon Abraham's Pond, one of the preserve's kettle holes. Though now filled with birds, turtles, water lilies, and lush wetland plants, it was originally created by industry. In the late 1800s, the site of the park was mined for its rich clay deposits—from which bricks were made—and the pits used to dig the clay have since filled with rainwater and turned into clay pit ponds.

HOW TO GET THERE: *By car: Take the Verrazano-Narrows Bridge to the Staten Island Expressway (Route 278). Continue on the expressway for 6 miles and exit onto Route 440 South. Follow Route 440 for 5 miles, to Exit 3. From the exit, turn left onto Bloomingdale Road. Then, turn right onto Sharrotts Road and right again after about 1 mile, onto Carlin Street, which leads into the park. By mass transit: From the Staten Island ferry terminal in St. George, take the S113 bus to Sharrotts Road. Turn right on Sharrotts Road, walk for ¼ mile, and then turn right on Carlin Street, which leads into the park.*

> ### Wild Fact
> ### FIRE-EATING TREES
>
> Clay Pit Ponds State Park Preserve is home to an unusual and isolated ecosystem found nowhere else in the city. Extremely sandy soil in parts of the park creates dry, almost desert-like conditions. Such an inhospitable environment, combined with a long history of wildfires, has led to the development of a forest—called a pine-and-oak barrens—that is virtually fireproof.
>
> Blackjack oaks and pitch pines, the most common trees in the barrens, are also among the most fire-loving plants in the world. Though they will burn black in a forest fire, they aren't actually killed by the flames. Within weeks of a conflagration, pitch pines sprout new buds from charred limbs, while blackjack oaks vigorously resprout from their roots. In spots where fires have historically been extremely frequent, the trees may further adapt by growing only in miniature and developing into a dwarf forest. In some areas of the Clay Pits Pond park, 30-year-old pines and oaks are only 5 feet tall.

GREAT KILLS PARK

Part of the Staten Island unit of the Gateway National Recreation Area, Great Kills Park is one of the city's best-kept secrets: a waterfront park with sandy beaches, baseball diamonds, and a sailboat-jammed marina. There is also a nature preserve on Crooke's Point at the park's southern end that features some of the prettiest and most unexpected scenery in the five boroughs.

Three miles from the main entrance on Hylan Boulevard, Crooke's Point was once an island and now is only connected to the park by a narrow neck of land. Its sandy shore is dotted with pink slipper shells, and its dunes are covered with bunches of beach grass, seaside goldenrod, and Spanish bayonet. Facing New York Harbor to the east, Raritan Bay to the south, and Great Kills Harbor to the west, Crooke's Point enjoys spectacular views of open sky (it's a great place to look at cloud formations), faraway lighthouses, flocks of birds flying over the bay, and of course, the sunset. Crooke's Point is also popular with nocturnal surf casters, who during late summer hit the shore for the annual "midnight blue" fishing frenzies.

HOW TO GET THERE: *By car: Take the Verrazano-Narrows Bridge to the Staten Island Expressway (Route 278). Follow the expressway to the Hylan Boulevard exit, and turn left (south) on Hylan. After 5 miles on Hylan, look for the Great Kills Park entrance on your left (opposite Buffalo Street). Follow the signs to Great Kills' main parking lot.* **By mass transit:** *From the Staten Island ferry terminal in St. George, take the S78 bus, which stops at Great Kills' Hylan Boulevard entrance. From here, it's a 3-mile trek out to Crooke's Point, so you may want to bring a bike or skates.*

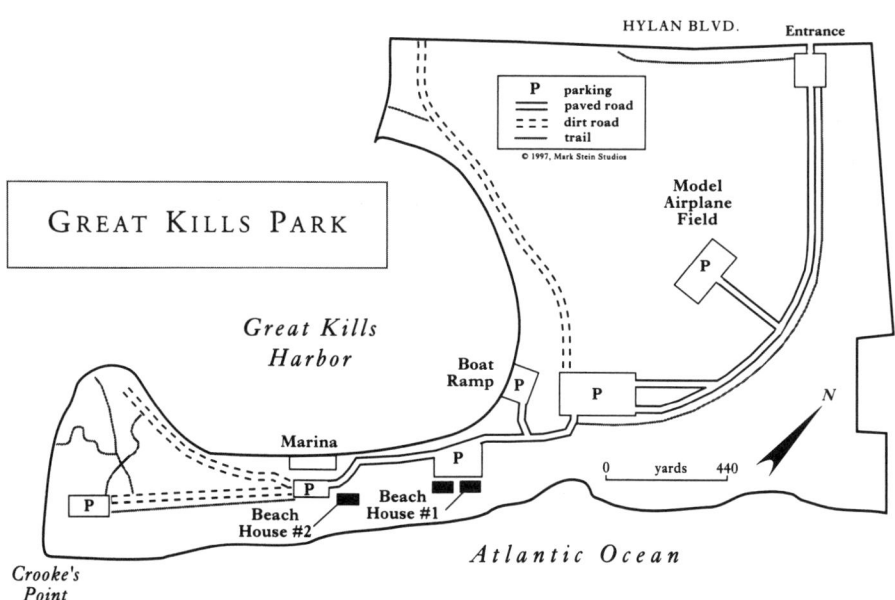

Wolfe's Pond Park

On Wolfe's Pond Park's 312 acres, kids play roller hockey in the parking lot, families picnic on wooden tables, and anglers cast for largemouth bass in the park's namesake pond. But it is the park's coastline—facing Raritan Bay on Staten Island's southern shore—that boasts the most natural highlights. From the parking lot, you can stroll three-quarters of a mile along the park's rubble beach, a promenade of dark sand that gives way to cobblestone-sized rocks at the water's edge. Amid this jumble, beachcombers will find green seaweed, broken oyster shells, live soft-shell clams buried in the sand, and bits of surf-smoothed green beach glass.

During the summer the beach is crowded with sunbathers. During the off-season, however, it is virtually empty, except for the occasional surf caster or dog walker. Out on the water you may see small boats tonging for clams, and in the distance you may be able to spot two national landmarks: the Coney Island Parachute Jump and the Sandy Hook Lighthouse, the nation's oldest continually operating lighthouse, on the opposite New Jersey shore.

HOW TO GET THERE: *By car: Take the Verrazano-Narrows Bridge to the Staten Island Expressway (Route 278) and get off at the Hylan Boulevard exit. Turn left on Hylan and continue for 6 miles. Turn left on Cornelia Avenue to reach the park's entrance. By mass transit: From the Staten Island ferry terminal in St. George, take the S78 bus to Luten Avenue and Hylan Boulevard. Walk 1 block west on Hylan to Cornelia Avenue and turn left.*

Clove Lakes Park

According to Staten Island lore, Clove Lakes Park in northern Staten Island was once a game preserve where hunters tracked wild bears. The park's original terrain—a stream-cut valley filled with swamps and woodlands—would indeed have been prime black bear country. However, during the 1930s, the park's 200 acres were significantly altered. The natural stream was dammed to create three separate lakes—Brook's, Martling's, and Clove lakes—and its freshwater wetlands were filled in to create playing fields.

Now these ball fields host countless high school and Staten Island league baseball games, and the lakes attract local anglers, who fish for largemouth bass, carp, and catfish. Although the wooded hillside overlooking the lakes no longer harbors bear, other native woodland animals, such as raccoons, opossums, and squirrels, still hide out here.

The trail through these woodlands is a pleasant hour-long stroll. The hillside offers solitude and views of the waters below, which occasionally can be glimpsed through the canopy of red and white oak trees. Beginning as a paved path at the parking lot (to the right of the public rest rooms), the trail first leads across Clove Lake over a scenic stone bridge. From there, the trail heads uphill into the woods.

HOW TO GET THERE: *By car: Take the Verrazano-Narrows Bridge to the Staten Island Expressway (Route 278). Follow the expressway for 4 miles, to the Clove Road exit. After exiting, stay on the service road until you reach Clove Road. Turn right on Clove Road, and after three traffic lights turn left into the public parking lot opposite Cheshire Place. By mass transit: From the Staten Island ferry terminal in St. George, take the S61, S62, or S66 bus to Victory Boulevard and Clove Road. From there, walk down Clove Road about 100 yards to the parking lot.*

INDEX

Allen, Woody, 63
Alley Pond Park, 57, 97, 99, 177–181
Amateur Astronomers Association of New York, 6
American Littoral Society, 53
American Museum of Natural History, 81, 109, 118
Amphibians, 81–84
archy and mehitabel, 86
Asbestos, naturally occurring, 29
Atlantic Flyway, 113–117
Atlantic Ocean: and fish, 88; and geology 23, 25, 34; view of, 151; and weather 7, 9, 11

Battery Park City, 19, 32, 141
Battery Park City Esplanade, 141–142
Bayswater State Park, 154–155
Beach ecosystems, 51–54, 70, 72, 151–154, 157–158, 193
Beebe, William, 116
Birds: bald eagles, 115, 153, 166; barn owls, 64; black skimmers, 151; brant geese, 45, 149; in Central Park Reservoir, 56; common terns, 151; double-crested cormorants, 146; egrets, 65–67, 144, 156; European starlings, 131; hawks, 153, 187; herons, 65–67, 156; herring gulls, 70, 71, 72; house sparrows, 117, 164; migration, 73, 113–117, 144, 153, 176; mockingbirds, 73; monk parakeets, 163; ospreys, 169; owls, 64, 145; peregrine falcons, 61–64, 141, 149; pigeons, 10, 63, 67, 117; piping plovers, 70–73, 151; red-bellied woodpeckers, 130, 131; red-tailed hawks, 63, 133; seagulls, 71; snow geese, 115; snowy owls, 58; spotted redshank, 68; and Statue of Liberty, 116; upland sandpipers, 57; warblers, 73–74, 114, 131; white-throated sparrow, 114–115; wood ducks, 171–172
Bird-watching, 73, 74, 122, 130–131, 144, 153, 183
Blizzards: of 1888, 10–11; of 1996, 8–9
Blue Heron Park, 51, 56, 189
Blue crabs, 43, 45, 90
Breezy Point Tip, 54, 70–73, 74, 83, 123, 151–153
Bridges, 42, 43, 65, 67, 69; as nesting sites for falcons, 62–64
Broad Channel, Queens, 15
Bronx River, 24, 54, 166, 173
Bronx Zoo, 54, 80, 116
Bronx, 140, 166–177; and coyotes, 80
Brooklyn Botanic Garden, 55, 95, 104, 105, 158, 159, 164–166
Brooklyn Bridge, 20, 62, 69
Brooklyn, 28, 35, 38, 158–166
Bryant Park, 70
Buffer the Bay, 155
Burg, David, 74

Cage, John, 109
Cameron's Line, 24
Caviar, 119
Central Park, 129–136; Belvedere Castle, 115, 130; birds, 73–74, 116, 130–131; Conservatory Garden, 133, 136; Conservatory Water, 56; Great North, 129, 133–136; Harlem Meer, 133, 134, 136; Henry Luce Nature Observatory, 130; jellyfish, 56; Lake, 129, 131; Loeb Boathouse and Cafe, 131, 133; Mall, 97, 103, 104; Pond, 94; Ramble, 74, 129–133; Reservoir, 55, 56, 105; rock outcrops, 25, 27, 29, 31, 130; Shakespeare Garden, 130; squirrel population, 76, trees, 99; Turtle Pond, 55, 130; Vista Rock, 130; Zoo, 79
Central Park Conservancy, 133
Cherry Blossom Festival, 165
Cicadas, see periodical cicadas
Citicorp Building, Queens, 32
Citicorp Center, 12
City Island, 92
Clay Pit Ponds State Park Preserve, 28, 104, 190–191
Clean Water Act, 44, 143
Clove Lakes Park, 193–194
Cockroaches, 85–88; and asthma, 87; and Combat, 87

Cohen, Mickey and Barbara, 155
Collect Pond, 56
Coney Island, 18, 51, 52, 53, 90
Cooney, Patrick, 104
Crooke's Point, see Great Kills Park
Cunningham Park, 50, 56, 57, 99, 183–184
Curran, Henry H., 86

Darsh, Lynn, 6
Dicker, Naomi, 104
Dubos Point Preserve, 155–156
Dutch elm disease, 103–104

Earthquakes, 18–20
East River, 14, 24, 42, 54, 65, 82
Ellis Island, 89
Empire State Building, 12, 31; and lightning, 16–18
Endangered species, 61, 70, 72, 149, 151
Exxon oil spill, 47

Fall colors, 110–112, 152, 164, 175, 187
Far Rockaway, Queens, 154
Fiddler crabs, 46, 47
Fish, 88–94; Atlantic Sturgeon, 119; blue fish, 92, 93; American eels, 54, 88; fluke, 93; killifish, 47, 48; in Bronx River, 54; in Hudson Estuary, 43, 45; menhaden or bunker, 45, 93; regulations, 94; shad, 117–120; striped bass, 43, 88, 92, 93; and salt marshes, 48; winter flounder, 149, 157
Fishing, 90–94, 149, 192
Flowers, see plants
Floyd Bennett Field, 6, 57, 58, 59, 74, 83, 148–151
Forest Park, 95, 107, 182–183
Forests, 48–51, 134, 136–137, 149, 153, 160–162, 169, 172, 173, 176–177, 180, 183, 184, 188, 189, 191; and fires, 100, 191; healthiest city forests, 49; restoration, 50–51, 134, 162, 176
Fort Tilden, 52, 123, 153–154
Fort Tryon Park, 142–143
Fossils, 28
Fresh Kills Landfill, 71, 65, 84
Freshwater ecosystems, 54–57; ponds, lakes, and swamps, 131, 134–136, 146, 149, 160, 163, 164, 172, 185–186, 188, 189, 191, 193–194
Fulton Fish Market, 117, 118

Gateway National Recreation Area, 70, 74, 83, 107, 143, 148, 151, 153, 158, 191
Gems and minerals, 33
George Washington Bridge, 42, 43
Giuliani, Rudolph, 9
Grand Central Station, 79
Grasslands, 57–60, 148–149, 172
Gravesend, 11
Great Kills Park, 6, 54, 123, 191–192; and Crooke's Point, 74, 191–192
Greenwood Cemetery, 158, 159, 163–164
Gribbles, 43
Grumet, Robert Steven, 128

Hake, Mary, 72
Harper's Magazine, 88
Hay fever, 109–110
Heat island, 7
Hoffman, Peter, 118
Horseshoe crabs, 120–122, 157, 158
Howard Beach, Queens, 19
Hudson Canyon, 34
Hudson Estuary, 42–45
Hudson, Henry, 2
Hudson River, 1, 3, 23, 34, 42, 54, 88, 116, 117, 118, 119, 120, 139, 140, 141, 142
Hudson River Foundation, 92
Hudson River Park, 141–142
Hurricanes, 11–14

Ice Age, 34–40; glacial boulders (erratics), 166; glacial grooves, 34; and golf, 35; knob and kettle terrain, 35, 183; neighborhoods affected by, 38, 40; outwash plain, 40; terminal moraine, 35, 38, 39, 162; Wisconsin Ice Sheet, 35–38, 56, 139, 162, 166, 179, 183
Inwood Hill Park, 46, 49, 50, 74, 97, 99, 106, 108, 136–139, 140
Islands, 65–67, 89, 167

195

Jacob Riis Park, 123
Jamaica Bay, 34, 46, 67, 88, 90, 143–156
Jamaica Bay Wildlife Refuge, 57, 74, 107, 111, 115, 122, 123, 143–148
Jocos Marsh, 71
John F. Kennedy Airport: animal escapees, 80, 163; marshland, 46; and migration, 116; and seagulls, 71; as wildlife habitat, 57, 58, 59, 64

Kettle ponds, 56–57, 179–180, 184, 185–186
Kinkead, Eugene, 76

La Guardia Airport, 8, 14
La Guardia, Fiorello, 86
La Tourette Park Golf Course, 35, 106, 188
Letts, Christopher, 92
Lightning, 16–18
Little bluestem, 58, 148
Long Island Jewish Hospital, 110
Long Island, 88

Madison Square Park, 76
Mammals: beavers, 2, 3; black–tailed jackrabbits, 80; coyotes, 80–81, 171, 172; gray squirrels, 75–76; harbor seals, 82; manatee, 82; marine mammals, 82; muskrats, 47, 155; Norway rats, 63, 64, 77–79; pilot whale, 82; raccoons, 158, 163; rat bites, 78
Manhattan, 126, 128–143; Beaver St., 2; Chambers St., 13; Dyckman St., 33; FDR Drive, 14; Greenwich Village, 31, 56; Harlem, 28; highest point, 39; Holland Tunnel, 19; Manhattanville Valley, 32; Marble Hill, 140; 96th St., 30; Riverside Drive, 103, 104, 140; 79th St. Boat Basin, 140; skyline, 30–32; topography, 27, 28; Times Square, 7; Wall Street, 14; World Financial Center, 32
Marine Park, 68, 121, 156–157
Mastodons, 34, 38
Migration, see Atlantic Flyway
Minetta Brook, 56
Monarch butterflies, 115, 122–124
Moore, Mary Tyler, 63
Moses, Robert, 146, 167, 187
Mosquitoes, 45, 48, 156, 179
Munsee dialect, 2
Mushrooms, 107–109, 180

National Parks Service, 57, 58, 59, 70, 72, 122, 144
National Weather Service, 14
National Hurricane Center, 13

Native Americans, 2, 88, 89, 128, 136, 137, 139
New Jersey Palisades, see Palisades, New Jersey
New York Aquarium, 52
New York Botanical Garden, 48, 49, 54, 101, 104, 173–175
New York City: astrological sign, 5; blackout, 3, 17–18; coldest day, 8; Department of Environmental Protection, 63, 90; Department of Health, 78; Department of Transportation, 10; Department of Parks and Recreation, 81; and Dutch settlers, 2, 88, 89, 104, 137; highest points of boroughs, 39; hottest day, 7; skyline, 30–32
New York City Audubon Society, 58, 59, 74, 149, 155
New York Harbor, 3, 43, 54, 66, 67, 88, 89, 93, 120, 192
New York Mycological Society, 109
New Yorker, 76
New York Times, 18, 69, 97, 125, 129
New York State Dept. of Environmental Protection, 119
Nor'easters, 14–16

Old Place Creek Marsh, 47
Olmsted, Frederick Law, 55, 129, 133, 140, 159, 160
Orchard Beach, see Pelham Bay Park
Ornitrol, pigeon contraception, 70

Palisades, New Jersey, 23, 139, 140, 166
Pangea, 23, 24, 28
Park Slope, Brooklyn, 18
Parsons, Samuel, Jr., 173
Pelham Bay Park, 46, 57, 166, 167–169; Hunter Island, 169; Orchard Beach, 82, 121, 167; Twin Island, 169
Periodical cicadas, 124–126
Piers, destruction of, 43
Plants, 95–112; birdfoot violet, 106; bloodroot, 106; common dandelion, 105; Dutchman's breeches, 106; exotic species, 95, 96, 105, 134; ferns, 184; Japanese honeysuckle, 105; Metropolitan Flora Project, 95–97; mugwort, 96; pinxter flower, 106; prickly–pear cactus, 107, 144, 191; ragweed, 110; vacant lot species, 97; weeds of the Upper West Side, 96; wildflowers, 104–107, 148
Plumb Beach, 54, 157–158
Poe, Edgar Allan, 140
Port Authority, 92

Potholes, 10
Prospect Park, 17, 42, 108, 159–163; Lookout Hill, 162; Lake, 55, 94, 163; Quaker Cemetery, 63
Prospect Park Alliance, 160, 162

Queens, 18, 126, 177–184
Queens County Bird Club, 183

Rare Bird Alert, 68
Reptiles, 81–84; diamondback terrapins, 83, 144, 156; Eastern box turtles, 83, 84?, 149; Fowler's toads, 83–84; snapping turtles, 84; turtles (general), 55
River Project, 141
Riverdale, Bronx, 26
Riverdale Park, 27, 176–177
Riverside Church, 62, 141
Riverside Park, 103, 105, 140–141
Rock types, 25–30; Fordham gneiss, 26, 137, 172, 176; Hartland Formation, 29–30; Inwood marble, 27–28; Manhattan schist, 26–27, 30, 140, 166; Palisades diabase, 23, 166; Staten Island serpentinite, 29, 187
Rockaways, Queens, 13, 96, 115, 151, 153, 155
Rockefeller, Nelson, 79
Roker, Al, 130
Roosevelt Island, 24, 26

Sadowski, Paul, 109
Salt hay, see *Spartina patens*
Salt marshes, 45–48, 137, 156, 157, 181
Salt marsh cord grass, see *Spartina alterniflora*
Savoy Restaurant, 118
Scheifflin, Eugene, 131
Shakespeare, William, 130, 131
Skyscrapers: affected by geology, 30–32; and earthquakes, 19; as nesting sites for peregrine falcons, 62–64; and wind, 12
Serpentine barrens, 59
Sharks, 52
Shellfish: fisheries, 88–90, 181; shell types, 51; surf clams, 53; *wampumpeag* or wampum, 89
Sheepshead Bay, 94
Shipworms, 43
Silvery checkerspot butterfly, 171, 172
Smith, Betty, 102
Smith, C. Lavett, 118
Snowfall, 8–11
Spartina alterniflora, 46, 47, 48
Spartina patens, 47
Spevak, Ed, 80
Spring peepers, 57, 146
Stargazing, 3–6
Staten Island, 185–194; cicadas, 124–126
Staten Island Greenbelt, 49, 95, 99, 106, 185–189
Staten Island Institute of Arts and Sciences, 126
Statue of Liberty, 34, 92, 116, 117
Stern, Henry, 97
Subway excavation, 32–34
Subway garnet, 33
Sunsets, 6

Tides, 42, 113
Torrey Botanical Society, 104
Travel & Leisure, 130
Tree Grows in Brooklyn, A, 102
Trees, 97–104; ailanthus, 102–103; American elm, 103–104, 140; arborcide, 97, 100; Bradford Callery pear, 99; Camperdown elm, 160, 162; cherry, 105, 165; ginkgo, 101; hemlocks, 49–50, 173–175; honey locust, 98, 111; London plane, 98–99, 111; native woodland species, 48–51, 99–101, 111; Norway maple, 99, 111, 134; papaw, 96; persimmon, 187; pin oak, 111; red oak, 100; sweet bay magnolia, 100; tulip, 100–101, 136, 137, 180
Trust for Public Land, 155

Udall's Cove, 46, 181–182
Union Square Park, 75, 107

Van Cortlandt Park, 26, 49, 57, 81, 97, 106, 166, 170–172; Vault Hill, 57, 60, 172
Vaux, Calvert, 55, 129, 159, 160, 173
Verrazano Narrows, 42
Verrazano–Narrows Bridge, 117
Verrazano, da Giovanni, 3

Waterways: Alley Creek, 179; Arthur Kill, 47, 48; Dead Horse Bay, 149–151; Gerritsen Creek, 156, 157; Gowanus Canal, 44; Harlem River, 42; Harlem River Ship Canal, 33, 136, 140; Kill Van Kull, 66, 82; Little Neck Bay, 89; New–town Creek, 44, 48; Prince's Bay, 89; Raritan Bay, 92, 192; Tibbetts Brook, 171
Wave Hill, 116, 176
Wildflowers, see plants
"Wildman" Steve Brill, 105
Wolfe's Pond Park, 193
Woodlawn Cemetery, 12, 80, 175
Woolly adelgid, 50, 175
World Trade Center, 2, 12, 27, 32